AF541701

BRITISH POLICY OF INTERVENTION AND EXPANSION

Encyclopaedic History of Indian Freedom Movement Series

BRITISH POLICY OF INTERVENTION AND EXPANSION

Edited by

OM PRAKASH

ANMOL PUBLICATIONS PVT. LTD.
NEW DELHI - 110 002 (INDIA)

ANMOL PUBLICATIONS PVT. LTD.
4374/4B, Ansari Road, Daryaganj
New Delhi - 110 002
Ph.: 23261597, 23278000
Visit us at: www.anmolpublications.com

British Policy of Intervention and Expansion
© Reserved
First Edition, 2004

ISBN 81-261-1512-2

[Responsibility for the facts stated, opinions expressed, conclusions reached and plagiarism, if any, in this book is entirely that of the Editor. The Publisher bears no responsibility for them, whatsoever.]

PRINTED IN INDIA

Published by J.L. Kumar for Anmol Publications Pvt. Ltd., New Delhi - 110 002 and Printed at Mehra Offset Press, Delhi.

Contents

Preface

'Golden bird' as India was known in yore days, rich in natural resources and well-developed cottage industries it was considered an affluent country. Indian spices, fabrics and other handicrafts were in great demand the world over. In the lure of having these goods and riches, many European powers made adventurous voyages to locate India.

The story of European expansions in Asia forms one of the great epics of modern times. India was the cornerstone of European imperialism in Asia. It was the lure of the lucrative 'Indian trade' which incited European adventurers to seek a new route to India, thus inaugurating a new era of contact between these two distant lands. Among the European empires in Asia, the British empire was the most enduring and prosperous one. And India was the finest jewel of the British dominion. It is worthwhile to remember that European exploration and adventure in the east were encouraged by the great demand in Europe for the products from Malabar like spices and calicoe cloth. Symbolically, the European age in Indian and indeed Asian history began with the landing of Vasco-de-Gama at Calicut on the 27th of May 1498. During this period, there was a continuous struggle between European traders and their native rivals and among the Europeans themselves. By the end of the eighteenth century this struggle for supremacy had been resolved in favour of the English.

The European traders were originally in the position of supplicants before the native rulers in India. For example, when William Hawkins arrived at the court of Jehangir with a letter from King James I asking for trade facilities, he had brought with him, a gift of 25,000 Gold pieces. As Lane Poole observes,

"There was nothing to suggest the most distant dream that in two centuries and a half the slight introduction Hawkins was then effecting between England and India would culminate in the sovereignty of a British Queen over the whole empire."

But unlike their European rivals like the Portuguese and the Dutch, the English made their bid for power in India only when the powerful Mughal empire had begun to decline. In any case the Portuguese and the Dutch had only small coastal settlements in India even at the height of their power and influence in this country.

By the end of the seventh Century, the Portuguese had been displaced by their Dutch rivals in Malabar and in the islands, of the East Indies. As for the Dutch, they were compelled by force of circumstances to regard the factories "which they established on the main land merely as marketing points for the products of an Empire which had its capital at Batavia in the East Indies."

Moreover, the Dutch power in India was largely jeopardised on European battle fields.

The wars with England and France drained the resources of this nation. Thus, it was left to the French to provide real opposition to the English in India.

The same pattern can be detected in the story of European activity in Malabar. Here the intensity of their rivalry was greater because of three main reasons. Malabar with its many fine harbours and backwaters was more accessible from the sea, increasing the scope for European interference.

Thus, European powers who came to India with the intention of trade snatched the political power and sovereignty from the local states, principalities and feudal lords. And established complete control over India. After over hundred years colonial rule, the feeling of national integration and freedom from the clutches of foreign power developed among the Indians. Thus, began the saga of freedom movement.

This encyclopaedic study is phased into two most significant and historic diversions having deep bearing on varied kinds of events which moulded the destiny of millions of people of Indian sub-continent. These events having complete political overtones, became a glaring phenomenon with the downfall of the Mughal Empire almost with the commencement of the 18th century. The ambitious piercing eyes of four European powers — the British, the French, the Portuguese and the Dutch—did cast upon several gainful economic successes in India.

Of these powers, the East India Company's government, with well organised force, bureaucracy and diplomats achieved phenomenal successes against their adversaries. The first phase,—therefore has been marked from Plassey to the Mutiny of 1857 (The First War of Independence) when the Company's role came to an end.

The second phase, naturally, came very much in the hands of the British Government functioning under the Whitehall and ended with the dawn of Swaraj on 15 August 1947.

This multi-volumes study would take up several themes, viz. political, socio-economic, religious, constitutional, educational, press, revolutionaries, local pioneers, legislation, revenues and judicial policy, on-going process of reaction — violent and non-violent, moderates and extremists, local and all India movements, reaction of the British Raj, efforts for conciliation, significant Acts passed by the Central Legislature, the impact of two global wars, 1914-1919 and 1939-1945; Congress, Muslim League, Hindu Mahasabha and the British Policy, a significant change in Britain soon after 1945, the Labour Government of Clement Attlee and Partition of India in August 1947.

In the first lot eleven volumes have appeared while in the present second lot ten volumes are being brought out namely the Marathas and their administration; Lord William Bentinck and Metcalf era of reforms; Raja Rammohun Roy: the reformer; Mutiny and its aftermath; History of Anglo-Sikh wars;

Emergence of Maharaja Ranjit Singh; Lord Hastings and his administrative measures; Ranjit Singh administration and British policy; British policy of intervention and expansion; and Lord Wellesley and policy of expansion.

This prestigious project is arranged, managed and looked after by a team of most dedicated and long experienced scholars of modern Indian history.

In gathering the authentic information, we have taken liberty to draw the material from the learned works of many great scholars in the field. We are deeply beholden to all those whose works are partially cited or substantially made use of in the project. I am indebted to Mr. J.L. Kumar, Managing Director, Anmol Publications Pvt. Ltd., New Delhi for his constant inspiration and moral support and finally to bring out this work. Last but not the least I am thankful to all those who have assisted me one way or other while preparing the manuscript.

—Om Prakash

1

Historical Background

To carry out the new policy of peace and moderation the prudent, cautious veteran Lord Cornwallis, the man of known and tried moderation, was sent out a second time, to rescue the Anglo-Indian Empire from the dangers and difficulties in which the last Governor General's grandiose schemes were supposed to have involved it.

A confidential litter from Lord Cornwallis to Lord Lake, of August 30th, 1805, is probably the best evidence of the state of public feeling and opinion in England at that time, and of the considerations which induced the Government to select him as Governor-General:

> "You will easily imagine that it was not slight cause that urged the ministers at home to press me to return once more to this country, and that I would not, without seeing very great necessity, have engaged at my time of life in so difficult and; I may say, so rash an undertaking. The real circumstances are, that it is not the opinion only of ministers or of a party, but of all reflecting men of every description, that it is physically impracticable for Great Britain, in addition to all other embarrassments, to maintain so vast and so unwieldy an empire in India, which annually calls for reinforcements of men and for remittances of money, and which yields little other profit except brilliant gazettes. It is in vain for us to conceal

from ourselves that our finances are at the lowest ebb, and that we literally have not the means of carrying on the ordinary business of government....

"I am sorry to find that the States who are most intimately connected with us, such as the Peshwa and the Nizam, are reduced to the most forlorn condition; that these powers possess no funds or troops on whom they can depend; that anarchy and disaffection prevail universally throughout their dominions; and that unless the British Residents exercised a power and an ascendancy that they ought not to exert, those governments would be immediately dissolved".

In a letter some days later he shows his anxiety to get rid of as much as possible of the territory acquired, and how his mind was occupied, "with a consideration of the means by which, without a positive violation of public faith, we may be relieved from the evils and embarrassments inseparably connected in my decided judgment, with the maintenance of the alliances with the several petty chieftains on the north of Hindustan".

Lord Cornwallis did not long survive his assumption of office, and a civil servant of the Company, Sir George Barlow, a man fully imbued with the policy and feelings which then governed the councils of Leadenhall Street, was appointed to succeed him.

His short rule was notorious for a starting episode—a mutiny of the native soldiers at Villore in the Madras Presidency, which at the time excited great alarm, and was the subject of much and angry discussion. There was a garrison at Villore, which consisted of 370 Europeans and about 1500 natives. At three o'clock one morning the latter suddenly attacked the Europeans, who suspecting nothing, were quietly at rest and unprepared. Thirteen officers and eighty-two European privates were killed, and ninety-one wounded, and several other Europeans were murdered by the mutinous Sepoys. The remaining officers and Europeans defended themselves gallantly and successfully in a corner of the fortress until help arrived; happily this was not long delayed. The news reached Arcot early in the morning and Colonel Gillespie, with a small but sufficient force of cavalry and mounted artillery, arrived before the fortress, and, joining the gallant remnant of the European garrison, soon overpowered the mutineers. Between 300 and 400 of the latter were slain, many taken, and the rest dispersed as fugitives in all directions over the country. But the promptitude and energy of these proceedings, the mutiny was at once effectually crushed before it had time to spread; and well it was so, for it was soon found that the disaffection was universal. It turned out that the Commander-in-Chief had issued orders as to the dress and painted marks of the Sepoys, offensive and alarming to their caste prejudices. The respectful remonstrances of some of them had been treated harshly as symptoms of a mutinous spirit, which stern discipline thought ought to be put down with a strong hand and without parley. The men were of course discontented, they became suspicious of their officers and the Government, and they saw in the dress regulations proofs of a deliberate scheme to deprive them of their caste and to make them embrace the Christian religion. They might well be excused for so believing, for how could it be supposed that sensible men, as the Frank Sahibs were admitted by all to be, would force a hated dress on their soldiers from a mere caprice of military tailoring and without some sufficient motive? What sufficient motive could be suggested but that of making them conform to Frankish notions of dress as preliminary to a forced conformation to the religion of the infidels? There were, moreover, not wanting, as there never will be wanting in like cases, agents of evil, dependents or partisans of dethroned princes, to stir up the passions of a discontented soldierly, by inventing and propagating the wildest stories, and attributing the blackest designs to the foreign rulers.

In looking back now at these painful events, the massacre and the slaughter of that day, we cannot but feel that the mutineers were men to be pitied, rather than to be condemned. It was moreover, a grave lessen to the civil and military authorities in the scrupulous respect which is due to the religious feelings of the soldiers, and the necessity of great caution and tact in endeavouring by the enforcement of military discipline to repress a genuine feeling of discontent. It is natural that an alien, infidel and outcast Government should occasionally, without any real cause, be suspected of designs against the faith and caste of their subjects, and the most innocent acts may be misunderstood and misrepresented. The true policy of the authorities under such circumstances is to believe that the men labouring under a delusion real and not feigned, and to deal with them as patients suffering from a temporary madness, not as criminals to be delivered up to the penalties of military law. The Madras soldierly were so dealt with, and in a few short months all fears of a wide-spread conspiracy, by which the English were haunted, were dispelled, and harmony and confidence were restored between the Sepoy and his master.

In consequence of this mutiny Lord Minto superseded Sir George Barlow as Governor-General, the latter being appointed Governor of the Madras Presidency. Lord Minto, who reached Calcutta in July, 1807, two years after Lord Wellesley's departure, had, as Sir Gilbert Elliot, taken an active part in the proceedings against Warren Hastings and Sir Elijah Impey, and was a warm supporter of the Indian policy of the Fox party, which had so strenuously and even passionately denounced all aggression on the native powers.

Shortly after his arrival, there occurred a mutinous combination of the English officers in the Company's service in the Madras Presidency. There was a dispute about some trivial matter, some regimental perquisites or allowances, between the civil and military authorities. There was a strange amount of blundering and intemperance on both sides, and the matter was at last taken up by the European officers, with such a violent *esprit de corps* that they entered into compacts to stand by each other in opposition to the Governor, and some of the regiments went so far as actually to seize on Seringapatam in open mutiny and revolt. It is difficult, and now needless, to follow the steps in this quarrel, by which English officers and gentlemen were led, not merely to the verge of, but into the actual commission of high reason, or to trace out how a mistaken sense of an honourable obligation one to the other should have led them to forget their most sacred obligations to their sovereign and their country. They, however, did become sensible, before it was too late, of the peril and the disgrace of the abyss into which they were about to plunge, and they recoiled from it. A golden bridge was made to enable them to return. To a great extent the quarrel had been a personal one with the Governor, Sir George Barlow, and the misguided officers were only too glad to make it appear to be wholly so. Therefore, when Lord Minto, the Governor-General, appeared personally on the scene the officers readily listened to his earnest appeals to their better feelings, and hastened to make to him the submission which they had refused to Sir George Barlow. The same indulgent moderation was shown—was shown wisely and successfully—to the folly of the European officers as had been shown to the delusion of the native Sepoys. The case was again dealt with as one of an epidemic madness, which had suddenly seized them. The officers had become conscious of their folly and their wickedness, and had found to sympathy. They were told by the highest and most esteemed military men, that the first duty of the army is submission to the civil power; and this painful episode in the history of the Company's army in Madras tended to strengthen and developed a sound public opinion in the universal body of their officers throughout all the Presidencies, which has probably rendered a repetition of such an outbreak impossible.

Lord Minto, like Lord Cornwallis and Sir George Barlow, had an honest and earnest desire to pursue the policy of peace, urged by the Directors and Proprietors, but the course of events could not be withstood.

It will be recollected that the Nizam and the Peshwa were submitted by the most stringent treaties to the British supremacy; but the other great powers, Scindiah, Holkar, and Berar, although much reduced and grievously mulcted by Lord Wellesley, had been left as the general peace still free and independent.

There were three groups of small states, the Rajhpoot states to the north-west, the Bundelcund states westward of the Jumnua and the Ganges, and the Sikh states between the Sutlej and the British territory. There was also, it will be recollected, the protected state of the Guicowar; and lying between Scindiah, Holkar, and Berar was the small Mohammedan state of Bhopal. There were the armies which the Mahratta powers had gathered for the late war, which they could neither pay nor disband, nor control; and there was especially a great body of mercenaries, half-soldiers, half-freebooters, known as the Pindarees, ready to take service with any one against any one, sometimes living in all the licence of free quarters on the subjects of the prince in whose service they nominally were, but more frequently engaged in marauding excursions into the neighbouring states, into which they carried fire and sword. There was no horror which they did not inflict, no atrocity of which they were not guilty. The Bundelcund states and the Rajhpoot states were especially the victims of the Maharatta powers and the Pindaree bands. Of the Rajhpoot states there was one, Jeypoor which the British were actually bound to protect by a treaty, the obligation of which the Calcutta Government evaded by asserting that the Rajah had not during the late war faithfully performed all the obligations on his part. Even the Court of Directors was ashamed of, and was constrained to rebuke, the pusillanimous abandonment of this prince to his powerful enemies. But independently of treaty obligations, the smaller states of Rajhpootana claimed the protection and interference of the British power on grounds the justice of which it is difficult, if not impossible, to controvert. There is a very striking despatch of Sir Charles Metcalfe, the Resident at Delhi, on this subject:

> "When I reply to these various applications, I find it difficult to obtain even a confession that the moderate policy of the British Government is just. People do not scruple to assert that they have a right to the protection of the British Government. They say that there always has existed some power in India to which peaceable states submitted, and in return obtained its protection. ... The British Government now occupies the place of the great protecting power, and is the natural guardian of the peaceable and weak; but owing to its refusal to use its influence for their protection, the peaceable and weak states are continually exposed to the oppressions and cruelties of robbers and plunderes, the most licentious and abandoned of mankind".

If the accounts given of the Pindarees are at all to be relied on, nothing could be more dreadful than the position of the provinces exposed to their ravages.

"Before the Pindarees set out on an expedition, a leader sent notice to the inferior chiefs, and hoisted his standard. By rapid marches they reached some peaceful region, against which their expedition was intended. Terror and dismay burst at once on the helpless population; villages were seen in flames. The plunderers dispersed in small parties, and spread themselves over the face of the country. Acting on a concerted plan, they swept round in a half circle, committing every sort of violence and excess, torturing to extort money, ravishing, murdering, and burning in the defenseless villages, but seldom venturing into danger, unless the prospect of booty was very certain. When they approached a point on the frontier, very distant from where they had entered, they united, and went off in a body to their homes. There was no refinement of torture which they scrupled to resort to, in order to extort the discovery of the treasures which the riots endeavoured to conceal from them".

Their ravages were chiefly confined to Malwa, Rajhpootana, and Berar, occasionally extending into the countries of the Peshwa and the Nizam, but for a time not venturing to provoke the British by attacks on their own subjects and territory.

The policy of abstention, under the plausible guise of moderation, was in fact a cruel and cowardly wrong. The power that Providence had given to the British, they were bound by every consideration of humanity, and by every motive of sound policy to exert for the suppression and extirpation of these enemies of the human race, and for the coercion of the powers by whom they were harboured. The principles of non-interference might as well be invoked to give impunity to the black flag of the pirate; and it is impossible to draw any sound distinction between these land-robbers and the marauders on the high seas, whom it is the acknowledged duty of every civilized power to hunt down. In truth, the policy of non-intervention was soon found impossible by Lord Minto; and the Court of Directors was compelled, by the irresistible force of circumstances, to acquiosce in its abandonment by him, in the notable instances which we have now to record.

Ranjeet Singh, who had established himself as the Sikh sovereign of Lahore, and had gradually subdued to his rule the Sikh chieftains and leaders to the north of the Sutlej, looked with covetous eyes on the Sikh states to the south of that river. He was a bold, ambitious unscrupulous, and astute chief; and if he had been allowed to extend and consolidate his power on the British frontier, he would have been a most formidable neighbour, a standing menace and danger. The Sikhs were physically far superior to the natives of Hindostan, and constituted as religious sect which regarded military courage as the first virtue, and the use of arms as the great duty of every man initiated into their fraternity or Khalsa. The commonest instinct of self-preservation made the British Government feel that it would be impossible to permit the extension of Ranjeet's power in their neighbourhood; they were obliged therefore, to listen to the applications which came to them from all the Sikh chieftains of the Cis-Sutlej territory, and to take them under their protection.

Ranjeet was warned that he could not be permitted to encroach. He chafed under the restraint; he remonstrated; he even protested against this as a violation of the amicable alliance between him and the British. He did not interfere between them and the Hindoo powers, and could not understand why they should interfere between him, a Sikh potentate, and the smaller Sikh chiefs, who were not British subjects or dependents.. The British, however, were firm. Ranjeet was made sensible of the risk he would incur by attempting the conquest of Sikhs, themselves as warlike as his own followers, if they were backed by the power of the British, the superiority of whose disciplined soldiers he was too sagacious not to appreciate. He came to an understanding with the British that he would, on his part, abstain from any further aggression in their direction, and that they would, on their part, confine their protection to the Cis-Sutlej chiefs, leaving him free to pursue his schemes of aggrandizement to the north and east.

Amicable relations were established, which have continued unimpaired to this day, with the Cis-Sutlej Sikh States, who accepted the protection, and willingly acknowledged the supremacy of the British. The latter undertook to abstain from all interference in their domestic affairs, but forbidding them all war between themselves or with their neighbours, and all external political relations assumed the absolute power of determining all disputes and questions. With respect to the right of succession, the British eventually claimed as sovereigns paramount the right to succeed by lapse to any state in default of lawful heirs. The Sutlej thus became the northern frontier of British India.

Lord Minto found himself also compelled to interfere to restore peace and order in Bundelcund. Advice and remonstrances having been fried in vain, he at length announced his determination to put an end to the intestine wars of the rajahs, and to compel them to submit their disputes and claims to the final arbitrament and decision of the supreme power. Most of them submitted without a struggle, when they found that he was in earnest, but he was compelled, in several instances, to use force to coerce the more refractory of the chiefs. The story of Lord Minto's administration is filled with details of military operations in and near Bundelcund which, although not devoid of interest, and creditable to the British arms, did not result in any acquisition of territory. After some years of warfare the strongholds of the high-land chiefs, the captains or patrons of the bands of marauders, in the most inaccessible fastnesses, were stormed; the most active leaders were, not withstanding the rapidity of their movements, by persevering pursuit at last run down; and the most obstinate of the rajahs were compelled to submit to the control of the Government as the supreme power. Peace and order were at length restored to the distracted provinces of Bundelcund, under the recognised supremacy of the British.

In Holkar's dominions troubles also arose. There was a man of great fame in those days, Amir Khan, an Afghan soldier of fortune, a Mohammedan who had risen to be Holkar's principal captain, and who was at the head of an army, which Holkar could not pay and which had to provide or itself. This was done for a while by means of contributions levied from the neighbouring Rajhpootana princes and the pillage of their unfortunate subjects; but his resource exhausted, it became necessary to find other sources of plunder, and under pretence of some old claim of Holkar's against the Rajah of Berar, Amir Khan marched with an immense force into the states of the latter. He was joined by great numbers of Pindarees, and his army is said to have consisted of as many as 40,000 horse, and 24,000 of his Pindaree allies. The Rajah was unable to offer any effectual resistance, and Jubbulpore, one of his principal towns, and all the surrounding country fell into the power of Amir Khan.

Lord Minto was again compelled to interfere. He was, it is true, bound by no treaty to protect the Rajah of Berar, and on the other hand, Amir Khan, professing to act in the name of Holkar, insisted that the British were absolutely bound by treaty with the latter not to interfere between him and the Rajah of Berar. It was, however, felt by Lord Minto, and felt justly, that it was impossible "that an enterprising and ambitious Mussulman chief, at the head of a numerous army, irresistible by any power except that of the Company, should be permitted to establish his authority, on the ruins of the Rajah's dominions, over territories contiguous to those of the Nizam, with whom community of religion, combined with local power and resources, might lead to the formation of projects probably not uncongenial to the mind of the Nizam himself, and certainly consistent with the views and hopes of a powerful party in his court for the subversion of the British alliance".

Encouraged by the certainty of the British support, the Rajah now took heart to defend himself, and disavowed a treaty of submission which had been made by his general. In some battles which ensued, the predatory leader was defeated by the Rajah's own troops, and being made aware of the powerful forces which the English had assembled, was fain to withdraw from his enterprise and to return to the states of Holkar. Thus the mere demonstration of force by the Calcutta Government, and the certainty that the demonstration was serious and would be followed by action if necessary, were sufficient to save the Rajah of Berar from the imminent perils to which he was exposed.

In the territories of the Peshwa, too, the British were obliged to interfere peremptorily to prevent the Peshwa from crushing some Jaghirdars or chiefs, who were under their protection, and to compel them, on their side, to perform the obligations to which they were by their terms bound.

In the south serious disturbances in Travancore and Cochin had even earlier called for coercive measures by the Madras army. The quarrel originated in the alleged inability of these Courts to discharge their pecuniary obligations to the Company, which had fallen greatly into arrears. Their finances were in a state of deplorable disorder, and money was raised by the most ruinous and oppressive of expedients, the assignment of whole districts in farms to the money-lenders. The revolt or mutiny was soon put down, and the Courts were, happily for them, induced or coerced into the appointment of the British Resident, Colonel Johan Munro, as Dewan or Finance Minister, under whose administration the whole aspect of things was soon changed. Order succeeded to disorder, the revenue was largely increased, while the most oppressive burthens were removed, and in a few years the administration was restored to the hands of the native rulers, every debt discharged, the exchequer full, the revenue increasing and easily collected, and the country peaceful and prosperous.

Thus everywhere throughout India the policy of non-interference with the native states and people was found to be impossible and the sincere and earnest resolution and effort to act upon it had only brought to the English danger and discredit, and to millions of natives evils which it is scarcely possible adequately to describe.

During Lord Minto's administration it became, moreover, necessary for the Indian Government to take part in the great struggle which was then pending between England and France. From the French colonies in the Asiatic seas the cruisers and privateers of France issued to prey on English commerce and the Company itself suffered enormous losses from the capture of its ships laden with valuable cargoes. Expeditions were accordingly planned and conducted by the Governor-General, which resulted in the reduction of all the French and Dutch possessions in those seas. Some formidable pirates were also hunted out of nests in which they had lodged on the western coast; and a still more formidable body of corsairs were attacked in a stronghold on the Arabian coast, and destroyed.

The course of the narrative has brought us to an event of great importance in the history of the East India Company itself. It in year 1813 their parliamentary charter was renewed, and a fresh lease was given to them of their Indian dominions for a period of twenty years. They were compelled, however, by the public opinion of the commercial community of England to abandon their trade monopoly, with one great exception. It was resolved by the House of Commons and so enacted that the existing restraints respecting the commercial intercourse with China should be continued, and that the exclusive trade in tea should be preserved to the Company during the aforesaid period of twenty years.

Some plausible reasons were assigned for this, derived from the nature of the Chinese Government and the evils which might result from the probable collision between the Chinese authorities and the English adventurers, who might be tempted to resort to China; but the real and substantial reason was the representation of the Company, that the profits of their China trade were absolutely necessary to enable them to defray their territorial charges and pay their dividend of 600,000*l.* a year. Again, there was the singular spectacle exhibited of the English people, the people who are supposed to have been actuated by the meanest motives and impelled by cupidity and shopkeeping interests to steal the fair domains of the much-wronged sovereigns and princes of India, actually submitting themselves to an oppressive monopoly and a heavy taxation, in order to provide funds for the Indian exchequer for the protection and government of India. While taking upon themselves the burthes of this restraint on their own commerce with China, they gave the most unreserved freedom of trade to their Indian Empire itself, the ports of which were open to all shipping, and the ships of which might trade freely with the whole world.

2

The Indian States

In the development of British relations with the Indian States from the time of Robert Clive to that of Lord Wellesley, the administrators of the East India Company in India did not follow a uniforms policy. Extension and consolidation of power, promotion of economic and commercial interests, weakening of the Indian powers, infiltration of British influence in their territories, elimination of hostile foreign elements from there and defence of British interests against any possible aggression, were the guiding principles of their inter-State political relations. In pursuit of these aims, periods of war and peace alternated, depending upon political circumstances in the country, the personality at the helm of British affairs at Fort William and the tone of the Home authorities in England. Very often, the policy of aggression and non-interference operated simultaneously in relation to different States and was largely based upon the dictates of expediency. Beginning with the policy of limited liability, determined by limited resources, want of experienced administrators and fear of creating Indian and foreign opposition to the bold enterprising and war-like schemes of Lord Wellesley, the keynote of the Company's policy was the progressive acquisition of commercio-political hold over India. The use of the term 'ring-fence' by Sir William Lee-Warner to connote all these trends is hardly comprehensive.

Lord Minto avoided the two extremes of the policy pursued by Lord Wellesley and his two successors and steered his way cautiously without giving up the British aims in India and also without arousing bitter criticism by any section of official opinion in Indian or England. In doing so he did not chalk out a set of pattern which can be defined in a nutshell. His policy had different phases, propitious to the circumstances, prevailing in each State and the exigencies of the Company's position. The instructions from the Court of Directors, the financial position of the Company and needs of consolidation of enormous gains already acquired during Lord Wellesley's regime, prevented him from contemplating a vigorous policy of annexation. At the same time, he found it difficult to adhere strictly to his predecessor's policy of non-intervention. His policy, therefore, ranged between non-intervention and intervention. While working within the framework of the former, at times, he interposed limited intervention by admonition and advice. In some cases, he effected active interference, compelling some of the small States to accept defensive alliances by which their foreign relations were controlled and several concessions affecting their sovereignty were secured. Herein lay the genesis of a new policy which blossomed during the time of his successor and by which the area under British protection in India was extended. To enforce the clauses of the Treaty of Bassein, relating to the Haryana tract between the Delhi territory and the Cis-Sutlej Sates, he had to use military force before he could bring it under direct British control. In Bundelkhand, some refractory usurper-chiefs were crushed by a military force and the fortresses were restored to the real proprietors. In relations to the Bhonsla Raja of Nagpur and the Peshwa of Poona, he strengthened friendly relations by rendering military assistance to the State of Nagpur against Pindaris and inculcating sense of obedience amongst the Southern Jagirdars towards the Peshwa by mediation. In short, his policy towards the Indian States formed a link between the systems of Lord Wellesley and Lord Hastings.

In relations to the Rajput States of Jaipur and Jodhpur and the Maratha State of Gwalior, Lord Minto adhered to the policy of non-intervention. Whereas in the former two cases, he refused to embroil the Company in the internal affairs of Rajputana, in the latter case, if disapproved the proposal of his Resident at Gwalior for preventing Sindhia's incursions in the neighbouring friendly States by military action. In May 1808, when the State of Jaipur became a helpless prey to the forces of Sindhia and Ameer Khan, Raja Jaswant Singh requested Archibald Seton, the British Resident at Delhi, for help in accordance with the terms of the Treaty of Amity and Alliance signed by him on December 12, 1803. But this request was politely declined on the plea that the British Government did not 'pretedn or wish to be considered as an arbiter of the differences between independent States'.[1]

In April 1810, when events took a serious turn on account of the renewed incursion of Ameer Khan in Rajputana, the rulers of Jaipur and Jodhpur sent their Vakeels to Delhi with a request to seek British help to ward off the menance. They put forth a proposal for the extension of British protection to their States which would ensure security against the dangerous inroads.[2] But the British Resident reiterated the old reply and discounted any idea of interference in their affairs with the Marathas and Pathan Chiefs in conformity with the declared policy of non-intervention.[3] This attitude was the outcome of the desire to avoid military involvement of Rajputana which might cause a heavy burden on the Company's exchequer.

Another instance of Lord Minto's application of the policy of non-intervention was in relation to whose troops made incursions in Jhansi, Duttia and Jalaun which had shown their fidelity and attachment to the British Government by signing Treaties of Friendship and Alliance on February 6, 1804,[4] March 15, 1804[5] and October 23, 1806[6] and had thus fallen under the category of the 'friendly States'. At this Maratha aggression on the Company's allies, Graeme Mercer, the British Resident at the Court of Sindhia, ordered

Colonel Martindell to despatch his forces against the invading forces and compel them to vacate aggression.[7] But Lord Minto did not agree to this step as he thought that such a measure would involve the Company's Government in a major conflagration. He, therefore, ordered to suspend the planned operation.[8] Thus the Governor-General did not wish to cross the bounds of his policy of non-interference, as far as possible, in his relations with the Indian States.

A slight shift in Lord Minto's foreign policy is visible in his relations with Holkar, Mysore and Gaekwar, where he adopted the policy of limited interference. The Company's interference in the affairs of the State of Indore arose from Jaswant Rao Holkar's indiscretion in affording protection, in May 1808, to Mahipat Ram, an influential member in the Nizma's Court and his two associates, Sripat Ram and Mohammed Raza Khan who left the State sensing danger to themselves, on account of their alleged anti-British and anti-Nizam inclination. Mahipat Ram was entrusted with the command of the infantry. This conduct of the Holkar Chief aroused suspicion in the British mind and a very serious view was taken of it. An allegation was advanced against him that he was aware of the anti-British proclivities of Mahipat Ram and the circumstances in which he was expelled from Hydrabad.[9]

The Governor-General, therefore, wrote to Jaswant Rao Holkar not to give any help or asylum to Mahipat Ram.[10] The Holkar Chief complied with this request and removed Mahipat Ram from his service as a measure to dispel British doubt and suspicion about his conduct. However, he did not share British doubts about Mahipat Ram's questionable loyalty towards the Nizam and the British; and communicated his own views about him.[11] This interference in the matter of an appointment in the State of Indore was legally not warranted by any Treaty relations with Indore, but a practice of this kind had started developing since the days of Lord Wellesley.

The second State to be dealt with under the policy of limited interference was Mysore. After the fall of Tipu, this State was allowed to exist under a descendant of the old Hindu ruling family under British protection. By the Subsidiary Treaty which its ruler signed in 1799, the British acquired the right to offer advice and to be consulted in matters of internal administration. When the young Raja came of age, a serious conflict for power arose between him and his Dewan, Purniya, who was accused of transgressing his authority and assuming powers not given to him by the Treaty.

The Dewan who had misappropriated a large sum of money from the State treasury, was ordered by the Raja to disgarb the illicit gain. But he questioned the Raja's right to make a demand of that kind from him.[12] The second point of dispute between the two arose from the Raja's desire to recover all the State letters received by the Dewan during his infancy from several authorities. The Dewan refused to deliver any one of these papers with the plea that they were of greater consequence ot him than to the young Raja.[13] The third point of dispute between them was the disrespectful treatment of the old Dewan towards the young Raja and his relatives and his disinclination to part with the power and authority he had enjoyed during the Raja's minority.[14] The Raja was only a nomical head. The overwinning conduct of Purniya created strained relations between him and the Raja who ardently wished to assume the administration of the state directly in his own hands.[15]

In these circumstances, Mr. A. H. Cole, British Resident, intervened to bring about amicable adjustment of differences between the Raja and his Dewan, and requested the latter to agree to settle accounts with the Raja.[16] Accordingly, a Commission of enquiry, consisting of three principal officials of Government was appointed. The Commission's findings revealed that the Dewan spent 389,600 pagodas in charity to Brahmans without authority and 342,378 pagodas on his household expenses from the public exchequer. There charges of misappropriation against the Dewan having been proved, the Resident agreed with the wishes of the Raja to dispense with the Dewan's services, but requested him to forego the amount lying against him as a measure of munificence and liberality towards him. The Dewan also attended upon the Raja, regretted his bad conduct, expressed his willingness to resign his post and requested for some subsistence allowance.[17]

The Raja responded magnanimously. He forgave him for his conduct, wrote off the amount of 631978 pagodas, he had misappropriated and sanctioned 500 pagodas as a subsistence allowance in token of his past services to the State.[18] This maturity of judgment, depth of understanding and magnanimity of spirit shown by the Raja in his dealings with his Dewan was highly praised by Lord Minto.[19]

The third State within the fold of the policy of limited interference was the Gaekwar State of Baroda which was allied to the Company's Government by subsidiary treaties of 1802[20] and 1805.[21] During the time of Lord Minto an intervention was effected in facilitating the collection of tribute from the rebellious feudatories of the State.

Major Alexander Walker, the British Resident at Baroda, exerted his influence upon the Gaekwar ruler to bring about discontinuance of Mulkgiri expeditions, he had launched against his feudatories in Kathiawar as they affected adversely the finances of the State and the peace of the region. To ensure the collection of tribute peacefully, he invited the chiefs to a meeting, where the amount of tribute to be paid by him to the Gaekwar was fixed and where 120 chiefs executed bonds to pay the mulkgiri tribute to the State of Gaekwar regularly and punctually.[22] This intervention was in conformity with the Treaty of 1805. It brought an increase of Rs. 414,433.00 to the revenue drawn by the State from Kathiawar and restored peace and tranquillity to that region.[23]

Another shift in Lord Minto's political relations with the Indian States took place in his dealings with the States of Delhi, Hyderabad and Awadh, where he interfered in matters of succession, selection of Chief Minister and change in the revenue administration respectively. In all these cases, the chief considerations motivating the British policy were the strengthening of British control over them and maintenance of law and order.

In Delhi, Emperor Akbar Shah II wanted to designate his third son, Prince Mirza Jehangir with his favourite consort, Mumtaz Mahal, for whom he had the greatest affection, as his heir-apparent in supersession of the more legitimate claims of his first two male issues.[24] Archibald Seton, the British Resident in Delhi, apprehended distractions in the imperial family and breach of peace in Delhi and in the neighbouring territories as a consequence of the provocation caused among the supporters of the superior claims of Abu Zafar, the eldest prince, by his unusual practice. He opposed the idea as it would occasion palace intrigue, cause suspicion and strife among the various princes and thus be a source of serious trouble in the palace.[25] Contrary to the wished of the Emperor, he favoured the nomination of Abu Zafar as the heir-apparent which would be effected without any fear of turmoil and in accordance with the law of primogeniture by which the eldest son was to be proclaimed as heir-apparent.[26] This issue brought the Emperor and the British Government at loggerheads, and British intervention in this matter sorely disappointed him. To his mind, appointment of the heir-apparent was a domestic matter, on which a decision could be taken only by him without any extraneous interference. But the Company's Government in Calcutta considered itself fully competent to interfere in matters, connected with the Emperor, either personal or political in nature.[27]

Notwithstanding these differences, the Emperor conferred the honours of the *Aftabee* on Mirza Jehangir in the open Court amidst the compliments and congratulations of his immediate dependents and the devoted servants of the prince's mother on December, 1, 1807, the day of the festival of *Id-ul-Fitar*. Lord Minto viewed this matter with serious concern and urged upon the Emperor to retrace his steps.[28] The Emperor resented this interference in his palace affairs, but after calm deliberations, though with considerable hesitation, agreed to the dictates of the Governor-General and withdrew the honours, he had conferred on Prince Jehangir.[29]

This episode was humiliating to the Emperor and gave a serious jolt to the palace junta. Egged on by ambition and disappointed by the withdrawal of honour, Prince Jehangir developed defiant attitude. With a body of retainers, loyal to him, he created confusion in the palace by keeping the immates in a state of alarm. When the Resident advanced to expostulate with him, he was fired at and had a very narrow escape. This conduct of the prince was retaliated by employment of the Residency troops which forced open the palace gates, dispersed the retainers, captured the Prince and sent him to the Fort of Allahabad as a State prisoner for life.[30] After this stern action, the Emperor was prevailed upon to nominate Prince Abu Zafar as *'Wullee Uhed'* on the eve of the festival of *Id-ul-Zohau* on January 16, 1810.[31]

In the history of the British relations with the Mughal Emperor, this was a momentous step, indicative of the position of the Emperor *vis-a-vis* the Company's Government. Among the palace circles, it created, the impression that the British decisions relating to Delhi were indomitable and upon the Emperor's mind, it pressed home the idea about the futility disregarding British advice.

The second State in which interference was effected was Hyderabad which was allied to British by a subsidiary alliance. Its ruler, the Nizam Sikander Jah lacked in qualities of an efficient administrator. On the demise of the Chief Minister, Mir Allum on December 9, 1808, the Nizam wished Munir-ul-Mulk, son-in-law of the late Chief Minister and a favourite of the Begum of the palace, whom he often consulted in State affairs, to be the Chief Minister.[32] But the Company's Government was interested in having a minister through whom it could control the executive branch of the administration of Hyderabad State.[33] It favoured the candidature of the Shamas-ul-Umra, the Chief of the military party in the State, and directed Captian Sydenham. Resident in Hyderabad, to tell the Nizam that among the *Umrahs* of his Court, he appeared to be qualified person to fill the vacancy and Raja Chandulal should continue as Peishkar.[34] Ultimately, after protracted negotiations, Munir-ul-Mulk was appointed as the Chief Minister of June 11, 1809 and Raja Chandulal as his Peishkar.

This arrangement could not function smoothly. The Chief Minister and the Peishkar did not look eye to eye with each other on important issue. It appeared that they were differently inspired. Munir-ul-Mulk was undoubtedly the Nizam's man. He raised doubts and suspicion in the Nizam's mind regarding the fidelity and attachment of Raja Chandulal and accused him of his attachment to the British Government and mal-administration in the State.[35] He was labelled as the stooge of the Resident. These accusations were treated by the Resident as the manoeuvres of the Chief Minister to oust the Peishkar. The plan to remove Raja Chandulal was foiled by the Resident. It appears that the Resident was interested in maintaining him in his post as an instrument of British policy. The Government of Calcutta took a strong attitude in this matter and wrote to the Resident that the very foundation of the subsidiary alliance with the Nizam would be exposed to hazards if Chandulal was removed from his office.[36] Hence Chandulal continued in his office against the wishes of the Chief Minister and the Nizam; and the British influence in Nizam's administration continued unabated.

The third State, where comparatively greater interference was interposed, was Awadh which had long been a nursery of every new aspect of Company's policy towards the Indian States. The last Treaty, on which its relations with the Company were based, was the famous Treaty of 1801 which virtually reduced its Nawab to a subordinate position by imposing upon him a clause that he would 'establish in his reserved dominions such a system of administration, to be carried into effect by his own officers, as should be conducive to the prosperity of his subjects, and calculated to secure the lives and property of the inhabitants, and that His Excellency would always advise with and act in conformity to the counsel of the officers of the Honorable Company'. British interference in this State during Lord Minto's time was based on this clause and related to land revenue administration which in the view of John Baillie, the British Resident, had degenerated, and necessitated an improvement. This caused strained relations between Nawab Saadut Ali and the Resident.

The first cause of the strained relations was the frequency in the employment of the Subsidiary troops by the Nawab for the collection of land revenue of the refractory taluqadars of Bhadri, Goura and Nanpara who defied his reforming measures. In the adoption of this measure, he was influenced by the considerations to establish an efficient centralized administration to increase his financial resources for the resumption of the rent-free-grants and to relieve the ryots from the tutelage of the landed aristocracy. In June 1810, John Baillie grew a little weary of Nawab's requisition of British troops to collect arrears of revenue from defaulting zamindars. The cause for this irritation was the friction between the British officers, and the Awadh Amils over the question of supplies for the subsidiary forces in the field.[37]

Another issue, on which differences arose, was the type of revenue arrangement to be made in Sultanpur and Partapghar, where trouble shot up between zamindars and the ryots in September 1810 and the order was restored with the help of the subsidiary troops.[38] On the restoration of peace, the Nawab decided to appoint Hakim Mehdi Ali Khan, one of the most efficient persons in his revenue administration, as the Amil of these districts. John Baillie did not appreciate this plan and suggested the revenue arrangement in the Ceded territories for adoption as a model for his districts. The Nawab did not accept this advice and proceeded with his original plan. This irritated the Resident and led to accusations and counter-accusations between him and the Nawab; each charged the other with a virtual infraction of the Treaty. The Resident accused the Nawab of disregarding the advice and the Nawab complained that he was not permitted to judge what was conductive to the efficient administration and prosperity of the people.[39]

This outspoken attitude of Saadut Ali was inconvenient to the Company's authorities. On December 28, 1810, Lord Minto addressed a letter to him in which he recommended a plan of revenue reform based upon a moderate assessment to be made with the land-holders as against the farming system. The settlement was to be made for a fixed term of year and the occupancy rights were to be recognized as long as the amount of the assessment was regularly realized.[40]

Nawab Saadut Ali did not receive the reform proposals with approval. He argued that his peasantry was contented and cultivation in his State was flourishing and any change in the system was unnecessary.[41] Thereupon, the Resident insisted on the adoption of the proposed scheme in conformity with the former Treaty. But the Nawab disputed the Resident's assertion on the plea that the Treaty contained no specific term binding him to accept any scheme of revenue referm proposed to him.[42] Thus a sort of dead-lock was created between the views of the Nawab and those of the British representative. Lord Minto treated the Nawab's conduct as a definance of his advice and addressed a letter of remonstrance to him on July 2, 1813, reminding him of the right of his Government in terms of the Treaty of 1801 and to propose reforms to him for the improvement of his administration.[43] He took a strong stand on the issue and firmly asserted that no lapse of time and no change of circumstances, would ever induce the British Government to relinquish a measure which it considered essential to the happiness and prosperity of Awadh, his reputation and the best interests of both States.[44] The Nawab was warned of the serious consequences of his refusal to accept the British advice and of the violation of the Treaty of 1801, and asked him to carry into effect the reform recommended to him without further opposition or delay.[45] This decisive attitude of Lord Minto was not without its effect upon the Nawab. Alarmed by it, he undertook to implement the suggested scheme of reform in revenue administration.[46]

This intervention of Lord Minto in the internal affairs of Awadh was a radical departure from the traditions of non-intervention which Lord Cornwallis and Sir George Barlow had tried to establish. He treated Awadh virtually as a subordinate power unable to resist British and the Nawab bowed to the inevitable out of sheer helplessness.

In Haryana and Bundelkhand which had not come under direct British control, inspite of their legal cession to the Company by the Treaty of Bassein, Lord Minto employed troops to enforce the British claims over the former and to establish peace and order in the latter. These regions were a constant prey to lawlessness and anarchy created by the predatory activities of some local tribes and chiefs who were not only a source of turbulence in the States, but had also endangered peace and security of the contiguous British districts.

The first territory to be dealt with was Haryana. Its administration was entrusted to Abdul Samad Khan in 1806 by the Company's Government as a reward to his military services to Lord Lake against the Marathas in 1803 in the hope that he would establish a stable Government. But he did not succeed in his attempt as he was involved in a protracted contest with the Bhutties, a war-like tribe of Sirsa. They created enormous difficulties for him and threatened to capture his fort of Hansi. Their turmoils diminished his influence and authority and involved him into debt. He could not pay his soldiers regularly on account of the depleted condition of his treasury and non-payment of revenue by the ryots.[47]

In these uncontrolled circumstances, Abdul Samad Khan approached Archibald Seton at Delhi for military help. But Seton declined any help. He, however, promised him a grant of Rs. 197,000.00 to enable him to relinquish the charge of the region. Hard-pressed by financial difficulties, he resigned his possession of Haryana in November 1807. For his maintenance, he was, however, allowed to retain his two ancestral estates of Dujana and Mahavane in the Rohtak district.[48]

The political settlement of Haryana baffled the British Government which desired to entrust its administration to some capable and trustworthy chieftain. Geographically, it was more convenient to assign this region to Sardar Bhag Singh, the Chief of Jind. But he expressed his inability to take this responsibility.[49] The Company's Government, therefore, decided to take over the administration of Haryana region directly into its own hands and discharge the responsibility of suppressing the lawless elements and providing peace, order and security in the disturbed areas. In taking this decision, the Company's Government was prompted by the considerations of security of the contiguous territories, already under its administration and the strategic importance of the tract in relation to the Sikh Kingdom under Maharaja Ranjit Singh. The region was sought to be used as an impregnable barrier against an attempt of the Sikh Chief to impose his authority over the Cis-Sutlej States.[50]

With these ends in view, Seton deputed Gardner, his Assistant, with instructions to quell the refractory elements. For this purpose, an army was put at his disposal. He reached Beree and called the leading men of the town and impressed upon them the liberal but firm policy of his Government, and asked them to desist from all acts of violence and accept British protection.[51] Little difficulty attended his proceedings. Most of the headmen of the village obeyed his summons, professed allegiance and promised the regular payment of a stipulated revenue and engaged to desist from intestine broils.[52]

A similar call was given to the refractory zamindars of Kahnaur and Deeghal. They responded favourably. From Beree, Gardner proceeded to Rohtak, where the leaders of the Roughar tribe of Negana, known for their turbulence, submitted to him and promised their obedience to the British Government. However, as a safeguard against their refractory habits, police stations were also established at their Centre.[53]

On May 14, 1809, Gardner reached Balliali, a village near Hansi, where the local Roughar tribe tried to thwart the extension of British hold in their region. But they were ruthlessly suppressed and a police station was established there to prevent any future outbreak. The Company's forces encountered another opposion at Bhiwani, where the inhabitants put up a stiff resistance. They carried off the camels and baggage of the British troops and fired upon them. But ultimately Col. Ball inflicted defeat on them and captured the town.[54] Seton considered this place to be the most important strategically and feared that but for its capture by the British troops, it might have become an asylum and a rallying point for the disaffected persons of the Hissar region.[55]

Thus Haryana was brought under direct British rule. The refractory tribes submitted to the British yoke which was beyond their power to be shaken off. For fear of extermination, they gave up their predatory habits and settled down as peaceful agriculturists. Effective watch was maintained on their activities.

The other region which presented a difficult administrative problem and necessitated British military interference was Bundelkhand. The Chiefs of Ajaigarh, Kotra and Kalinjar in this region, were found to be contumacious in their behaviour. Among them, one of the most audacious killadar was Lakshman Dawa who had usurped the fort of Ajargarh from Raja Bakht Singh. On December 9, 1806, by an engagement with Sir George Barlow, he promised to surrender the fort to the Company's Government after two years and to hold in Jageer the adjacent lands on payment of an annual sum of Rs.

4000.00.[56] Raja Bakht Singh also signed an *Ikrarnamah* on June 8, 1807, promising the Company's Government allegiance and military help, if he was restored to his original position.[57]

During the time of Lord Minto, the British sources alleged that Lakshman Dawa never paid the tribute and even after two years showed disinclination to retore the fort to the Company's Government despite repeated reminders to him.[58] This was tantamount to a violation of the article V of his engagement with the Company's Government. Besides this, by his frequent military incursions in the neighbouring British territory of Mirzapore, he incurred the displeasure of the inhabitants.[59] This was another violation of article I of his former engagement. Therefore, a military force under Col. Martindell was despatched to curb his activities and to force him to conform to his engagement. For this expedition, a sum of Rs. 40,000.00 was sanctioned.[60] Batteries were opened against the fort and its fortifications were demolished. Left with no alternative, the killadar surrendered.[61] On the occupation of the Ajaigarh fort, two Proclamations were issued to weed out his influence and to cripple his resources. By the first, the Bundellas were asked to withdraw help to him.[62] By the second, his jageers and property were confiscated and the zamindars and cultivators of these jageers were ordered to dissociate themselves from him and pay the land revenue to the Company's Government.[63] The killadar was, however allowed to remain at large on parole. He repented his conduct in a petition addressed to the British Agent and sought British pardon and his restoration to original position.[64] But his request was refused as he was not considered worthy of any provision or protection.[65]

This strict and firm British attitude made Lakshman Dawa desperate. He broke his parole on May 25, 1809 and proceeded to Calcutta in the guise of a *faqir* to seek interview with Lord Minto.[66] He reached Calcutta on July 4, 1809, where he represented his case to the Persian Secretary, Government of India, through whom he expressed his desire to meet the Governor-General. He was not given any favourable response and was immediately taken under police vigilance.[67] He even endeavoured to manage his flight back to Bundelkhand, but failed. He was detained there till his death in November, 1828.

The fortress of Ajaigarh and its adjoining territories were handed over to Raja Bakht Singh by a *Sanad* on his assurance of allegiance and loyalty and the promise of fulfilment of the same obligation from his heirs and successors.[68]

Similarly Kotra was another Pargana, originally under Raja Bakht Singh, Gopal Singh a free-booter and an adventurer, had usurped it from the Bundella Chief in 1801. In course of a few years, he increased his forces to two thousand foot and seven hundred horses and began his predatory incursions into the adjacent British districts, setting fire to a few villages.[69] His destructive eruptions became a source of terror to the population during the Governor-Generalship of Lord Minto. The British Agent at Banda proclaimed a reward of Rs. 10,000.00 for his apprehension. But there was no response to this effect. Consequently, a British force under Col. Martindell attacked his fort and made his resistance futile.[70] Many of his adherents deserted him and offered their services to the British Government.[71] To save his life, he took to flight to the hills southward along with his family. Pursued by the British troops, he ultimately surrendered himself to the British and acknowledged submission.

By an *Ikrarnamah*, he made a solemn promise that he or his brothers or children or any of his adherents would not longer resort to plundering expeditions and lead peaceful life.[72] For his support, he was granted a jageer in the district of Panwari in Bundelkhand. Like Ajaigarh, the pargana of Kotra was also restored to Raja Bakht Singh on his assurance of allegiance and fidelity to the Company's Government.

The final establishment of order and tranquillity in Bundelkhand was in a greater degree dependent upon the reduction of Kalinjar which was under Dario Singh Choubey, a Bundella Chief. During the time of Lord Minto, he began to aid and abet the refractory elements hostile to the British. The British sources alleged that with his connivance, his vassal, Dilgunjan Singh, committed numerous acts of depredations and outrages in the Company's territory of Mirzapur in cooperation with the Pindari leader, Badil Khan, who was afforded shelter in the fortress of Kalinjar after his incursions in Rewa, from where he kidnapped the son of a Rewa grandee.[73] The Raja of Rewa solicited British help for the recovery of the kidnapped boy. In response to the request, when the British demanded the restoration of both the boy and Badil Khan from Dario Singh, he complied with the former demand, but evaded the latter.[74] Having leagued with a rebel, he was treated as guilty of the breach of Article I of his engagement of September 25, 1806 with the Company's Government.

Therefore, an effective action was taken against him. The fort of Kalinjar was stormed by the British troops and after a brief resistance, he was compelled to surrender and sign an *Ikrarnamah* on June 19, 1812.[75] The fortress of Kalinjar and its adjoining territories were taken under British control. In lieu thereof, Dario Singh Choubey was given a grant of fourteen villages in the British Parganas of Bhettree, Koonhuss and Burghur and seven villages each to his two deceased brothers' sons.[76] He also promised to abide by the pledges contained in the previous *Ikrarnamah* and undertook to live peacefully in his jageer and not to move out of it without British permission.[77] His new jageer would be subject to the jurisdiction of British laws and regulations.[78]

In relation of Rewa and Cohin, Lord Minto adopted the policy of 'Friendship and Defensive' alliances. This policy was necessitated by the growth of refractory anti-British elements in these States and their location contiguous to British territories. The seriousness of the situation was realized and steps were taken to bring them into subordination.

Rewa, the largest State in Baghelkhand, occupied a place of great strategic importance. Its boundaries touched

Bundelkhand, the Bhonsla's territories of Nagpur and British territories. The attitude of the ruler, Raja Jai Singh Deo, towards the Company was not clearly defined. He was suspected of being in collusion with Gopal Singh a freebooter of Bundelkhand and inimical to British interests.[79] Besides, in March 1812, 25,000 Pindaris under Ameer Khan penetrated into the British territory of Mirzapore through the Rewa territories without committing any depredation in that State or molesting its Raja John Richardson, the British Agent at Banda, therefore, alleged that the pindari incursion was with the connivance of Raja Jai Singh Deo.[80] The Raja was also suspected of aiding and abetting Dilgunjan Singh, a freebooter and an ally of the Pindaris in his sporadic incursions in the Company's dominions.[81] The Raja denied his connections and affiliations with any anti-British elements.[82] But John Richardson could not feel convinced of his bonafides and decided to deal with him effectively.

Consequently, by the threat of a military demonstration of Company's troops under Col. Martindell which took positions on the Rewa borders, Raja Jai Singh Deo who was not strong enough to resist the British successfully was compelled to accede to a Treaty of Friendship and Defensive Alliance on October 5, 1812[83] by which the British Government promised not to commit any hostility against his State, if he faithfully discharged the stipulations of the Treaty; and undetook to protect and defend his State against foreign aggression with its forces. The expense of such forces would be defrayed by the Raja. The Raja's territorial disputes with the other Indian Powers were to be adjudicated by the British Government. Both of them engaged not to affored asylum or refuge to the persons inimical to any one of them, and would immediately deliver tham to the respective Governments. The British Government engaged not to consider any anti-Raja's representation from his relatives without probing into facts and would respect and honour the authority of the Raja. The Raja promised to permit the Briths force, in intercepting the Pindaris in his territories and arrange for their supplies at the current rate. He also engaged to conform to the British advice and to fulfil the obligations of friendship and attachment towards them.

This treaty greatly limited the freedom of action and reduced the prestige of the Raja. Hard-pressed by the circumstances, he had accepted the Treaty, but was not happy with it. When a British detachment under Capt. Patrickson was posted in his territory in accordance with Article IX of the Treaty for intercepting the Pindaris, he did not provide supplies to it as required and stipulated.[84] He did not permit the establishment of dawk system between the Company's detachment in Rewa and its Agent at Banda.[85] Moreover, he did not allow Persid Ray, the Company's news-writer, to reside in his capital and impolite treatment was accorded to him.[86]

The conduct of the Raja was inconsistent with the Treaty and was viewed seriously by Lord Minto. He was threatened with dire consequences and was made to acquiesce to another Treaty of Mutual Friendship and Defensive Alliance on June 25, 1813[87] by which he was required to abide by all the stipulations of the previous Treaty and had to concede new concessions: such as the establishment of a newswriter in his capital grant of passage to British dawk through his territory permission to British troops or police force and supply of provisions to the British forces operating in his territories.[88] For the enforcement of the Treaty, he was required to maintain his Vakeel either at Banda or with the Commanding Officer of the British troops, to apprehend offenders taking shelter in his State.[89] Besides, he had to pay Rs. 45,173.00 as damages to the Company's Government which it had spent on its troops to enforce the stipulations of the previous Treaty.[90]

This Treaty, though friendly and defensive in character, circumscribed the freedom of the Raja of Rewa more than the previous Treaty. The control of foreign relations, requiring him to fulfil fresh obligations, frequent entrance and movements of British military detachments and police officers and establishment of a newswriter and dawk system in Rewa territories, damaged his independent existence. On the other hand, the superiority of British power came to be recognized in Rewa.

The second State with which the policy of 'Friendship and Defensive Alliance' was adopted, was Cochin, a tributary to the Company's Government since 1791. During the time of Lord Minto, the relations between the Company and Cochin were strained on account of exciting disturbances by Paliat Achin, the Dewan of Cochin, in Travancore and conniving with its Dewan's anti-British activities. After the rebellion in Travancore had been nearly suppressed and the British Government had gained a superior position, the Dewan of Cochin, feeling his position and authority weakened, requested Col. Macaulay, the British Resident, for pardon and promised obedience to the Company's Government.[91] At this, the Resident asked the Dewan to pledge himself under his hand and seal to withdraw and separate himself from alliance with the Dewan of Travancore, to make common cause with the Company, permit its troops to enter his territories freely, supply them with provisions on payment and assist them in their operations against their enemies.[92]

On receipt of a favourable response,[93] Col. Macaulay gave assurance of protection to the person and right of the Raja of Cochin upon the foundation of subsisting Treaty and of protection to the person, family and property of Paliat Achin.[94] However, the cause of the Raja and that of his Dewan could not be separated. To the British mind, it was clear that the Raja had failed to check his Dewan in his hostile proceedings against the Company's Government. The Government-in-Council considered the British Government entitled to require the Raja to enter into such engagement as would prevent his authority and resources from being again employed in the promotion of designs injurious to the Company's interests.[95] Hard-pressed by the Company's

Government the Raja acquiesced, made his Dewan to resign and signed an engagement which was concluded on May 6, 1809.[96]

It was agreed that the friends and enemies of the contracting parties would be considered as friends and enemies of each other, and the Company engaged to defend and protect the territories of the Raja of Cochin against all enemies whatsoever.[97] The Raja agreed to pay a sum equal to the expense of one battalion of Native Infantry of Arcot Rs. 176,037.00 annual to the Company in addition to the usual subsidy of one lac rupees.[98] He also agreed to pay the increased-expense, should it become necessary to employ a large force for the defence and protection of his territories against foreign invasion.[99] He promised to abstain from interference in the affairs of any State in alliance with the Company and also not to communicate and correspond with a foreign State without the knowledge and previous sanction of the Company's Government.[100] He also agreed not to admit any European into his service without the concurrence of the Company,[101] and promised to pay, at all times, the utmost attention to the British advice in connection with the economy of his finances, better collection of his revenues, administration of justice, extension of commerce and encourагement of trade, agriculture and industry.[102] The British Government was empowered to dismantle or garrison fortresses and 'strong places' within the territories of Cochin.[103]

This alliance enhanced the prestige of the British Government in the State of Cochin and virtually crippled the political power of the head of the State both in the internal and external affairs of his administration. No spirit of freedom remained with him to give any further embarrassment to the British power.

In Nagpur and Poona, the Company's Government offered its support to Raghoji Bhonsla and Baji Rao Peshwa in order to intercept elements against their interests and prevented them from taking an ugly and embarrassing situation in their States. Whereas the Pindari menace was silenced with a strong British military force in favour of Nagpur, the southern jagirdars were brought to subordination of the Peshwa with the mediation of Elphinstone, the British Resident at Poona. Although British intervention was motivated by self-interest, its timely help proved of much consequence to the two Maratha States.

In case of Nagpur, Lord Minto afforded liberal military assistance against the Pindari leader, Ameer Khan, who, after exhausting the resources of the Rajput Princes, had made Indore his headquarters for plunders in the neighbouring Indian States and the British territories. In January 1809, Ameer Khan crossed the Narbada and threatened the Raja of Nagpur on the borders of his State.[104] The resources of Raghoji Bhonsla had been so reduced by the effects of war of the 1803 which deprived him of Berar and Cuttack, that he was scarcely strong enough to defend his own dominions from the aggression of the predatory bands. Besides, he had no subsidiary alliance with the British under which he was entitled to claim their protection. On the principle of non-interference, therefore, he ought to have been left to his fate. But in practice, he could not contemplate with indifference the army of Ameer Khan swelled by the Pindaris and ready to overwhelm the State of Nagpur. Though aware of the inconsistency, he placed this problem on broader grounds than that of any routine policy. Expressing his sentiments in his Minute on October 10, 1809, he opined that the question was not whether it was just and expedient to aid the Raja in the defence and recovery of his dominions, but whether an ambitious chief like Ameer Khan irresistible by any power except that of the Company, would be permitted to establish his prowess in the territory contiguous to the Company's borders. The Governor-General held that there could be 'but one solution' of the question and therefore decided that Ameer Khan must, at all hazards, be repelled.[105]

To enforce his decision the Governor-General tendered gratuitious military assistance to the Bhonsla Raja. A force under Colonel Close proceeded towards the eastern frontier of the State, and another under Colonel Martindell was ordered to cooperate with the former. Although the Raja had not formally applied for this assistance, he gratefully accepted it, when an assurance was given to him that no compensation, pecuniary or territorial, was expected of him. On the approach of the British troops, Ameer Khan and his followers lost heart and took to flight. They, first, proceeded towards Seronge and on being pursued, Ameer Khan abandoned his own troops which ran helter and skelter, and he himself escaped to Indore.[106] Therefore, the British forces were recalled. In this way, the Nagpur territories were saved from a terrible incursion. The Court of Directors approved the policy of Lord Minto towards the State of Nagpur and expressed satisfaction at the prompt and effective measures taken by him to foil the aggressive exodus.[107]

In Poona, Peshwa's relations with his subordinate southern jagirdars was a matter of anxiety to the Company's Government which neither wished the Peshwa to act according to his own free will nor to leave the matter as an open source of trouble and strife. Elphinstone, therefore, exerted his pressure to bring about a friendly understanding between the Peshwa and his jagirdars who yielded him neither service nor obedience. In doing so, he was prompted by a desire to prevent the Peshwa from effecting the consolidation of his hold in the southern territories by crippling the jagirdars with his superior military forces. This was in consonance with the British policy of maintenance of peace on British borders. Moreover, these jagirdars were, as a class, useful to the British Government in the past.[108] They had rendered military service to the Duke of Wellington during his expeditions.[109] Hence the Company's Government could not see them wiped out by their vindictive sovereign. To subserve British interest, it was necessary to make an arrangement between the Peshwa and his jagirdars under British guarantee, assuring the rights and privileges of the jagirdars and making them fulfil the conditions under which they held their lands from the Peshwa.[110] The arbitration of disputes in 1812 at Pandharpur between the two parties, and British guarantee of personal security to the recalcitrant jagirdars, so long as they served the Peshwa, conformably to the original conditions of their holdings and traditional custom, brought the desired results.

This settlement[111] brought to an end the source of disturbance in the Poona territories. While it raised British prestige among the jagirdars subordinate to the Poona Court, it prevented the Peshwa from becoming too strong in that region.

PART II

In the year 1807, on the landing of Lord Minto on the Indian shores, the British Empire in India was barely fifty years old. The dual character of the East India Company was well-marked. Its commercial and political activities were parts of a consolidated plan of Empire-building in all its senses. Starting with the commercial end, it had jumped into political arena after about one and a half centuries, largely due to a historical inevitability, for safeguarding its commercial interests but not without the ambition of having political hold over the country. The benefits once drawn from politics, it became difficult to distinguish one from the other till 1813, when its commercial monopoly with India was withdrawn by a Parliamentary legislation as the consequence of an organized agitation by the adventurous English mercantile interests to reap benefits denied to them till then.

The first phase of the Company's career in India lasted until the complete disintegration of the Mughal Empire by the middle of the eighteenth century and the death of Nawab Ali Wardhi Khan of Bengal in 1756. During this period, the commercial prosperity of the Company was based on its peaceful commerce under the patronage of the Indian rulers which was ungrudgingly extended to them and also on their fair dealings with the Indian merchants which they continued in their own interests. Its first aim was to obtain concessions and to by cheap from India. Its other motive was to secure exclusive commercial opportunities for itself as against its European rivals. On the death of Ali Wardhi Khan, the Company's servants showed no scruples to defy the authority of the Nawab for advancing their own interests. They openly abused the commercial privileges and built up military strength, fulfilling their long cherished ambition which Aurangzeb had effectively crippled. In 1757 they removed the inconvenient Siraj-ud-Dowlah from the *musnud* of Bengal and set up a puppet, Mir Jaffar. In the same year they crippled the French and, in 1759, they destroyed the Dutch influence in Bengal. As a result of three Carnatic Wars from 1746-63 the French were ousted from the commercial markets of India.

The period from 1757-64 forms a turning point in the history of the East India Company in India. It is marked by the establishment and expansion of its political influence, military power and firm economic hold over Bengal. The East India Company attained a high political stature by the defeat of the combined armies of Bengal, Awadh and Delhi at Buxar. Consequently, Diwani of Bengal was acquired; control over the Northern Circars was secured, and friendship with Awadh was established. Bengal came under the dual administration of the Company and the Nawab.

The period commencing from 1765 was the worst period in the history of the Bengal *subah*. During this period of power without responsibility, the political and economic life of Bengal was virtually ruined, and mal-administration of the East India Company reigned supreme.[112] In spite of the new advantages secured, the financial position of the Company became hopelessly bad largely due to the illegal private earnings of its employees. All these necessitated parliamentary interference in the affairs of Bengal in 1773, when by the Regulating Act, the political status of the Company was recognised by the Parliament and its affairs were regulated.[113] It acquired a legal status as a semi-sovereign political body acting under the direction and authority of the British

Parliament without loss of its preeminent commercial ascendancy. Henceforth Parliamentary control over the East India Company's affairs began to take shape and eleven years after by the Pitt's India Act of 1784, it was considerably strengthened.

As a consequence of the loss of American colonies, Lord Cornwallis was instructed to adopt a pacific and defensive policy as laid down in Pitt's India Act. In his political relations with the Indian powers, he is popularly known as a non-interventionist. But in actual practice, expediency rather than any set principles guided his deliberations and policies. He considered Tipu Sultan of Mysore as the greatest enemy of the British interests in India, and apprehended the possibility of an anti-British alliance between him and the French in the event of an Anglo-French conflict in Europe. Determined to ward off this dangerous possibility and convinced fully of the inevitability of a war with Mysore as a part of the British struggle for survival and expansion in India, he successfully negotiated an anti-Mysore alliance with the Nizam and the Marathas, apparently for defensive purposes, but really with offensive intentions. At a suitable opportunity, this alliance led to the Third Anglo-Mysore War in violation of the friendly Treaty of Mangalore and the guiding principles of state policy, contained in Pitt's India Act. As a consequence of this war, Tipu had to sign a humiliating Treaty at Seringapatam by which his power was crippled. This was the greatest political achievement of Lord Cornwallis by which British resources and prestige increased, and the chances of anti-British French intrigues became remote.

Sir John Shore was a thorough-going non-interventionist. He carried out literally the instructions of the Court of Directors at the cost of friendship with the Nizam who, on being beaten by the Marathas, lost faith in the British and reorganised his forces under the control and supervision of French officers. This unfriendly attitude of the Nizam and the revival of French influence in the Deccan were the legacies Sir John Shore left for his successor.[114]

Lord Wellesley was a bold and enterprising imperialist. He abandoned the policy of non-intervention, considering it as inexpedient and no longer a guarantee for British security in India. The first Indian prince to be crushed effectively was Tipu Sultan, then known to be the most formidable enemy of the Company, Suspecting his anti-British intrigues with the French and fearing Nepoleon's invasion of India, he defeated and destroyed Tipu in the Fourth Mysore War and brought his State under the Company's control, thus putting an end to the uneasy situation that had so long disturbed British minds in South India.[115]

After this military success, Lord Wellesley turned his attention towards the Marathas whose formidable power stood as a challenge to British expansion in India. Taking advantage of the growing dissensions among their confederates, he persuaded the peshwa to accept British protection by the Treaty of Bassein. This annoyed the other Maratha leaders and led to the Second Maratha War in which Bhonsla, Sindhia and later on Holkar were defeated and compelled to sign humiliating treaties at Devgaon, Surji Arjan Gaon and Rajpur Ghat. The Gaekwar of Baroda who had not participated in the war, accepted British protection by the Treaty of Combay.[116] The Raja of Nagpur agreed to the clauses of the subsidiary alliance and ceded Cuttack to the Company.[117] Sindhia ceded the territories between the Jamuna and the Ganges. By these Treaties, the Maratha confederacy was torn asunder; its political weakness was exposed[118] and its final end seemed to be certain by another military stroke. Besides, Tanjore, Carnatic and Surat were annexed to the Company's territories.

Besides these two wars and annexations, Lord Wellesley dexterously developed an imperial policy based on the subsidiary alliances made with the Indian princes in immediate contiguity to the Company's territories. This was a cleverly drawn-out scheme for an indirect extension of the Company's sovereignty and an effective method of defence without expenditure.[119] He brought the Nizam's Kingdom,

Travancore, Cochin, Awadh and 'temporarily' the Rajputana States under the operation of the subsidiary system.

His successor, Lord Cornwallis came to India to pacify the enraged Maratha leaders by a more considerate policy towards them. But his career was cut short by his sudden demise within a couple of months. However, he outlined a plan for revoking the objectionable policies of Wellesley and appeasing Maratha princes without giving up the major gains.[120] This policy was carried out by his successor, Sir George Barlow, who adhered to non-intervention as a policy of expediency in order to consolidate peacefully the territories acquired by Wellesley. This was the political state of affairs in 1807 when Lord Minto arrived in India as Governor-General.

In the sphere of administration, land revenue and justice were the two most important activities. Since the early years of the East India Company, the land problem had been the central problem of India economy. It was the most important source of the state's revenue. The chief considerations of the Company in its revenue administration were, (1) acquisition of the largest amount of income from land; (2) collection of entire revenue within time and, (3) creation of loyal landed interests.

Till the acquisition of Diwani by the East India Company in 1765, its territorial revenue was limited to Zamindari of Calcutta, the twenty four parganas and the assigned districts of Burdwan, Midnapore, and Chittagong.[121] After seven years, under the irresponsible Double Government of Clive, Verelst and Cartier, the old system was continued without any structural changes, and the highest possible amount of revenue was collected to keep Indian administration self-supporting as well as profitable.[122] From 1772 to 1789, a number of short-term revenue arrangements, unscientific and defective in character, such as quinquennial and annual settlements were made by auction bids. These measures wrought much damage to the existing indigenous land system; proved disastrous to Bengal, Bihar and Orissa and could not serve the British ends in view. Hence, the British attempts to collect revenue by the farming system could not be successful. The quinquennial and the annual settlements proved a failure. Consequently, agriculture and trade decayed, ryots and zamindars sank into poverty and money-lenders flourished. Cornwallis found the result of more than 20 years of unscientific and vacillating land revenue policy as highly unsatisfactory. He, therefore, introduced the Decennial System in 1789 preparatory to the Permanent Zamindari Settlement as was already advocated by several authorities and laid down in Pitti's India Act.[123] He made it permanent on March 22, 1793 against the advice of Sir John Shore and without waiting for the results of the Decennial Settlement.[124]

As far as possible, this settlement was made with the existing zamindars as a deliberate administrative policy. They were vested with legal proprietory rights over land, subject to the payment of revenue on a fixed date and adherence to the revenue law. The assessment of revenue was unduly high, ten-elevenths being the Government share. The Government reserved to itself the right of selling the estates of defaulting zamindars for arrears of revenue. Under the operations of this sale law, a large number of estates were put up to sale as a result of which some of the oldest and most respectable families were deprived of their Zamindaris. The worst feature of the settlement was that the rent which the cultivators were required to pay to the zamindars, was not fixed and their interests and rights were not sufficiently safeguarded. Hence, their traditional relations with the landlord were annihilated; there tenantry-rights were neglected and the zamindars freely ejected them from their lands. In 1799, the zamindars were invested with larger powers to rackrent the tenantry. It led to the reduction in the number of occupancy tenants and increase in the number of tenants-at-will and the agricultural labour. Prior to the arrival of Lord Minto, the inevitable results of the East India Company's efforts to get the highest revenue from land were economically and socially ruinous to the zamindars as well as the ryots. While the former managed to minimize its evil consequences accruing to them, the latter found themselves helpless, and remained exploited for a long time.

In the Ceded and Conquered territories, Lord Wellesley introduced short-term periodical settlements on the principles of the Bengal system with a view to making it permanent after a *decade*.[125] The authority of the Calcutta Board of Revenue was extended to those territories. Here also the assessment was excessive and very often unfairly distributed. The increasing arrears of revenue and the difficulties of its collection and management prompted Sir George Barlow to appoint a Board of Commissioners on June 11, 1807, consisting of R. W. Cox and Henry St. George Tucker to superintend the settlement and collection of revenue. By this time, the reports about the defective working of the Permanent Settlement of Bengal and the favourable reports about experimental Ryotwari System in the Presidency of Madras, made the Court of Directors sceptical about the good results of the Permanent Settlement and reduced its importance in their estimation.

In the Northern Circars of Madras Presidency, where local Chiefs existed, the Bengal system of land revenue was introduced in 1802.[126] In its southern part, where there were no zamindars, Captain Read introduced Ryotwari System with the assistance of Munro, Macleod and Graham in 1798 as an experimental measure.[127] Subsequently, it was introduced in Canara, Tanjore and territories between the Krishna and the Tunghbhadra.[128] Economically and administratively, this system appeared to be more gainful to the Company as it was made directly with the ryots; and the middle man's profit which accrued to the zamindars elsewhere, could enrich its coflers. Although, this system required a large number of revenue officers, it enabled the Government to have direct contacts with the people. By the time of the departure of Sir George Barlow, advantages of this system were hardly very clear in the British mind and a controversy had started among the supporters of this system and those of the village system, headed by Mr. Hodgson.[129] In this system also, the land was over-assessed and pecuniary considerations were dominant.

Besides land revenue, customs duty was also an important source of income to the East India Company. The Company's Government levied customs of two kinds, *viz.*, the 'Calcutta Customs' or town duties and the 'Government Customs'. The former were collected by the Company in virtue of their factorial rights and were leviable on all goods imported into Calcutta and the latter fetched 2½ per cent realized on articles exported from or imported into Bengal, Bihar and Orissa. To inspect, regulate and control the customs, Warren Hastings appointed a Board of Customs, which established five custom-houses at Dacca, Calcutta, Hugli, Murshidabad and Patna. In addition to these, a chain of *chowkeys* were erected to collect the duty on goods exported to the westward through the passes of the hills bounding Midnapore, Birbhum and Raniganj. But these measures had no great effect in removing the prevailing anomalies in internal trade. Complaints of undue and illegal exactions from merchants at the *chowkeys* were frequent. Cornwallis abolished these *chowkeys*, five custom-houses, and Government customs duty. But there remained the Calcutta town duties. He established a new custom-house at Manji, a place at the confluence of the Ganges and the Gagra for collection of duty of 2½ per cent on goods exported from or imported into the Company's territories in Bengal, Bihar and Orissa by that route.[130]

These measures, however, did not remove the restraints on internal trade in the Bengal Presidency. Lord Wellesley reestablished the Government customs July of 2½ per cent on the exports from and the imports into the parts of Calcutta.[131] But with all these, the merchants continued to be hampered in their trade on account of vexatious practices on the part of the customs-officers who often made illicit gains in releasing the goods of the merchants. The whole system, therefore, needed overhauling; and steps, in this connection were taken by Lord Minto.

Another important aspect of British administration in India was the dispensation of justice. During the regime of power without responsibility, the existing judicial system degenerated, and necessitated European superintendence in 1769. But this could not be effectively done as the Europeans were strangers to India and its way of life. Warren Hastings reorganized the system by establishing two courts of superior judicature at Calcutta under the name of the Sadar Diwani Adalat and Sadar Nizamat Adalat, with powers to hear appeals from civil and criminal courts in the districts. A Supreme Court was established at Calcutta by the Regulating Act, with a Chief Justice and three other judges. It was declared to have full power and authority to exercise and perform all civil, criminal, admirality and ecclesiastical jurisdictions'. Besides these courts of judicature, the head farmers of *parganas* were allowed to exercise a local jurisdiction in all petty disputes of property, not exceeding the value of rupees ten and decrees were considered final in all such cases. But in spite of these efforts, the inhabitants of the provinces were groaning under the wrongs inflicted upon them by officers in whom the fiscal and judicial powers had been combined. According to J. W. Kaye, "The whole administration of the country was well-nigh brought to a stand-still".[132] These evils were, however, remedied to some extent by his successor.

Lord Cornwallis laid a super-structure on the system established by Warren Hastings and provided it with a broader basis. He separated the revenue collection from the administration of justice.[133] He reorganized the administration of justice by establishing four Provincial Courts of Appeal in the vicinity of Calcutta, at Patna, Murshidabad and Dacca which also acted as Courts of Circuit for the administration of criminal justice. For the guidance of the officials and the people, a Code of Laws was introduced.[134] The punishment of mutilation was replaced by imprisonment, for a maximum of 14 years. Justice was made cheap, and the judgment seat accessible. This was not a complete remedy. With the passing of years, the judicial business accumulated fearfully and the people wrung their hands in despair to think, 'what a laggard was English justice with the weight of the Regulations on its back'.[135] The new system was hardly sufficient to cope with the growing need for a large number of more efficient judicial courts. Lord Wellesley appointed Assistant District Judges in 1803 at stations working under an unusually heavy load of business. The Court of Directors questioned the expediency of the measure as the amount spent was greater than the business transacted. The judicial administration remained in this state will the appointment of Lord Minto as Governor-General of India.

The police was largely associated with the criminal justice. Its chief functions were to assist the revenue authorities in revenue collection, maintaining public tranquillity, prevent crimes, apprehend criminals and disturbers of peace, and prosecute them before the criminal courts. The Company's territory was infested with dacoits, gang-robbers and *thugs*. For their apprehension, Warren Hastings entrusted police functions to the influential zamindars.[136] Cornwallis found this system hopelessly inadequate and highly unsatisfactory. He, therefore, took away police functions from the zamindars and reorganized the system with a *thana* as a unit and a *Darogah* as its head. But this system also could not work efficiently and effectively. The *Darogahs* were not respectable men of education. They were found ill-paid and indulging in corrupt practices to increase their income. Extortion of huge sums as bribes became a regular feature with them, and opportunities for it were not infrequent.[137] They were viewed with fear by some, with jealousy by others and ignored by most of the inhabitants. They could not maintain law and order within their jurisdictions. Hence the police system needed a complete shake up.

In the establishment of postal services, the Company was impelled by the need for a regular supply of information regarding the conduct of their officials, movement of their enemies, and market conditions. It maintained *harcaras* for communicating information between one settlement and another. But the regular postal system was introduced by Clive in 1766 for conveying the official communications of the Company as well as private letters of Europeans. Warren Hastings improved this system by establishing postal divisions in the Bengal Presidency under a Postmaster-General. Cornwallis further regulated the postal system and established overland postal system, and established postal links with Bombay and Madras.

Lord Wellesley established district *dak* establishments under the superintendence of the Collectors. At each stage of the postal route, two runners and a *massalchi* were maintained. Parcel posts were also started during him time. Heavy despatches were carried by runners in the *bahangis*. On the acquisition of the Ceded and Conquered territories, he extended the postal system to these areas. Notwithstanding these postal arrangements, the postal system in India was in its rudimentary stage. Delay and expensiveness marred the efficiency of the existing system. The crude *dak* system of the Indian traders was much more efficient than the Government postal system.

In the field of education, the East India showed no interest. It pursued a policy of indifference and non-interference. Pre-occupied as it was mostly with commerce and politics, it neglected the essential responsibility of educating its Indian subjects and did not take the place of the Indian patrons of education, whom it had supplanted. Hence education did not find a place in its official programme till the end of Lord Minto's administration. Consequently, that existing system of education was left free to take care of itself. However, education was not without its supporters among English men in India. Private individuals, officials in their private capacity and the Christian missionaries did show some interest in education within their limited capacity and resources. They worked as pioneers in this field. In 1718, Rev. Richard Cobbe, Chaplain of St. Thomas's Church, established a school for the education of poor Protestant European children; in 1719, Schultze, a great Danish missionary, opened two schools in Madras; in 1772, Frederick Schwartz founded a school in Trichinopoly for European and Eurasian children; in 1794, William Carey founded a school at Dinajpore, and in 1804, the London Missionary Society opened numerous schools in Vishakhapatnam and Chinsura.[138] Besides, Warren Hastings opened the Calcutta Madrassa in 1781. In 1784, Sir William Jones, the Judge of the Supreme Court, was instrumental in founding the Royal Asiatic Society of Bengal to promote Asiatic studies and researches. Jonathan Duncan, the Resident at Banaras, established a Sanskrit College at Banaras in 1791. Lord Wellesley founded the College of Fort William in 1800 for the training of civil servants. The professors of this institution made valuable contributions to Indian languages. But there was no separate fund for the promotion of education and learning, and the need for it was realized only during the time of Lord Minto.

An important corollary to British rule in India, was the Christian missionary activity for the diffusion of the Gospel and the spread of Christianity. The missionaries first came to the Malabar Coast in the wake of the Portuguese in the early 16th century. They made the Church of Rome unpopular by their religious intolerance and persecutions, forcible conversions and inter-racial marriages, and their bitter criticism and condemnation of Indian religious and social life. But their work was largely confined to the Presidency of Madras, till the Baptist Missionaries of England settled down at the Danish settlement of Serampore and carried on their work under William Carey, Marshman and Ward. The work of these Protestant missionaries was persuasive and propagandist rather than aggressive.

During the Governor-Generalship of Lord Wellesley, the missionary work increased in British India. His administration, on the whole, proved propitious to their activities. He appointed William Carey as one of the professors in the College of Fort William. This direct encouragement was fully exploited by the missionary leaders. Their work excited uneasiness among the people of Bengal during the time of Sir George Barlow. In South India, they were watched with distrust suspicion and doubt on account of the Vellore Mutiny which was dubbed by the Court of Directors as a reaction against their religious propaganda to preach Christianity in the streets and villages and distribute controversial religious tracts.[139] This stiff attitude of the Directors created resentment amongst the Christian missionaries against the unsympathetic official policy towards them. In England, it revived a vigorous movement in favour of uninterupted freedom for the missionary work in India under Wilberforce, Sir Charles Grand and Rev. Claudius Buchanan, leading to Parliamentary intervention in 1813.

All these activities of the East India Company could not remain unnoticed by the Parliament of England, the sovereign political institution of the English people. Certain events and affairs in India, such as Clive's victories; acquisition of the rich provinces of Bengal and Northern Circars; overthrow of political influence in the rival European companies and mal-administration of the East India Company in Bengal, bringing a bad name to the English people, drew the attention of the Parliament to the Company's affairs. A section of British public opinion, very vocal in Parliament, emphasized the incompetence of a trading corporation to handle Imperial matters satisfactorily and doubted the wisdom of allowing it to assume the role of a state.[140] Its disordered finances and approach to the Government for a loan provided an excuse for interference in its affairs. In these circumstances, the regulation of East India Company was brought from the personal and nominal arena of the Royalty to the broader and more effective sphere of the national politics of England.

The Regulating Act of 1773 constituted an epoch-making stepping stone in the history of the Parliamentary control over the affairs of the East India Company. Since then, the Company carried on the administration of India in all its phases including its commercial activities under the superintendence, direction and control of the parliament and was ultimately responsible to it for all its acts and policies in India. In the name of the Crown, the Cabinet of England nominated the first Governor-General of Bengal and a Council of four to assist him and accorded them the status of Central authority over the Presidencies which were declared subordinate to it in foreign relations. This was a faint beginning of the centralized administration of the East India Company in India. A Supreme Court of Judicature was also established in Bengal to regulate the conduct of European British subjects in India and to guard against the dangers of the Governor-General becoming absolute in the Company's territories.[141]

Due to the lack of the clear definition of the powers of the Governor-General, his Council, the Presidency Governments and the Supreme Court, the Regulating Act could not function smoothly and satisfactorily. Consequently, the Parliament redefined the powers and jurisdictions of the Supreme Government and the Supreme Court in the Amending Act passed by it in 1781, and removed the existing elogs.[142]

With the passing of Pitt's India Act in 1784 commenced the second stage in the establishments of Parliamentary control over Indian affairs. It established more effective control of the British Cabinet over the Company by the appointment of an official body, called the Board of Control and a Secret Committee. In practice, the authority of the Court of Directors was considerably diluted and a sort of double government was established. Though the new system of superintendence, direction and control by the Home Government over the Indian affairs proved to be dilatory and cumbersome, the Parliament felt satisfied that its wishes would ultimately prevail in matters of Indian administration.

Twenty years after the passing of the Regulating Act, the Parliament took up again Indian affairs for renewal of its Charter in 1793. During this time, the advocates of the *laissez faire* commercial ideal and champions of missionary work laboured hard to get the doors of India open for their free commercial and religious enterprises. Due to the stiff opposition of the Company, the concessions could not be conceded to the merchants and missionaries of England. The Company was allowed to carry on its commercial and political work for another period of twenty years without any well-marked change in the policy of the Parliament, beyond regulating its finances, asking it to pay the expenses of the Royal forces serving in India, extending jurisdiction of the Supreme Court and powers of the Governor-General-in-Council. The motion defeated in the Parliament could not suppress the issue raised. On the questions of freedom of trade with India and missionary work in that country were organized powerful movements in England which were destined to engage the attention of the Parliament during the Charter debates in 1813.

REFERENCES

1. Seton to Edmonstone, Aug. 17, 1808, For. Deptt. Pol., Cons. Sept. 12, 1808, Cons 28.
2. Setons to Edmonstone, June 6, 1810, For. Deptt. Pol., Cons. June 21, 1810, Cons. 42.
3. Seton to Edmonstone, June 16, 1810, For. Deptt. Pol., Cons. July 7, 1810, Cons. 37.
4. Aitchinson, C. U., *op cit*, vol. V., pp, 64-66.
5. *Ibid.*, pp. 89-91.
6. *Ibid*, pp. 53-56.
7. Resident to Edmonstone, June 20, 1813, For. Deptt. Pol., Cons. July 7, 1813, Cons. 25.
8. Edmonstone to Resident, July 9, 1813, For. Deptt. Pol., Cons. July 9, 1813, Cons. 33.
9. Seton to Edmonstone May 30, 1808, For. Deptt, Pol., Cons. June 13. 1808, Cons. 16.
10. Lord Minto to Hokar, July 15, 1808, For. Deptt. Pol., Cons. July 18, 1808, Cons. 1.

11. Holkar to Lord Minto, Oct. 5, 1808, For. Deptt. Pol., Cons. Oct. 5, 1808, Cons. 49.
12. Resident to Chief Secretary, Madras, July, 14, 1811, For. Deptt. Pol., Cons. Nov. 8, 1811, Cons. 4.
13. *Ibid*.
14. *Ibid*.
15. *Ibid*.
16. Resident to Chief Secretary, Madras, Sept. 18, 1811, For. Deptt. Pol., Cons. Nov. 18, 1811, Cons. 5.
17. *Ibid*.
18. Resident to Chief Secretary, Madras, Sept. 18, 1811, For. Deptt. Pol., Cons Nov. 8, 1811, Cons. 5.
19. Lord Minto to Barlow, Nov. 8, 1811, For. Deptt. Pol., Cons. Nov. 8, 1811, Cons. 6.
20. Aitchinson, C. U. *op. cit*., Vol. VIII, pp. 32-33.
21. *Ibid*, pp. 61-66.
22. Major Walker to Chief Secretary Bombay, Dec. 10, 1807, For. Deptt. Pol., Cons. Jan. 18, 1808, Cons. 14 and Major Walker to Governor of Bombay, Feb. 7, 1808, For. Deptt. Pol., Cons. Apr. 18, 1808, Cons. 5.
23. Governor of Bombay to Lord Minto, Feb. 4, 1809, For. Deptt. Pol., Cons. Aug. 5, 1809, Cons. 51.
24. Seton to Edmonstone, Nov. 26, 1806, For. Deptt Secret, Cons. Dec. 18, 1806, Cons. 21.
25. *Ibid*.
26. Seton to Edmonstone, Nov. 26, 1806, For. Deptt. Secret, Cons. Dec. 18, 1806, Cons. 21. (There was no Law of Primogeniture among the Mughals in India. However, it had become an established practice to designate the eldest son as the heir-apparent.)
27. *Ibid*.
28. Lord Minto to Emperor of Delhi, Dec. 26, 1807, For. Deptt. Pol., Cons. Dec. 28, 1807, Cons. 1.
29. Seton to Edmonstone, Feb. 13, 1808, For. Deptt. Pol., Cons. April 25, 1808, Cons. 40.
30. Seton to Edmonstone, Oct. 7, 1809, For. Deptt. Pol., Cons. Oct., 24, 1809, Cons. 11.

31. Seton to Edmonstone, Jan. 16, 1810, For. Deptt. Pol., Cons. Feb. 6, 1810, Cons. 4.
32. Resident Capt. Sydenham to Edmonstone, Dec. 20, 1808, For. Deptt. Secret, Cons. Jan. 16, 1809, Cons. 37.
33. Edmonstone to Resident, Capt. Sydenham, Dec. 31, 1808, For. Deptt. Secret, Cons. Jan. 2, 1809, Cons. 104.
34. Edmonstone to Resident, Capt. Sydenham, Feb. 17, 1809, For. Deptt. Secret, Cons. Feb. 20, 1809, Cons. 21.
35. Capt. Sydenham to Lord Minto, Aug. 4, 1810, For. Deptt. Pol., Cons. Sept. 6, 1810, Cons. 23.
36. Edmonstone to Capt. Sydenham, Sept. 20, 1810, For. Deptt. Pol., Cons. Dept. 25, 1810, Cons. 44.
37. Awadh Papers, Jan. 1808—Dec. 1815, pp. 74-75.
38. *Ibid.*, pp. 94-97.
39. *Ibid.*, pp. 94-107.
40. *Ibid.*
41. Awadh papers, *op. cit.*, pp. 209-10.
42. *Ibid.*, pp. 215-16.
43. *Ibid.*, pp. 506-7.
44. *Ibid.*
45. *Ibid.*
46. *Ibid.*, pp. 506-7.
47. Seton to Edmonstone, May 8, 1807, For. Deptt. Pol., Cons. May 28, 1807, Cons. 25.
48. Seton to Edmonstone, Nov. 22, 1807, For. Deptt. Pol., Cons. Dec. 14, 1807, Cons. 42.
49. *Ibid.*
50. Lord Minto to Seton, dated Nil, For. Deptt. Pol., Cons. Feb. 6. 1809, Cons, 104.
51. Military Commander in Haryana to Seton, March 17, 1809, For. Deptt. Pol., Cons. April 10, 1809, Cons. 56.
52. *Ibid.*
53. Military Commander in Haryana to Seton, March 17, 1809, For. Deptt. Poly Cons. April 10, 1809, Cons. 56.
54. Military Commander in Haryana to Seton, March 17, 1809, For. Deptt. Pol., Cons. April 10, 1809., Cons. 56.

55. Seton to Edmonstone, July 15, 1809, For. Deptt. Pol., Cons. July 22, 1809, Cons. 45.
56. Aitchinson, C. U., *op. cit.*, Vol. V, pp. 151-53.
57. Aitchinson, C. U., *op. cit.*, Vol. V, pp. 151-53.
58. Agent to Edmonstone, Dec. 1, 1808, For, Deptt. Secret, Cons. Dec. 19, 1808, Cons. 8, & Pol. Letter to Court of Directors. Sept. 27, 1808.
59. Agent to Edmonstone, Dec. 4, 1808. For. Deptt. Secret Cons. Dec. 19, 1808 Cons. 9.
60. Agent to Col. Martindell, Jan. 16, 1809. For, Deptt. Pol, Cons. Feb. 16, 1809. Cons. 36.
61. Pol. Letter to Court of Directors, April 19, 1809.
62. Proclamation issued by John Richardson, Jan. 29, 1809, For. Deptt., Pol Cons. Feb. 20, 1809, Cons. 33.
63. Second Proclamation dated Nil, For. Deptt. Pol. Cons. Feb. 20, 1809. Cons. 34.
64. Killadar to Agent, March 27, 1809; For. Deptt. Pol. Cons. April, 29, 1809 Cons. 5.
65. Agent to Killadar, March 27, 1809, For. Deptt Pol. Cons. April 29, 1809 Cons. 6.
66. Agent to Edmonstone, May 26, 1809, For. Deptt. Pol., Cons. June 6, 1809 Cons. 22.
67. Report from Chief Secretary's Office July 5, 1809, For. Deptt. Pol., Cons. July 8, 1809, Cons. 40.
68. Aitchinson, C. U. *op. cit.*, Vol. V. pp. 159-60.
69. Agent to Edmonstone, Aug. 26, 1807. For. Deptt. Pol., Cons. Sept. 8, 1807 Cons. 41.
70. *Ibid.*, Nov. 10, 1810. Cons. 107.
71. Agent to Edmonstone, Dec. 16, 1810 For. Deptt. Pol., Cons. Jan. 4, 1811. Cons. 25.
72. Translation of an Ikrarnamah entered into by Gopal Singh, dated Nil, For. Deptt. pol., Cons. April 3, 1812, Cons. 49.
73. Manifesto addressed to all Chiefs of Bundelkhand by John Richardson, Nov. 22, 1811, For. Deptt. Pol., Cons. Nov. 22, 1811, Cons. 3.
74. Agent to Killadar, Jan. 12, 1812, For. Deptt. Pol., Cons. Jan. 12, 1812, Cons. 5.

75. Aitchinson, C. U. *op. cit.,* Vol. V., pp. 322-24.
76. *Ibid.*
77. Article V of the Treaty.
78. Article IX.
79. British Agent at Banda to Edmonstone, March 10, 1812, For. Deptt. Secret, Cons. May 7, 1812, Cons. 6.
80. *Ibid.*
81. British Agent at Banda to Military Commander, March 22, 1812, For. Deptt. Secret, Cons. April 13, 1812, Cons. 10.
82. British Agent at Banda to Mily. Cdr., March 22, 1812, For. Deptt. Secret, Cons. April 13, 1812, Cons. 10.
83. Aitchinson, C. U., *op. cit.,* Vol., V, pp. 250-53.
84. Secretary, Secret and Pol. Deptt. to all British Resident, March 29, 1813, For. Deptt. Secret, Cons. April 9, 1813, Cons. 22.
85. *Ibid.*
86. Agent at Banda to Secretary Secret and Pol. Deptt. April 29, 1813, For. Deptt. Secret, Cons. May 9, 1813, Cons. 22.
87. Aitchinson, C. U., *op. cit.,* Vol. V, pp. 253-56.
88. Articles I and III.
89. Articles IV and VI.
90. Article IX.
91. Dewan to Col. Macaulay, Feb. 7, 1809, For. Deptt. Secret, Cons. March 13, 1809, Cons. 24.
92. Col. Macaulay to Dewan, Feb. 8, 1809, For. Deptt. Secret, Cons. March 13, 1805, Cons. 25.
93. Translation of a Note of Dewan to Macaulay, Feb. 8, 1809, For. Deptt. Secret, Cons. March 13, 1809, Cons. 24.
94. Resident to Dewan, *Ibid.*
95. Chief Secretary, Madras to Macaulay, April 19, 1809, For. Deptt. Secret, Cons. May 20, 1809, Cons. 15.
96. Aitchinson, C. U., *op. cit.,* Vol. X, pp. 161-164.
97. Article I of the Treaty.
98. Article II.
99. Article III.
100. Article VI.

101. Article VII.
102. Article IX.
103. Article XIII.
104. Resident to Persian Secy., April 22, 1809, For. Deptt. Secret, Cons. May 15, 1809, Cons. 10.
105. Minute of Lord Minto, dated October 10, 1809.
106. Resident at Nagpur to Lord Minto, Jan. 12, 1810, For. Deptt. Secret and Separate., Feb. 6, 1810, Cons. 8.
107. Secret letter from Court of Directors, Sept., 18, 1811.
108. Minute of Colebrooke, April 10, 1812, For. Deptt. Secret. Cons. Aug. 28, 1812, Cons. 26.
109. *Ibid.*
110. Elphinstone to Lord Minto, July 9, 1812, For. Deptt. Secret, Cons. Aug. 14, 1812, Cons. 6.
111. Aitchinson, C. U., *op. cit.*, Vol. VII, pp. 230-35.
112. Parkinson, C. N., *Trade in the Eastern Seas*, p. 199.
113. Keith, A. B., *A Constitutional History of India*, pp. 68-76.
114. The Directorate of the Chamber's Social Organisation: *The British Crown and the Indian States*. p. 18.
115. Lovet, Verney, *India*, p. 102.
116. Panikkar, K. M. *Indian States and the Government of India*, pp. 11-12.
117. Aitchinson, C. U., *A Collection of Treaties, Engagements and Sanads*, Vol. VII, p. 56.
118. Mehta, M. S. *Lord Hastings and the Indian States*, p. 7.
119. Panikkar, K. M. *op. cit.*, p. 10.
120. Embree, A. T., *Charles Grant and British Rule in India*, p. 232.
121. Baden-Powell, B. H. *The Land System of British India*, Vol. I, p. 393.
122. Gupta, H. L. *Land System Under the East India Company*, an article in Journal of Indian History, April, 1964, p. 171.
123. Gupta, H. L., *op cit.*, P. 172.
124. Kaye, J. W., *Administration of the East India Company*. p. 183.
125. Baden-Powell, *op. cit.*, Vol. II, p. 16.
126. Dutt, R. C., *The Economic History of India*, p. 86 (The general standard by which the revenue demand was regulated appears

to have been two-thirds of the gross collection from the cultivators).

127. *Ibid.*

128. *Ibid.* pp. 84-93.

129. Mukerjee, N., *Ryotwari System in Madras*, p. xiv.

130. Dutta, K. K. *Survey of India's Social Life and Economic Condition in the 18th Century*, pp. 58-63.

131. *Ibid.* p. 63.

132. Kaye, J.W., *op. cit.*, p. 330.

133. *Ibid.*

134. Aspinal, A., *Cornwallis in Bengal*, pp. 95-98.

135. Kaye, J. W., *op. cit.*, pp. 340-41.

136. *Fifth Report of the Select Committee on the Affairs of the East India Company*, Vol. II, p. 71.

137. *Ibid.*

138. Nurullah, Syed and Naik, J. P. *A History of Education in India*, pp. 62-64.

139. Mill and Wilson, *History of British India*, Vol. VII, p. 342.

140. Banerjee A. C. *Indian Constitutional Documents*, Vol., I. pp. 19-21.

141. Banerjee, A. C. *op. cit.*, pp. 25-29.

142. Banerjee, A. C., *Indian Constitutional Documents*, Vol. I, pp. 66-67.

3

Administrative Measures

With the acquisition of a large territory in India by the East India Company, the need for its retention and consolidation engaged the attention of its administrators. This required a sound administrative policy. However, the administrative measures adopted were largely intended for the welfare of the governed. For the maintenance of peace, order and tranquillity, necessary for affording stability to the Empire, in the collection of revenue without coercion, dispensation of justice, without harassment and irritation, organization of police for ensuring safety of life and property and institution and maintenance of public utility services, were essential prerequisites of a sound administration. In the beginning, exercise of power without responsibility was the greatest drawback of the Company's Government in Bengal which had caused havoc to the people and brought bad name to it. Subordination of principles of administration to commercial considerations had been the chief defect in its administration. Consequently, the administration in Bengal had become productive of abuses and oppressions. The permanent zamindari system of Lord Cornwallis could not be carried out in the spirit in which it was formulated. The soundest views of its authors which were not given the form of legislation were conspicuous more by their negligence than for their observance by his successors. The zamindars and officers of the revenue department exercised judicial powers for which there was no legal provision. Legal proceedings varied with individuals and circumstances. Judicial system under the European judges, with their inadequate knowledge of Indian traditions and laws, had its own inherent limitations. The police was only an instrument in the hands of the administrators for creating conditions conducive to the British interests. The powers of the Government were undefined and were all muddled together. These basic troubles affected the unity and strength of the Company's Government in Bengal.

The defects of the administrative organization could not escape the attention of Lord Minto. As Governor-General, his main work was preservation and promotion of the East India Company's interests. In his work in India, he was not altogether a free agent. He was required to carry out the policies laid down for him by his superiors at the Leaden-Hall Street. Effecting a balance between the multiple conflicting interests, he proceeded cautiously in his administrative activities in the Home Department to avoid uncharitable criticism of his work. In the sphere of administration, his period was merely a link between his predecessors and successors. An estimate of his comprehension, outlook and judgment can be had from his measures of internal administration such as revenue, judiciary, police, customs, postal system, education and missionaries.

Revenue

India being predominantly an agricultural country, land revenue administration constituted an important item of internal administration. On his arrival in India, Lord Minto found inefficiency in the Permanent Settlement existing in Bengal. It was fixed assessment made with a certain class of landholders who were considered as the legitimate owners of the soil. The amount payable to Government from each estate was fixed in perpetuity. The productiveness of the land might increase a hundred per cent, but the zamindar carried the same amount of revenue to the office of the Collector. He might lease it out as he pleased in large or small holdings. Cultivators were reduced to the worst condition as the zamindars could extort from them as much as they desired. Hence the prevailing system in Bengal needed a complete shake-up. Besides, Lord Minto found a controversy raging between the Government of India and the Court of Directors about the land revenue system to be finally introduced in the British territories, where revenue collection was being done on an experimental basis and definite settlement was yet to be introduced. Such territories were the Ceded and Conquered districts in the north and the territories taken from Mysore in the south. The influential members of the Bengal and Madras Governments, trained in the school of Lord Cornwallis, tenaciously adhered to the principles of perpetual settlement and favoured its adoption. The Home authorities, however, did not agree to this view. Influenced by new and more favourable experiments carried on in certain parts of the Madras Presidency, they, first, suspended and finally prohibited the inclusion of an assessment in perpetuity in the provinces to which it had not been extended.

Lord Minto noticed that the Board of Revenue could not exercise effective control over the outlying districts of the Diwani Provinces. He, therefore, took an important step in this direction under Regulation XIII of 1811 which authorized the Board of Revenue to depute one of its members temporarily to any part of the country, if necessary, to superintend the formation of settlements or the conduct of officers employed in the revenue collections. The members so deputed could individually exercise all such duties, powers and authority in the places to which they were deputed.[1] During the period of appointment, a single member of the Board at the Presidency exercised all the duties, powers and authority collectively vested in it for remaining parts of the provinces of Bengal, Bihar and Orissa. On the termination of the period of appointment, all correspondence and papers relating to the subject were to be deposited in the office of Secretary to the Board of Revenue.[2]

The rules regarding the grant of *patahs* by the proprietors of land to their tenants were revised as it was found that considerable abused and oppression had been committed by zamindars, talukdars, and farmers of land with respect to the attachment of the property of their tenants for the recovery of the arrears of rent. In their place, new rules were promulgated by which some of the clauses of Regulations of 1793, 1795 and 1803 precluding the zamindars from granting leases for a period exceeding 10 years were rescinded. By the Regulation V of 1812, they were authorized to grant leases for any period, considering the convenience to themselves, to their tenants and improvement of their estates. The Courts of Judicature were made competent to give effect to the clauses of the engagements contracted between the parties and enforce payments agreed upon between them.[3]

Some measures were also undertaken to ameliorate the depressed condition of the cultivators who were unscrupulously exploited by the new proprietors of land. The existing Regulation permitted the persons purchasing land at the public sales to annual engagements, contracted between the late proprietors of the lands and his under-tenants, with the result that the cultivators were required to pay enhanced rent to its new proprietors at their will. This caused heavy financial burden to the tenants. The Government discouraged this practice without depriving the new land-holders of the right to enhance rent by declaring enhancement of rent legally cognizable, if there was a specific contract to that effect. Under no other circumstances could the rent be enhanced nor could the enhancement by illegal means be recoverable by suit in the law-court. If, however, the proprietor levied more from the cultivators, they were entitled to a refund of the excess with damages through the Court of Justice.[4]

The law of distraint was amended to ensure recovery of rent. A Zamindar, a talukdar or a revenue farmer intending to distraint the property of his tenant for the recovery of rent was required to serve on him a demand-notice containing the *jumma wassil baukee*.[5] No distraint without a formal notice was deemed legal and valid. If the notice could not be served personally on him, it was to be affixed on the gate of his residence. Distraint proceeding against him could, however, be stayed, if he questioned the validity of demand and executed a bound before a judge or District Collector or the Pargana Kazi or the distrainer with 'good' security binding himself to institute a suit in the law-court within fifteen days or agreeing to pay the amount adjudged to be due from him with all costs of suit. To safeguard the legitimate interests of a tenant, his ploughs, implements of husbandry and cattle employed in agriculture were not subject to distraint on account of areas of rent.[6]

In this respect, Regulation V of 1812, known as the Panjam, looked apparently better than the notorious 'haftam' of 1799, but in practice could not serve as an adequate safeguard to the interests of the tenantry. As most of them could not make use of the law-courts owing to their ignorance and poverty, and those, who could manage to approach the law-courts, were not granted quick and inexpensive justice. Consequently, land-alienation by rack-renting continued. The new purchasers of the zamindaris managed to enhance the rent in violation of the spirit of the Regulation V of 1812. These proceedings of the zamindars continued to affect adversely the economic condition of the peasantry who suffered from hardship and misery. To remedy these defects, drastic rules and regulations were needed, but could not be adopted.

Revenue Arrangements in Ceded and Conquered Territories

In accordance with the plan formulated in 1803, the permanent settlement in the Ceded and Conquered territories was to be introduced in 1813. Lord Wellesley was so strongly impressed with a conviction of the advantages of the Permanent System and was so eager to promise those advantages to the North-Western zamindars, that he omitted in his Regulation XXV of 1803 to make the permanency of the settlement conditional on the confirmation of the Court of Directors.[7] The omission was subsequently repaired by Sir George Barlow who declared in his Regulation X of 1807, that the *Jumma* which might be assessed in the last year of the temporary settlements then ensuing should remain fixed for ever provided the arrangement received the sanction of the Court of Directors. He also appointed a special land commission to superintend the settlement operations. Lord Minto accelerated the work of the Commission appointed by his predecessor. It was instructed to report on the condition of land and state of cultivation to enable the Government to conclude the proposed settlement. In short, the object of the Government was to secure a 'local report' to confirm its policy.[8]

After a comprehensive enquiry on the spot by visiting all the collectorates and consulting the revenue collectors, the commissioners submitted their report on April 13, 1808,[9] which did not conform to the expectations of the Government. They did not find conditions favourable for the immediate introduction of permanent settlement and did not make categorical recommendations in favour of the proposal. They stated that the resources of the Ceded and Conquered districts were not assessed; one-fourth of the arable land was uncultivated; most of the lands were held by farmers, but proprietory rights were being contested by other claimants, and Government had not taken a decision on this ticklish issue. In the absence of any precise laws regarding the proprietorship of land, a perpetual settlement with the occupants of the land was likely to be resented by the disputants and might lead to ruinous litigations. There was also a fear of currency depreciation in the market which was destined to entail losses to the Government, if land was fixed in perpetuity.[10] Besides, the Court of Directors' attitude towards the permanent settlement was undecided. They feared if the Home authorities withheld their confirmation to the proposed settlement, the landholders would lose their faith in the Government and would begin to suspect that advantages of permanency were held out to them to extort a higher revenue. They therefore, considered permanent settlement to be inexpedient at that time, and recommended the extension of short settlements and further inquiries with detailed surveys before a final decision could be taken.[11]

The report of the Commissioners did not find vavour with the Government of India, but the Leaden Hall-Street appreciated their arguments and seriously doubted the wisdom of implementing the plan of 1803.[12] They had already begun to doubt the soundness of the permanent settlement in theory as well as in practice within a decade of its actual operation in Bengal. Its failure to achieve all the objectives envisaged by Lord Cornwallis, viz, a regular and steady flow of revenue, security and protection of the rights of all the agricultural classes and the permanency of the demands of landed proprietors on the ryots, was exercising their minds. They looked for an alternative mode of revenue settlement by which the inconveniences of the permanent settlement could be avoided, its 'mistakes', 'evils' and 'injustices' eliminated, its basic advantages retained and larger revenue assured.

With this current of thought flowing into their minds, the Court of Directors accepted the recommendations of the Revenue Commissioners and wrote to the Governor-General-in-Council on February 27, 1811 that it would be premature to fix in perpetuity the land rents at so early a stage of their connection with those territories, when their knowledge of the revenue actually derived was imperfect.[13] They were of the opinion that prior to the extension of permanent settlement, a careful investigation of local peculiarities and a minute and detailed survey of those territories were indispensable. Nine months after, on November 27, 1811, they addressed another letter to the Governor-General in which they reiterated their previous note of caution citing the example of Bengal where permanent settlement was introduced thirty years after its occupation. They stated that unless the Government were sufficiently acquainted with the resources of the Ceded districts and with the rights and ancient customs of the different classes of landholders inhabiting there, it was not feasible to venture open a step of so much importance.[14] Positive instructions were, therefore, given to the Governor-General not to commit the Government to a perpetual settlement, he had in view, till he had obtained their sanction.[15]

The most important reasons for this change in the climate of opinion on the nature of settlement of the Ceded districts were the considerations of fiscal and commercial interests. The East India Company was interested in the enhancement of its economic resources to finance the expenditure on its empire-building activities. Its income from the Indian trade had been dwindling and its land revenue resources had not been increased since the introduction of permanent settlement. Moreover, the news about the new land revenue settlement in the Madras Presidency had shown them better prospects of revenue. It was, therefore, quite natural for the Home authorities to reconsider the 'expediency' of extending a settlement of doubtful advantages before exhausting all possibilities of finding out a system financially more advantageous to them.

To meet the temporary expediency, they suggested a short-term settlement not exceeding five years which the Government of India carried into effect.[16] The final decision on the land revenue settlement for the Ceded and Conquered districts was, however, postponed for consideration at a more opportune time.

Revenue Arrangements in Madras Presidency

The land revenue settlement in the Madras Presidency also engaged the attention of the Government. The Permanent Zamindari Settlement was already extended to the Northern Circars and the Jagir lands around Madras, and the Ryotwari System was introduced in Baramahal. Salem, Ceded districts, Coimbatore, Malabar, Canara and Carnatic as an experimental measure. Eventual settlement in these districts and a type of settlement to be introduced in other parts of the Presidency had yet to be decided.

After Munro's departure to England on leave in 1807, prior to the arrival of Lord Minto, his favourite system began to be subjected to criticism. Hodgson, a member of the Tanjore Committee initiated a controversy pointing out the defects of the settlements experimented upon by Capt. Read, Macleod, Graham and Munro; and advocated village lease settlement in their place.[17] The Tanjore Committee agreed with his views and wrote to the Madras Board of Revenue that the ryotwari settlement held no promise of financial benefit either to the ryot or to the Government proportionate to the risk of loss due to the uncertainty about the extent of cultivation, amount of produce and market fluctuations.[18] As against it, the village lease settlement appeared to the Committee to be more advantageous to the Government and less burdensome to the ryot who were to share equally profits and losses accruing from the land. They felt convinced that the system, they favoured, would improve agriculture, afford greater security to the ryots due to the fixity of rent minimize the chances of an over assessment.[19]

The Board of Revenue endorsed the view and the Governor-in-Council was impressed by the arguments in favour of the village system. Consequently, on the orders from the Government, the Board of Revenue decided on July 11, 1808 to introduce village-lease-system for three years in Nellore, Palnad, the Ceded districts, the Northern and Southern Divisions of Arcot, Trichinopoly, Coimbatore and Tinnevelly, preparatory to a permanent village settlement.[20] Under this system, the village tent was to be assessed after due consideration of the area under cultivation, the quantity of produce and of actual collection of each village. In the event of extraordinary calamities, the Government had discretion to grant abatement of rent. In the *mirasi* districts, where the hereditary landed property existed, the settlement was to be made with mirasidars who were jointly responsible for the payment of rent. In nonmirasi districts, the Collectors were emprowered to make settlements with Patels, Maharajans or heads of villages. For the security of the ryots, the renters were required to grant pathans to them.[21]

The Court of Directors approved this system, but preferred leases for five years. They considered three years period as too short a term preliminary to a permanent one. Very soon they became septic about the advantages of a permanent settlement and were disinclined to support its adoption without fully ascertaining the actual state and resources of the lands; their capacities of improvement and the tenures and rights of individuals. They were of the view that the people would not receive the benefits of a settlement unless influence of the village chiefs over the cultivators was destroyed and those prejudices which had contributed to the prevailing evils, were removed. They, therefore, restricted the Government from declaring the village-lease-settlement permanent, without their specific sanction.[22]

Thus village rent scheme was launched with an amount of uncertainty about its future. In actual working, the scheme showed little signs of success. Neither larger areas of land could come under cultivation nor large amount of rent could be collected by the renters. To some extent, the competition among the renters tended to produce this effect. In many cases, the renters would have failed to fulfil the terms to ryots. The Collector of the Northern Division of Arcot noticed frequent disputes between the ryots and the renters, the one complaining of unjust demand and the other of unnecessary and evasive delay in the payments of the rents. The Collector of the Southern Division of Arcot reported that in many cases, the ryots were made to pay more rent and in most cases, the full rent, even for the waste lands cultivated by them for which they were entitled to a remission for the first three years according to the former system. He predicted that if the new system continued, the resources of the district on the expiry of the lease would be found far more deteriorated than they were.[23]

Similar conditions prevailed more or less in all the districts in which the introduction of village rents had been attempted. This was destined to seal the fate of the village-lease-system. The Madras Government, however, ascribed the defective working of the village-lease-system to the 'degraded and impoverished state' to which the people had been reduced under the previous Government and to the ryotwari system of land revenue administration which had hitherto prevailed in those areas. To have renewed the lease for another term of three years would have been acting in opposition to experience as the short period of the triennial lease had been productive of much mischief and hardly a few of the land-holders would have consented to a renewal of the lease for similar terms without reductions of land revenue. It only remained, therefore, either to relinquish a large portion of the land-revenue or to devise some other principle in its place. This necessitated fresh thought on a system, suitable for the Madras Presidency. After due consideration to all shades of opinion, the Board of Revenue recommended a Decennial Settlement to become eventually permanent in the belief that somewhat longer prospect of enjoying the produce of their improvements, would stimulate the industry of the ryots and also secure the due payments of the revenue. The Government concurred with this recommendation and the settlement for ten years was concluded with the heads of the villages collectively or in their absence with some respectable inhabitants of the village to become perpetual with the approval of the Court of Directors.[24]

The Court of Directors expressed surprise at the establishment of the village system as a measure for permanency conditional on their sanction, when they had not been apprised of the result of the triennial leases. They had ample evidence from Bengal that great errors had been committed in concluding the permanent settlement there. In their letter dated December 16, 1812, they criticized the conduct of the Madras Government in having the recommendations of the Board of Revenue acceded to such a settlement in opposition to their orders.[25] They ordered that in all unsettled districts, the ryotwari system should be adopted and in places where the village rents had been already established, the leases should be declared terminable at the expiration of the period for which they had been granted.[26]

These views of the Court of Directors were largely influenced by Munro who impressed all who met him in England with the 'depth and range' of his knowledge of the land revenue administration in India. He was a strong critic of the Cornwallis system and an ardent champion of the ryotwari settlement. In his evidence before the Select Committee of the House of Commons on Indian affairs in 1812, he made a strong case for the land revenue system, he favoured. The Court of Directors felt convinced by the arrangements contained in Munro's evidence and took a firm stand on the revenue settlement to be adopted in the Madras Presidency. The Select Committee also held similar opinion.[27]

The scheme of the Court of Directors was received by Lord Minto in June 1813, but it could not be implemented during his regime as he was to retire within a few months. Consequently, this work devolved upon his successor in whose time arrangements were made to effect the change-over from the village lease to the ryotwari system. In the districts, where Decennial Settlement had already been made, the Government had to wait till the expiry of its term.

Judiciary

The judicial system introduced by Lord Cornwallis was growing obsolete. Its inherent defects were clearly visible by the time of Lord Minto. It appeared from its defective working that it was not in keeping with the needs of the time. Justice was not expedited. Dilatoriness in deciding cases, expensive character of judicial proceedings and uncertainty of justice were the pronounced features of judicial administration. Justice was virtually impeded and its object was almost defeated. Arrears became so numerous and decisions were so long delayed as to amount to a virtual denial of justice. Attempts were made from time to time to remedy these imperfections. Charges and fees were imposed in order to render justice more expensive and discourage litigation; additional courts were established; additional powers were given to the judges and the privilege of appeal was subjected to new limitations.[28] But the accumulation of arrears still continued to constitute a serious evil. The judicial system had become so cumbersome and unwieldy that serious apprehensions were entertained of its breakdown. The outcome of it was loss of public confidence in the British judicial system. Under these circumstances the need for a better system and more efficient judicial personnel was badly felt.

Civil Justice

The decaying judicial system engaged the attention of Lord Minto. Removal of its defects, prevention of the abuse of power, introduction of economy, and efficiency in judicial system exercised his mind. These objects were sought to be attained by promulgating new Regulations which introduced changes in the constitution of the Civil Courts and jurisdiction and authority of the judicial officers.

By Regulation XIII of 1808, all causes of a civil nature, except those specifically referred by the Governor-General-in Council or by the Sadar Diwani Adalat for trial in the first instance by the Provincial Courts, were instituted in the zilla or city courts. Suits for property not exceeding Rs. 50.00 were tried by the Native Commissioners vested with the authority of the Munsiffs.[29] All causes exceeding 5000 sicca rupees which were ultimately appealable to the Sadar Diwani Adalat, were now to be instituted in the Provincial Courts of Appeal in order to relieve the people of unnecessary delay and financial embarrassment.[30] To relieve the Sadar Diwani Adalat of some of its work-load, a provision was made for a heavy security deposit for filing an appeal in the highest court of civil judicature. This had the tendency to discourage litigious and groundless appeals by the defeated party for the sole purpose of retaining the disputed property to the prejudice of the real proprietor so long as door for an appeal was open.[31] It also saved the expenses and botheration of real proprietor.

After two years, by Regulation XIII of 1810, an attempt was made to expedite the dispensation of justice at the level of the superior courts by increasing the powers of the single sitting judges of the Provincial as well as the Sadar Diwani Adalat in the absence of other judges. They were made competent to hold a sitting of the Court and pass orders as they might deem just and consistent with the Regulation, respecting the admission of evidence and examination of witnesses.[32] In this way, the single sitting judge began to exercise all powers connected with the trial of the suit. In the Provincial Court, he could receive miscellaneous petitions decided by any zillah or city Court. This measure was necessitated because of the prevailing defect in the working of the higher courts where cases were to be decided by the majority decision and on many occasions, it was not possible for the majority of the judges to assemble to hear an appeal.[33] The consequence was that the flow of business was often obstructed in the absence of the requisite majority. For instance, in the Provincial Court of Appeal at Patna, justice remained suspended for over nine months in 1809, because of the absence of the second judge on circuit and of the third judge on deputation to enquire into charge preferred against the judge and magistrate of Saran.

Criminal Justice

Delays of a similar nature, although not to a like extent, prevailed in the administration of criminal justice. Owing to the heavy load of judicial work, District Judges, better devoted to civil work, could hardly pay timely attention to the disposal of criminal cases. Owing to this defect, an interval often intervened between the apprehension of a prisoner and his actual commitment to the law-court, detaining in confinement for an indefinite period a person against whom no charge could be substantiated and thus subjecting the innocent to the punishment of the guilty. Some enactments were also passed for the effective conduct of investigation by the local officers and provision was made for admission to bail of persons not charged with crimes of heinous nature and for the dismissal of frivolous complaints and the avoidance of unnecessary delay between the apprehension of the accused and his examination before the Magistrate.

Under Regulation XIV of 1810, the judges of the Courts of Circuit were empowered to instruct the zillah and city magistrates to accept sufficient bail from the accused charged with offences not bailable.[34] They were further made competent to direct the magistrate to admit to bail any prisoner whose trial might be referable to the Court of Nizamat Adalat.[35] In cases, where the prisoner could not find bail, the judge of the Circuit Court was to transmit, with the least possible delay the proceedings relating to him, to the Sadar Nizamat Adalat. The judges of that court were required to deliver their 'futwa' as soon as possible. This Court could revise a sentence passed by the lower court depending upon the evidence and circumstances of the case. In every case of revision, the reasons for it were to be recorded.[37]

A new addition to the wheel of judicial administration was the appointment of Assistant Magistrates and Joint Magistrates in the districts for the despatch of public business, under Regulation XVI of 1810. They were made subordinate to the District Magistrates in the discharge of their judicial duties and were guided by the instructions of the Court of Nizamat Adalat Assistant Magistrates when not stationed at the same place with the District Magistrates were authorized to correspond directly with the Governor-General-in-Council, the Court of Nizamat Adalat, the Court of Circuit and other public authorities. But all their monthly and periodical reports and accounts were passed through the District Magistrates.[37]

These judicial enactments were undoubtedly an improvement on the existing judicial system from the point of view of administrative organization. But they could not prove to be of any marked benefit to the seekers of justice at the law-courts. Justice continued to be delayed and expensive. Multitude of legal formalities continued making expeditious justice impossible. The evils of distraint were neither removed nor restricted. Practically, no provision was made for the protection of the indebted ryots against the attachment of his means of agriculture by his creditors. Thus the minor judicial changes made during Lord Minto's time were of little consequence to the convenience and welfare of the governed.

Tanjore: Surat: Duncan's settlement of Kathiawar: Wellesley and Oudh: annexation of the Carnatic: Wellesley's asperity in despatches to native States: his wisdom in the matter of the Company's trading monopoly: Wellesley recalled.

It was Wellesley's 'conscientious conviction, that no greater blessing can be conferred on the native inhabitants of India than the extension of the British authority, influence and power'. Dundas, however, wrote (March 21, 1799) of the States which had enjoyed longest the advantage of intimate supervision of their affairs, with a studied moderation which should not deceive us as to the thorough contempt entertained, even in late eighteenth-century England, for the Company's administration and morals:

> 'The double Government existing in the Carnatic has long been felt as a serious calamity to that country. It enfeebles the natural resources of the country and, above all, tends to continue that system of intrigue and consequent corruption which has been imputed to the Madras Government so much more than to our other settlements. It is singular to remark, that the country of Oude is the other part of India, where the purity of the Company's servants has been most suspected, and that

> the same circumstance of a double government has always been assigned as the cause... . Tanjore... is exposed in a certain degree, to the same inconveniences which have been injurious to the government of the Carnatic'.

In the case of Tanjore, it would be depressing to recall even a few of the events that justify Mr. Roberts, who never exaggerates, in his conclusion that 'our connection with the country had not, on the face of it, been particularly creditable either to our statesmanship or our good faith'.[38] To take the story up in its closing chapter in 1786 the Company, acting by the advice of pundits, chose a villainous lunatic as Raja. He was deposed after some years of michief, and Wellesley inherited a disputed succession:

> 'After a most tedious enquiry, I brought the several contending parties to a fair discussion (or rather to a bitter contest) in my presence; and after an argument which lasted three or four days. I proceeded to review the whole case... . At length the contending parties unanimously concurred in the expediency and justice of the treaty,'[39]

which ended Tanjore's existence as even nominally a sovereign State (October 25, 1799) and pensioned the candidate formerly passed over in the madman's favour.

Earlier in the same year the Nawab of Surat died. The Company, by arrangement, since 1795 had defended Surat Fort. So Wellesley annexed the State under a justification anticipating Dalhousie's 'lapse' doctrine; he ruled that, when the Company displaced the Mogul Empire in any district, it acquired the right to settle the fate and successions of principalities formerly under Delhi.

The Governor of Bombay, Jonathan Duncan, carried out the annexation unwillingly. His own practice went to the other extreme; by recognising 'princes' all *Zemindars*, however petty, who paid tribute to the Mogul, he studded Kathiawar with the multitude of kinglets that are one of the most striking anomalies in the princes' question to-day; His Highness of Bikaner is reported to have stated that one of the Kathiawar 'princes' is sovereign of nothing but a well. Historians condemn Wellesley's action.

> 'The whose proceeding was characterised by tyranny and injustice';[40] the most unceremonious act of dethronement which the English had yet performed as the victim was the weakest and "most obscure",[41] 'the procedure was certainly high-handed'.[42]

But it was justified by results, and also by the situation of Indian affairs. When maintenance of a legal right means the community's abiding disadvantage, the paramount Power does well to act illegally.

Oudh was a more complex problem. Its defence was a Company liability; and in India, as the Duke of Wellington observed there was no frontier. In Wellesley's early despatches, the threat of Zaman Shah, ruler of Kabul, recurs frequently. He established himself in Lahore, 1796: returned to Afghanistan the next year, but in 1789 reappeared and notified the Nawab of Oudh and the Governor-General that they were to assist him in restoring the Emperor and rescuing him from the Marathas.

> 'he should consider our not joining his royal standard, and our not assisting him in the restoration of Shah Allum and in the total expulsion of the Mahrattas, in the light of an act of disobedience and enmity'.[43]

Insurrections in his rear caused this hectoring gentleman to retreat again; and in 1800 he was dethroned and blinded by his brother, and became a refugee in British India. Ranjit Singh, later famous as 'the Lion of the Punjab', presently succeeded to more than his power.

Meanwhile Oudh compelled attention from Wellesley. For years it had been drained of 'the maximum tribute which it could afford,'[44] it was overrun by rascally Europeans, and 'behind the all too powerful screen of British bayonets[45] was oppressed and pillaged. The subsidiary system 'meant the sacrifice of independence, of national character, and of whatever renders a people respectable'.[46] But Wellesley's main concern was not for the misery of the people of Oudh; hardly any statesman of the period bothered about the flesh and blood actuality which abstract maxims of statesmanship concealed. His main concern was the menace from Afghan invasion, to which the rabble which formed the Oudh army was a first line of defence. Therefore, though Oudh was bled white by what it had to pay already—for

> 'the subsidy demanded from Indian rulers was totally out of proportion to their revenue. In the subsidiary armies the scale of pay was lavish, and the cost of quarters and equipage high—'[47]

he demanded that the Nawab entertain a much larger body of Company's troops, sufficient to be 'at all times adequate to your effectual protection,' whose charges could be easily met: 'nothing further is requisite than that you should disband the numerous disorderly battalions at present in your service'.[48]

The cool, breath-taking ignorance behind that advice justifices a minute's pause'. All the Nawab had to do, to settle all his difficulties finally, was to 'sack' all his own retainers! The Governor-General's brother Arthur on the other hand, comments continually on what was notorious to every intelligent inhabitant of India, British or Indian—the hardship and harms following from Indian loss of all honourable or lucrative employment:

> 'Conceive a country, in every village of which there are from twenty to thirty horsemen who have been dismissed from the service of the state, and who have no means of living except by plunder. In this country there is no law, no civil government... . This is the outline of the state of the countries of the Peshwa and Nizam' (1804).

Even the Governor-General in less lucidly self-complacent moods could see something of the undercurrents of resentment as when he writes to the Directors (April 22, 1799), on a conspiracy nipped in time at Bonares:

> 'You will observe that the persons concerned in this reason are almost exclusively Mahomedans, and several of them of high rank. It is a radical imperfection in the constitution of our establishments in India, that no system appears to have been adopted with a view either to conciliate the goodwill or to control the disaffection of this description of our subjects, who we found in possession of the Government and whom we have excluded from all share of emolument, honour, and authority, without providing any adequate corrective of those passions incident to the loss of dignity, wealth, and power'.

What 'adequate corrective' *could* be applied, and what thought (if any) lies behind such verbose and confused lucubrations as these (so characteristic of authority when its attention is vaguely drawn to some stirrings of dissatisfaction in the administered sections of mankind), it would be idle to stop to enquire.

By 1799 Wellesley's mind was set on annexing Oudh. Unfortunately, the Nawab somehow or other managed to keep up his huge payments of tribute, and though endowed with every possible fault from his subjects' side, was embarrassingly loyal. Wellesley therefore merely badgered him to accept 'an improved system' of government; the proposer's power and pertinacity made this suggestion an order' though the Nawab knew it meant additional costs for 'protection'. In November, 1799, he said he wished to abdicate—he meant, in favour of one of his sons. Wellesley was delighted. His Excellency, he told the Directors,[49]

> Your honourable Committee will observe that His Excellency declares this resolution to have originated in the reciprocal aversion subsisting between himself and

> his subjects (an aversion, which on his part, he declares to have grown into absolute disgust), and in his sense of his own incompetency....'

If His Excellency 'should ultimately persevere in this declared intention'—and

> 'it is my intention to profit by the event to the utmost practicable extent; and I entertain a confident hope of being able to establish, with the consent of the Vizier, the sole and exclusive authority of the Company within the province of Oude and its dependences, or at least to place our interests in that quarter on an improved and durable foundation'

then 'it must be deemed entirely and absolutely his own voluntary act'. The Company had long been past-masters of the art of making some vacillating Indian potentate, anxious only to evade decision, sign the order for his own execution. But that Governor after Governor should be capable of such contradictory tangles of argument and while plainly flaunting his own vivacity of pursuit and inflexibility of will should nevertheless assert that everything was done by the victim's free will, so that his after-wriglings were arrant treason and 'Oriental' duplicity, helps us to understand why our dealings on the imperial stage have so often been misunderstood by foreigners as hypocritical. What followed was a repetition of earlier pages in Company history. The Nawab was offered a treaty; he pointed out that nothing was said about his successor; he was informed that there would be no successor, whereupon he 'formally withdrew his offer of abdication,'[50] and the Governor-General was 'extremely disgusted at' his 'duplicity and insincerIty'. The delinquent received a letter remarkable even from the most arrogantly sure of his rightness of all Indian Governor-Generals. Waterloo, no doubt, was won on the Eton milling-grounds: but the Empire's administration was certainly learnt in a less public but even more terrible place. Wellesley, in a letter after letter, rules like the indignant headmaster about to flog a boy after scathing exposure first of his sinfulness:

> 'The duty imposed on me by my public station, and the concern which I take in your Excellency's personal honour and welfare, as well as in the prosperity and happiness of the inhabitants of Oude, compel me to communicate to you, in the most unqualified terms, the astonishment, regret, and indignation which your recent conduct has excited in my mind.

The reader will note that nothing of the time-honoured formula is omitted; the castigation is for the castigatee's good, and is obviously going to hurt the castigator worse.

> 'The conduct of your Excellency ... is of a nature so unequivocally hostile ... that your perseverance in so dangerous a courage will leave me no other alternative than that of considering all amicable engagements between the Company and your Excellency to be dissolved, and of regulating my subsequent proceedings accordingly. I am, however, always inclined to hope that your Excellency may have been inadvertently betrayed into these imprudent and unjustifiable measures by the insidious suggestions of evil councillors, and being ever averse to construe your Excellency's actions in such a manner as must compel me to regard and to treat you as a Prince no longer connected with the Company by the ties of amity and of a common interest; I trust that my next accounts from Lieutenant-Colonel Scott may enable me to view your Excellency's conduct in a more favourable light, but best my wishes in this respect should be disappointed, it is my duty to warn you I excellency in the most unreserved terms...'.

His Excellency was urged to see to the two really important matters:

> 'namely, the reform of you military establishment and the provision of funds for the regular monthly payment of all the Company's troops in Oude.
>
> 'The least omission or procrastination in either of those important points, must lead to the most serious mischief'.

The troops, at any rate, he was to have, whether he wanted them or not. They were sent, 'and he was simply ordered to find money for paying them,' He was told that he could not alter this decision, though he might,

> 'present reasoned objections, to which he replied, not without dignity: "If he measure was to be carried into execution, whether with or without his approbation, there was no occasion for consulting him".[51]

This, the reader will see, was impertinence; and he completed the offence by pointing out that the disbandment his own army threw the soldiers out of employment, and was ill-advised enough to reinforce his argument by appeal to his treaty with Sir John Shore. Wellesley found this behaviour 'highly deficient in the respect due to the first British authority in India'. The culprit was accordingly hauled back to the headmaster's study, and told to be very, careful. If,

> 'in formally answering his lordship's letter, His Excellency should think proper to impeach the honour and justice of the British Government in similar terms... the Governor-General would consider how such unfounded calumnies and gross misrepresentations... deserve to be noticed'.

In such documents as these (a good many of them exist) the paramount Power does not condescent to anything so essentially base as argument. The conduct in question is always 'unjustifiable', objections are 'calumnies', and of course 'unfounded'. 'If the party injured, observes Mill,'[52]

> 'submits ... his consent is alleged. If he complains, he is treated as impeaching the honour and justice of his superior, a crime of so prodigious a magnitude as to set the superior above all obligations to such a worthless connection'.

The upshot of a prolonged and tortuous business, in which the Nawab showed surprising sprit and a hunted animal's sense of territory where he stood some chance of safety, was that in November, 1801, he had to cede the territory that Oudh had obtained by the Rohilla War:

> 'By a singular reverse of circumstances the Company were able, after having pocketed the price, to seize the territories, and thus obtain possession both of price and subject,'[53]

'extremely rich and valuable territory... known henceforth as the Ceded Provinces,' which Henry Wellesley was sent to govern, an appointment which the Directors considered nepotism, though we can believe that the Governor-General's aim was not merely to give his brother a lucrative post, but to be himself in specially intimate touch with the district. The remainder of Oudh became a State more abjectly vassal than any other in India; but there was this gain, that the subsidy ceased. The Company's gains were immense, in security of financial advantages, in strategy, in quietness.

No serious writer has ever pretended that the episode was from first to last anything but a bullying exercise of overwhelming strength. Wellesley did what little was possible to make things easy for the dispossessed soldiery, and even for the Nawab, to whom he had written so insultingly. But it is hard to follow Mr. Roberts when he says that the Governor General,

> 'looked through the immaterial barriers of treaties and agreements to the wretched condition of the administration Oudh, which he so eagerly desired to rectify'.[54]

It is true that he refused to regard Indian States as genuinely independent Powers, and with some reason. But there is no justice in yourself 'looking through the immaterial barriers of treaties and agreements' when you explode with fury at every divagation of others from the rigid letter of any and every promise; and as to the 'eager desire to rectify' the miseries of Oudh—after the richest regions had been carved off and added to Company territory:

'The scandalous and shameless misgovernment of the country continued unabated without the slightest improvement until 1856, when the authorities in England insisted on annexation'.[55]

Wellesley's conduct would have been both more honourable and more profitable to both the Company and the people of India (whose interests still had to wait some time before they were considered by the high contending parties) if he had acted straightforwardly on his convictions and made annexation more sweeping and thorough instead of trying to persuade himself and others, to assert—with prohibition of any contradiction by the Nawab—that he was keeping promises and engagements.

On July 25, 1801, the Carnatic at last passed to the Company, one fifth of the revenues being settled on the Nawab as a pension, the annexation was overdue and justified by every moral consideration; even Mill thinks that, done frankly, it would been an excellent action,[56]

'we should have deemed the Company justified in proportion as the feelings of millions are of more value than the feelings of an individual, in seizing the government of the Carnatic long before and on the same principle, we should rejoice that every inch of ground within the limits of India were subject to their sway'.

But it was not done frankly or decently. At the taking of Seringapatam Wellesley, to his intense glee, secured documents which he held proved treacherous collusion between the Nawab and Tipu. They proved nothing of the sort, and were merely flowery compliments; and the Nawab was so inconsiderate as to die while his conduct was under discussion. This evasion, however, did not disconcert the Governor-General; his son had,

'succeeded to the condition of his father, which condition was that of a public enemy...consequently ... the British Government remained at liberty to exercise its rights,

> founded on the faithless policy of its ally, in whatever manner might be deemed most conducive to the immediate safety and to the general interests of the Company in the Carnatic".[57]

Wellesley's despatches form what be the most question-begging and self-righteous body of literature in existence. 'Rights' 'founded on what? On alleged behaviour strenuously denied by the accused and at this very time under alleged investigation. Clause follows clause, every phrase specious and opposed by pleading protest; the protest is not even noticed, the doubtful statement rises instantaneously into a principle established and beyond query and deductions or supports to it are thrust forward—in the same infallible and unfaltering fashion!

He put round the Nawab's palace a ring of troops, and on the very day of his death demanded that his successor a boy under age (who 'had succeeded to the condition of a public enemy') should abdicate the sovereignty. Himself always loud in denunciation of the impropriety he found in the conduct of Indian princes, he acted consistently as if they were blocks of unfeeling wood, queerly warped into wickedness, but having no other semblance of response or responsibility. It is better to drop a matter so depressing to remember.

There remained the ever-overhanging cloud of the Nawab's 'debts', which we have examined in Book III. Chapter II.

To continue to quote the Governor-General's missives to inferrior Powers will only exasperate the reader. It was not easy for the Resident at Haiderabad to carry out his orders (June, 1799) to rebuke 'in the most public and pointed manner' a noble who had spoken disrespectfully of the Company's government. Wellesley thought that the culprit should perhaps be deprived of his pension. The Nizam was commanded to be awakened 'to a just sense of the extensive advantages' his connection with the British had brought him. His enemies had been destroyed at little expense to him, and 'from a weak, decaying, and despised state, he has recovered substantial strength and resumed a respectable posture among the princes of India'. His dominions, 'formerly the most vulnerable,' were now secure. All true; but hardly tactful. Fortunately, the Residents at the two courts most subject to the Governor-General's asperity were men whose revulsion from the duties so overbearingly inculcated upon them would induce them to soften his speech in deliverance. Major Kirkpatrick at Haiderabad lived and acted as an Indian; Colonel Palmer at Poona constantly condemned the score of Indians, which was now the rule. They were treated, he said (1802), 'with a mortifying *hauteur* and reserve,' 'in fact, they have scarcely any social intercourse with us'.

When he moved out of the domain of the Company's relations with Indian States, Wellesley could show a detached wisdom in advance of his time. He tried, without success, to persuade the trading concern who remployed him, to abandon a spirit of narrow monopoly that was extremely harmful to British interests. A very small proportion of India's trade with the West was by means of Company vessels; foreign countries, and America in especial, were thrusting into it. English traders, forbidden to do what traders of any nation but their own could do, worked through this foreign shipping. So did Company employees, secretly. Wellesley and Dundas urged that the Company should set aside some vessels for the use of non-Company British trading, to keep immense sums now being lost to aliens. Thus might that pre-eminence of wealth and power' (in India) 'which has proved so important to the general interests of the British Empire' be preserved and increased. But selfish views prevailed, especially those of the shipping interest, 'under a most false and erroneous idea that it is prejudicial to their interests'. His far-sighted policy offended the Directors almost more than the expense of his wars did.

Warren Hastings, watching with mixed feelings while Wellesley did all that he had desired to do but for which he had lacked the means and personal position, noted the unwisdom of the latter's habitual scorn of the Company Directors: 'If I was in his confidence I would tell him that civility costs little'. England has never been able to regard India as a matter which came close to her own necessities, except in 1857; and the British Government, occupied with the Continental struggle, could not bring itself to believe that large armies and glorious wars were necessary in India. Assaye faded before the sun of Austerlitz: even Tipu was not the Corsican: the defeat of French men-of-war off Malacca by merchantmen that they intended to plunder, though gratifying to national pride, was not Trafalgar. These Indian wars were costly. These princes that we engaged to support seemed more deserving of being left to such fate as the devious twist of events might bring them. Wellesley was recalled (1805) under a cloud, even amid mutterings of impeachment. But no one wanted to renew the idle show which the persecution of Hastings had provided. The Directors concurred in his observation that 'the disturbances occasioned by Jeswant Rao Holkar and his adherents have proved a vexatious and painful interruption of tranquillity;'[58] saw through his half-hearted assurances that matter was now practically settled; and were weary of the whole business. Lord Cornwallis was sent back, though in age and failing strength, King Log in place of King Stork.

Lord Cornwallis, whose return had been fitfully imminent ever since he left, and whom Pitt 'regarded as an infallible cure for all ills,'[59] governed for two months, dying October 5, 1805, at Ghazipur, where be has buried in accordance with his injunction, 'Where the tree falls let it lie'. An excessively sick men, he sought only peace, for which it is the custom to censure him. But the man who has himself seen the squalor and ugliness of war, how wretched in defeat, how melancholy in triumph, is less enthusiastic about it than, the man who knows it merely as a sequence of exciting rumours and happy intrigues. The old warrior was so weary of pomp and the trappings of regality, that the rejected the titles of 'Excellency' and 'Most Noble', and all the grandeur of Wellesley's time.

The charge of pusillanimity is brought against him and his immediate successor, Sir George Barlow (who had been senior member of his Council), for abandoning the Rajputs to the Marathas (as Cornwallis and Sir John Shore had formerly abandoned the Nizam, and for the same reasons). It is a shameful enough story: yet these inevitable recoils follow on policies of aggression and vigour beyond a Government's power to sustain. In essentials it does not differ from such later abandonments as those of Assyrians or Druses, after they had been encouraged to show friendliness to British effort in the World War. Wellesley had sown native India with distrust, and piled up indebtedness. It is generally overlooked that it was actually in his time that the process of withdrawal began, in those last days when there was a distinct flagging of energy and outward thrust. When the Maharaja of Jodhpur did not choose to accept the Governor-General's conditions of protection, Sindhia had received what looked uncommonly like a direct invitation to handle him in his own way—the Raja being delivered over to Satan, that he might be taught not to blaspheme:

> 'The British Government has no intention to interfere in any a manner between your Highness and the Rajah of Jodepore ... . Your Highness will act according to your pleasure towards the Raja'.[60]

His Highness did.

Even more did Holkar and his Pathan ally, Amir Khan, act according to their pleasure towards the Rajput chiefs. Holkar after being harried into the Punjab—the Sikhs neither helped his pursuers nor molested him, but watched the double incursion and drew conclusions which kept peace between Ranjit Singh and the Company until his death (1839)—was given generous terms by Barlow. His persecutors withdrew to their own territory leaving the Marathas, hemmed in between Sikhs and Company, to pour out their profligacy of pillage on the confined Rajput area. The oppressed only put up the plea that the Company had in fact succeeded to the paramountcy of the Moguls, and were under obligation to succour the weak. But the plea went unheeded. Inward decay worked with outward pressure, as commonly in such circumstances. The Rajput rulers were degenerates, and all the barbaric cruelty miscalled Rajput chivalry—such as widow-burning, often on a terrific scale (the saner and humaner Marathas disdained while not actually prohibiting the rite—was allowed to keep this attractive race on a childishly savage level.

There is generally some one incident, when the affairs of any nation have sunk into squalor, which to men's imaginations seems to fling a torch up against the truth. It came now, in the death of Krishna Kumari, the lovely Udaipur princess, in 1807. When internecine war, fomented by Sindhia and Amir Khan, broke out about the hand of the girl-princess, her father accepted the suggestion that she should drink poison and in that fashion bring his people peace. Her patience and valour and the pity of her passing—though to us this will seem a merciful anticipation of death on some warrior's funeral pyre—have never ceased to stir Indian memory.

Sir George Barlow, after some vacillation, was not permanently appointed. He is usually considered (and was considered at the time) to prove once more the utter unfitness of any Company man to take up the supreme authority. A Governor-General of these antecedents was apt to be ill served, from the jealousy of his late equals above whom his new authority had raised him. Also, the Company's administration was already shedding—except in 'frontier' regions, such as the annexed parts of Mysore and Malabar (as, later, in the Punjab of the Lawrences)—its earlier improvised and vigorous character, and was accumulating all the merits and shortcomings ascribed to 'bureaucracy'. The Company man now, said Thomas Munro,

> 'learns forms before he learns things. He be comes full of the respect due to the court, but knows nothing of people. He is placed to high above them to have any general intercourse with them. He has little opportunity of seeing them except in court. He sees only the worst part of them, and under the wort shapes; he sees them as plaintiff and defendant, exasperated against each other, or as criminals; and the unfavourably opinion with which he too often, at first, enters among them ... is every day strengthened and increased. He acquires, it is true, habits of cautious examination and of precision and regularity but they are limited to a particular object and are frequently attended with dilatorincess, too little regard for the value of time and an inaptitude for general affairs, which require a man to pass readily from one subject to another'.[61]

Barlow had willingly seconded Wellesley's imperial schemes; he was equally ready to support the Directors' new opposite policy of retrenchment and retreat.

The main event of his brief administration was the Vellore Mutiny. The Madras Commander-in-Chief ordered the sepoys to wear a special and obnoxious turban, trim their beards as directed, and give up caste marks. These 'ill-judged regulation[62] were considered important enough to risk empire for; Munro told the Governor, Lord William Bentinck:[63]

> 'However strange it may appear to Europeans, I know that the general opinion of the most intelligent natives in this part of the country is, that it was intended to make the sepoys Christians'.

To us, conscious of our absolute impartiality in religious matters, this general opinion seems silly in the extreme. But in a country which remembered Tipu Sultan's measures to make Hindu Mussulmans it spread easily. A regiment declined to obey the new orders; and when two ringleaders were awarded 900 lashes apiece, the sepoys rose and massacred two European companies. Gillespie raced in with his galloper guns, stormed Vellore, and rescued the besieged survivors. The inevitable crop of executions followed. In every detail the episode is a little rehearsal of the Mutiny of 1857, and it thrilled British India with a horror unparalleled until that later event swept it into oblivion. Since Tipu's family and the concomitant swarm of hangers on of Indian royalty and semi-royalty resided at Vellore their complicity was suspected, and they were certainly an aggravating factor in what was partly a Hindu revolt.

Lord Minto, the new Governor-General passed through Madras when the business was finishing. Like most men who have ever come to India fresh from the outside world, he was surprised by the atmosphere which he found:

> 'The mutual ignorance of each others' motives, intentions, and actions, in which Europeans and natives seemed content to live, had forcibly struck Lord Minto during his short residence in Madras in 1807. "I do not believe that either Lord William or Sir John Cradock had the slightest idea of the aversion their me assures would excite. I fully believe that their intentions were totally misapprehended by the natives".[64]

He considered that the Directors made a mistake in recalling the Governor and his Commander-in-Chief; since the chiefs of army and administration were dismissed, the sepoys executed under their orders would be regarded as justified and be made into martyrs. Here, again, we hear a familiar argument; and are reminded that in every period of British-Indian history all strata of opinion have been simultaneously present the 'diehard' and the 'bolshy', the modern and the medieval.

A devoted friend of Burke, Minto had been one of the managers of Warren Hastings' impeachment. He was a quiet humane, experienced man: 'of as courtly manners as Lord Wellesley: but though he is less lively, he is far more finished and elegant'.[65] His term was one of steady progress. He modified the policy of non-intervention carried to extremes but never resumed Wellesley's high-handness. When Amir Khan in 1809, invaded Berar, he observed, with that dryness and cool lack of emotion which make his despatches such a change from Wellesley's:

> 'It has not perhaps been sufficiently considered that every native State in India is a military despotism; that war and conquest are avowed as the first and legitimate pursuit of every sovereign or chief, and the sole source of glory and renown; it is not therefore a mere conjecture deduced from the natural bias of the human mind, and the test of general experience, but a certain conviction founded on avowed principles of action and systematic view that among the military states and chiefs of India the pursuits of ambition can alone be bounded by the inability to prosecute them'.

After what may be felt to be this 'glimpse into the obvious' he goes on to note that British interests should be the factor deciding,

> 'whether it was expedient ot observe a strict neutrality amidst these scenes of disorder and outrage which were passing under our eyes in the north of Hindostan, or whether we should listen to the calls of suffering humanity,'

and referred to the Directors, who replied that they thought non-interference could be carried a great deal too far, a change from their feeling of only a year or two back. Minto had meanwhile chased Amir Khan out of Berar, and occupied his homeland and capital. The company then relaxed its grasp, and the freebooter was left at liberty to harry people not actually its allies.

Minto's rule was marked by a number of 'little wars', reducing tubulent chiefs in Bundalkband, and punishing a Travancore out-break (due to offended religious susceptibilities) in which thirty European soldiers were murdered. He had next to give some attention to Ranjit Singh, who had established a Sikh State in the Punjab and, after conquering the smaller Sikh chiefs north of the Satlej, was threatening those on its southern bank. Charles Metcalfe was sent to him to negotiate an understanding. Metcalfe, in the last Maratha War, when only nineteen, had been General Lake's political officer. Now, at twenty-four,[66] he had won golden opinion, including Lord Minto's; 'he really is the ugliest and most agreeable clever person—except Lady Glenbervie—in Europe or Asia'.

The Sikh Power was regarded as an extension into India of the block of great Central Asian States, vaguely known and distrusted, Afghanistan, Persia, the Turkestan Khanates. Russia was beginning to emerge as the main foreign bugbear, but had not yet ousted France from this position, despite Napoleon's naval disasters. The Company kept nervously looking towards Persia and the frontier lands. Malcolm was twice sent to Persia the first time making a good impression, the second time erring by arrogant demand that the envoy of France and Russia (the latter obviously in a far better position to damage Persia than the far-off Indian Government) be dismissed. It is only fair to remember that in his second visit he was hampered by the presence of a rival embassy, sent direct from England; the Shah not unreasonably kept asking which embassy he was to attend to. Elphinstone (who was one of the great four who are England's glory in the next twenty years—Malcolm, Metcalfe, and Munro (who belonged to an earlier generation) are the other three) was sent to Kabul, 1808, but, merely reached Pewhawar, where he set up with Shah Suja, the Afghan Amir, who was dethroned shortly afterwards, cloudy but friendly relations which had a deplorable sequel in Lord Aucklands' time.

Metcalfe's embassy proved the most difficult and most successful of all. Ranjit Singh was jealous and suspicious; it was true that his aggrandizement had been swift and great, but it was nothing to the progress he had seen made by the

Company. Thigh the young envoy impressed him, he plainly hinted that he did not want him. Metcalfe followed the Sikh ruler about; and his patience and firmness, seconded by Minto's firmness, won, after immense dues. In December, 1808, when Ranjit Singh was sunk in a prolong debauch, he sent him a severely worded warning that the British Government insisted on taking under their protection the Cis-Satluj Shikh States. Nabha, Jhind, Faridkote, Patiala. Reading it, the India staggered as from 'sudden shock', the dreaded foreigners were henceforward camped on his doorstep. He spoke humbly to the buyer. Metcalfe's confidential *munshi;* but immediately fled from polity to a Mussulman dancing-girl, conduct which so pained the priest of the Golden Temple at Amritsar that they laid the shopkeepers uncern inferdict (*hartal*): 'There was a great strife between the Tenoral and the Spiritual power; and the former was worsted in the enumter'.[67] Ranjit fled to Lahore, followed by the pertinacious youngenvoy. Ranjit grew 'careworn and thoughtful,' Hindus were sitting *anna* at his gates his people were beseeching a peaceful settlement. H. uministers,

> 'tried to reconcile Metcalfe to the eccentricities of their chief; by the English gentleman had answered with becoming firmness that although eccentricities were sufficiently apparent, he could not admit that they firmed any justification for his conduct'.[68]

Brought to bay, Ranjit demanded *why* he should me to give up places he had already captured. Metcalfe told him because the British Government intended to protect them. After final interview, Metcalfe to his astonishment saw the Raja, was 'surprising levity', a phrase which indicates the psychological dulness which went with such high qualities in so many Company's men, ring his favourite horse, round and round his courtyard. The *Times* in December, 1839, gave this incident the proper journalistic picuresqueness by making him gallop madly over the confined space Metacalfe said 'prancing'. Ranjit Singh by his body was trying to exn the demons of anger and perplexity. More interviews followed. Metcalfe lost temper and prepared to leave. General Ochterior appeared on the Satlej; other troops were moving up in support this contingent. Again Ranjit Singh turned to his courtesan from which 'pleasant forgetfulness Metcalfe roused him by accussive which flashed the sunlight into his sleeping face':[69]

> 'The Maharaja is revelling in delight in the Shalimar gaens, unmindful of the duties of Friendship. What friendship requires is not donor is it doing'.

He demanded his dismissal. Ranjit replied humbly 'the delights of the garden of Friendship far exceeded the delights of a garden of roses,' and Metcalfe got his treaty, a treaty of immense value, since it kept the peace over so many years between the two greatest armies in India.

In 1765 Clive had put down a mutiny of the officers of the Bengal army; since then 'scarce a decade had passed without an open struggle between the military and the civil power'.[70] Mutinies were periodic, and the mutineers usually won, which 'justified the belief that representations made by numbers and supported by clamour would not fail'.[71] In 1808 the Bombay officers almost mutinied because it was found that a cavalry regiment might be more conveniently raised at Madras. In Madras next year the government, driven by the Directors who 'threatened to take the pruning knife into their own hands,'[72] asked their Quartermaster-General to draw up a report on a system which gave the commanding officers of regiments tent allowances for their men, whether they were in the field or in cantonments. He found the system was regularly abused, whereupon the officers called on the Commander-in-Chief to bring him 'to a court-martial for aspersions on their character as officers and gentlemen'.[73] The Commander-in-Chief complied; but Barlow, who had gone to Madras as Governor, countermanded his action. Then the former, whose soreness at his exclusion from a place on the Council made him unwearied in forming a party for himself, confronted Barlow with a mutiny. The officers in many large stations.

> 'talked of fighting against a tyrannical Government in defence of their rights to the last drop of their blood. Seditious toasts were given at the mess tables, and drunk with uproarious applause. From day to day tidings went forth from one excited station to another—tidings of progressive insubordination which fortified with assurances of sympathy and support the insane resolves of the scattered mutineers.... The moral intoxication pervaded all ranks the colonel to the ensign'.[74]

At Masulipatam the officers put their commanding officer under arrest and seized the fort; Seringapatam followed suit. Malcolm, sent to Masulipatam, wrote back,

> 'that there was not a Company's corps Cape Comorin to Ganjam that was not implicated in the general guilt—that is not pledged to rise against Government unless what they call their grievances are redressed'.

Haidarabad next rose. 'All concealment was thrown off,' and 30,000 men, it was threatened, would march on Madras. Public funds were seized, correspondence interrupted—'in a word, civil war had commenced'. Then Barlow for once acted with some approach to vigour. He demanded from all officers a signed pledge to obedience, on pain of being sent inland if they refused. When not one-tenth consented to sign, he appealed to the sepoys to stand firm to their allegiance; they did so, and though Sir James Mackintosh wrote to John Malcolm that[75] 'were he asked whether the deposition of a Governor by military force or an appeal to private soldiers against their officers be the greater evil, I am compelled to own that I must hesitate,' the sepoys' loyalty left the mutineers stranded. They had never allowed themselves to doubt that they would have their regiments with them. Lord Minto on going to Madras received 'a penitential letter'. As every decade proved, there was a wide difference in the punishment meted out to mutineers, according to whether they were sepoys or British officers; only a handful of ringleaders were now court-martialled having first been offered their choice of trial or dismissal. The court-martial resulted in several being cashiered. Much bitterness remained and the Company officers sent to Coventry the King's officers, who held them 'might cheap,'[76] Barlow's handling of the episode was considered unsatisfactory. It finished whatever chance he had of being appointed Governor-General, and he went home in 1812.

Inside India, Minto's regime was one of quiet consolidation, with vigorous action against turbulent chieftains. The ablest of these, Jeswant Rao Holkar went mad in 1808, and for three years was kept bound with ropes and fed with milk, dying October, 1811. Outside India, Lord Minto's government was one of brilliant conquest. As part of the war with Napoleon, he captured the islands of Bourbon and France (Mauritius). Whenever Napoleon compelled a European State into his system, England 'took charge' of that State's foreign possessions. Thus she possessed for a few years the Moluccas and Java, the Governor-General himself accompanying the latter expedition and being present at the Dutch rout at Fort Cornelis, near Batavia. Gillespie of Vellore led the storm, which Minto describes (August 28, 1811):[77]

> 'It really seems miraculous that mortal men could live in such a fire of round, grape shells, and musketry long enough to pass deep trenches defended by pointed palisades inclining from the inner edge of the ditch outwards, force their way into redoubt after redoubt, till they were in possession of all the numerous works, which extend at least a mile... . The slaughter was dreadful, both during the attack and in the pursuit... . We have upwards of 5000 prisoners, including all the Europeans left alive... . There never was such a rout'.

Java passed into British keeping and the great Stamford Raffles was appointed lieutenant-Governor. These dark slavery-ridden East Indian regions certainly needed cleaning up. Minto abolished execution by torture, and the brutal custom of compelling the families of the condemned to witness the malefactor's death, and afterwards selling them into bondage. Java entered on a period of prosperity and humane administration. It was returned to the Dutch when general peace was made, at the end of the Napoleonic wars.

Lord Minto's most criticised action was that which he took against missionaries. The Company's territory being closed to them, they were established in the Danish settlement at Serampur, whence they issued pamphlets which were distributed in British India. Minto forbade propagandist preaching in Calcutta, and William Carey, the great Baptist leader, agreed to a censorship of their publications. In the latter demand Minto was not as unreasonable as clamour in London represented. To the Chairman of the Directors he wrote:

> 'Pray read especially the miserable stuff addressed to the Gentooes, in which without one word to convince or to satisfy the mind of the heathen reader, without proof or argument of any kind, the pages are filled with hell fire, and hell fire, and still hotter fire, denounced against a whole race of men for believing in the religion which they were taught by their fathers and mothers, and the truth of which it is simply impossible it should ever have entered into their minds to doubt. Is this the doctrine of our faith? ... . If there are two opinions among Christians on this point, I can only say that I am of the sect which believes that a just God will condemn no being without individual guilt ... . The remainder of this tract seems to aim principally at a general massacre of the Brahmins of this country. A total abolition of caste is openly preached. A proposal to efface a mark of caste from the foreheads of soldiers on parade has had its share in a massacre of Christains...'.

As that last sentence reminds us, Vellore had gone deep and into bitter remembrance.

In 1808, when England and Denmark were at war, Serampur was occupied by the Company. The Serampur missionaries were Baptists, and the Governor-General found them easier to persuade to be reasonable than he found the Rev. Claudius Buchanan, one of his own Presidency chaplains. Buchanan printed a memoir urging:

> 'An archbishop is wanted for India—a sacred and exalted character, surrounded by his bishops, of ample revenue and extensive sway... . We want something royal in a spiritual and temporal sense for the abject subjects of this great Eastern empire to look up to... . When once our national Church shall have been confirmed in India, the members of that Church will be the best qualified to advise the State as to the means by which from time to time the civilisation of the natives is to be effected'.

So firmly did Mr. Buchanan believe in the efficacy of the mere sight of his sacred and exalted characters, that he was said to have exclaimed, 'Place the mitre on any head. Never fear, it will do good among the Hindoos! Clearly, long before Keble's sermon on 'National Apostasy' gave a date for the start of the Oxford Movement, there was a widespread *preparatio evangelica*.

Minto dealt also with characters whom no one has called sacred or exalted. In Mogul times, in Warren Hasting's time, in Lord Curzon's time, in our own time, dacoity—robbery with violence—had been rife in Bengal especially in East Bengal, where natural conditions make it almost ineradicable. Dacoits are people who heed not excite our pity:

> 'It is impossible to imagine, without seeing it, the horrid ascendancy they had obtained over the inhabitants.... They had established a terrorism as perfect as that which was the foundation of the French republican power, and in truth the *sirdars*, or captains the band, were esteemed and even called the *hakim* or ruling power, while the real Government did not possess either authority of influence enough to obtain from the people the smallest aid towards their own protection.... Men have been found with their limbs and half the flesh of their bodies

> consumed by slow fire, who persisted in saying that they had fallen into their own fire, or otherwise denying all knowledge of the event that could tend to the conviction or detection of the offenders. They knew, if they spoke they would either themselves or the remaining members of their families be despatched the same evening. By these measures such as vigorous efficient government was erected by the banditti in these districts, that they could sent a single messenger through the villages with regular lists of requisitions from the different houses and families—some to furnish grain, some forage, some horses some two sons to join the gangs, some labourer to carry the plunder or to bear torches, or to act as scouts; some were to sent a wife or daughter to attend the gangs'.[78]

Governor-Generals occupied with disposal of partonage or with vast imperial design had been too busy to be vext. But Minto,

> 'was not a little shocked, and could not help feeling some shame, when I became fully apprised of the dreadful disorders which afflicted countries under the very eye of Government; and for many months past it has been one of the principal objects to put this monstrous even town… . I am happy to say that hitherto the success has even exceeded my expectations. In Nuddeah, which was the principal seat of this evil, therefore has not been a single dacoity during the last months; and it is in that one district that the computed average of persons put to death in torture was seventy a months. Nine sirdars have been executed at one spot, and the impression of that example was remarkable. The people had come to think it impossible that the leader of an established gang should be punished or at least capitally punished, and they exceed on with fully as much awe as satisfaction on this proof of the supreme power of Government'.

The 'gangster' operates very similarly in East and West, and requires the same conditions for success and impunity.

This quiet, unassuming man has had much less than his due of praise. He was firm when firmness was wanted: he tightened up Government when it had been rendered intolerably lax, and yet there was no return to the bullying arrogrance of Lord Wellesley. He was amused by the pettifogging pompousness which he found enwrapping his position, and 'in the log kept for the benefit of the family circle at home' (who we may hope, were worthy of it) he redicules it with mild ribaldry it merits:

> 'The first night I went to bed at Calcutta I was followed by fourteen persons in white muslim gowns into the dressing-room. One might have hoped that some of these were ladies; but on finding that there were as many turbans and black beards as gowns, I was very desirous that these bearded handmaids should leave me… . which with some trouble and perseverance I accomplished, and in that one room I enjoy a degree of privacy, but far from perfect. The doors are open, the partitions are open or transparent also, and it is the business of a certain number to keep an eye upon me, and see if I want the particular service which each is allowed by his caste to render me. It is same in bed; a set of these black men sleep and watch all night on the floor of the passage, and an orderly man of the body-guard mounts guard at the door with Sepoys in almost all the rooms, and at all the staircases. These give you a regular military salute every time you stir out of your room or go up or down stairs, besides four or five with maces running before you. I have gradually got rid of this troublesome nonsense, but enough remains and must remain to tease me and turn comfort out of doors… .

An ease and informality of intercourse came into Government correspondence between the Governor-General and his higher officers. Government House became a habitable region; 'no other circle in Calcutta contained prettier women or abler men'.[79]

Young Charles Metcalfe, in April, 1811, entered on his great work as Resident at Delhi, where he found the Mogul's family a heavy trial. As with Tipu's family at Vellore, there were rumours that the young bloods committed murder and robbery; they were reported to have killed an old woman behind the walls of what Kaye calls 'that great sty of pollution,'[80] and we are given this glimpse of what must be called their amusements:[81] 'oiling their naked persons, then rushing with swords among the startled inmates of the Zenana, and forcibly carrying off their property'.

Ought the place to be allowed to continue the slave-trade, which Metcalfe had prohibited in Delhi (where also he prohibited suttee)? 'The truth struggled out but dimly from the murky recesses' of the labyrinth of buildings where a swarm of several generations of the royal family co-existed, plotting and fighting among themselves. Blind, old Shah Alam was dead, and his successor complained that 'the tribute' paid him by the Company was insufficient. The young Englishman who had to reconcile his responsibility for a great city with his anxiety to respect fallen majesty found support in an administration so cordial and so full of common sense and sense of the absurdity of the whole Indian scene (that comforting reflection which has kept the wiser Indians and wiser British alike sane). When Metcalfe lost two valued assistants promoted elsewhere, Minto answered his protests by a 'ragging' which showed how complete was the confidence in the Resident who was left to carry on with new and raw help:

> 'You will perceive that I entertained none other' (intention) 'than that of promoting the views in the service of two young gentlemen, whom, without knowing either personally, I esteemed and admired extremely... . With regard to the *Resident at Delhi*, I may as well confess that, having always had a very mean opinion of his abilities, and thinking him a very unamiable character and dull companion. I did entertain a secret wish to bring him into disrepute, by depriving him of his most able and experienced coadjutors... .

REFERENCES

1. Regulation XIII of 1811.
2. *Ibid.*
3. Regulation V of May 1, 1812.
4. *Ibid.*
5. *Ibid.*
6. Regulation V of May, 1, 1812.
7. Kaye, J. W., *op. cit.*, p. 236.
8. *Selection of Papers from the Records of East India House*, Vol. I, pp. 6-44.
9. *Fifth Report from the Select Committee on the Affairs of the East India Company*, Vol. II, pp. 52-53.
10. *Ibid.*
11. *Selection of Papers from the Records of East India House*, Vol. I, pp. 6-44.
12. *Ibid.*
13. Fifth Report, *op. cit.*, p. 53.
14. *Ibid.*
15. Fifth Report, *op. cit.*, p. 53.
16. Fifth Report, *op. cit.*, pp. 53-54.
17. Firminger, W. K., *Fifth Report*, Vol. III, pp. 517-518.
18. *Ibid.*
19. Madras Revenue Selections, p. 463.
20. *Ibid.*
21. Select Committee Report, Vol. II, p. 151.
22. Madras Revenue Selections, p. 587.
23. Select Committee Report, Vol. II, p. 1.4.
24. Madras Revenue Selections, pp. 589-91.
25. Revenue letter from the Court of Directors, Dec. 16, 1812.
26. *Ibid.*
27. The Fifth Report, Vol. I, p. 300.
28. *The Fifth Report from the Select Committee on the Affairs of the East India Company*, Vol. II, pp. 63-65.

29. Bengal Regulation XIII of 1808.
30. *Ibid.*
31. Bengal Regulation XIII of 1808.
32. Bengal Regulation XIII of 1810.
33. *Ibid.*
34. Bengal Regulation XIV of 1810.
35. Bengal Regulation XIV of 1810.
36. *Ibid.*
37. Bengal Regulation XIV of 1810.
38. *India under Wellesley*, 111.
39. Wellesley to Dundas, March 5, 1800 (M. Martin, *ii*. 247).
40. H. Beveridge, *A Comprehensive History of India ii*. 717.
41. Mill, *History of British India iv*. 207.
42. Roberts, *India under Wellesley*, 114.
43. Wellesley to Sir J. H. Craig, September 16, 1798 (Martin, *i*. 262).
44. Robers, *India under Wellesley*, 117-18.
45. *Life of Sir Thomas Munro*, 249.
46. Robers, 37.
47. November 5, 1799 (Martin, *ii*. 134).
48. November 28, 1799 (Martin, *ii*. 154-6).
49. Roberts, *India under Wellesley*, 124.
50. Roberts, 125.
51. *History of India, vi*. 155.
52. H. Beveridge, *History of India, ii*. 371.
53. *India under Wellesley*, 135-6.
54. *Oxford History of India*, 519.
55. *History of British India, vi*. 232.
56. The words are those of the Governor of Madras, 'by and with the authority of the Governor-General' (Martin, *ii*. 553 ff.).
57. Letter, March, 1805.
58. *Oxford History of India*, 604. The same comment is made by Marshman (*History of India*, 279): 'Lord Cornwallis was Mr. Pitti's invariable refuge in every Indian difficulty'.

59. April, 1805.
60. Gleig, *Life of Sir Thomas Munro*, 279-80.
61. Munro.
62. August 11 and September 4, 1806.
63. *Lord Minto in India, i.* 369.
64. Elphinstone, August, 1807.
65. Ranjit Singh was three years older.
66. John William Kaye, *Life of Lord Metcalfe, i.* 289.
67. Mr. Gandhi's method of putting pressure on those who offer from him, by fasting until they see their error.
68. *Life of Metcalfe*, 290.
69. *Op. cit.* 306.
70. *Lord Minto in India*, 197.
71. *Op. cit.*, 202.
72. Marshman, *History of India, ii.* 240.
73. *Lord Minto in India*, 207.
74. *Op. cit.*, 197.
75. J. Kaye, *Correspondence of Sir John Malcolm*, quoted in *Lord Minto in India*. 216.
76. Lord Minto.
77. *Lord Minto in India (Life and Letters...from 1807 to 1814)*, edited by his greatniece the Countees of Minto, 291.
78. Letter to Lady Minto, 1809.
79. *Lord Minto in India*, 349
80. *Life of Lord Metcalfe, i* 351.
81. *Op. cit. i.* 34.

4

Francophobia and British Attitude

In the later half of the eighteenth century, when England and France were serious rivals of each other in the fields of overseas trade, commerce and Empire, the British mind remained in a perpetual state of alarm till French rivalry was finally eliminated and England's unchallenged supremacy was virtually established. Though the three Carnatic Wars had damaged the French interests in India almost beyond repair, their formidable leaders such as Dupleix, Bussy and Count Lally no longer existed and the year 1763 marked the close of the most dramatic phase of Anglo-French rivalry in India, still their rivalry did not end abruptly and continued for another half of a century. During this period, the feeling of danger from France did not completely disappear from the British mind. With the growing French fraternisation with the anti-British potentates of India, like Haider Ali and Tipu Sultan; and the increasing activities of the individual French adventurers, the Francophobia in the minds of the British statesmen in India and England re-emerged as a tangible reality. In the post-French revolutionary era, with the rise of Napolean Bonaparte to power and prominence as the greatest and the strongest enemy of England, with his dreams of Asiatic conquest and destruction of England in Europe and outside, it took a definite, articulate and alarming shape like a hydra-headed leviathan.[1]

Towards the end of the eighteenth century and in the beginning of the nineteenth century, when the British position in India was not too strong; and their Indian antagonists were not too weak, Francophobia dominated the Foreign Office of England and the imagination of the British statesmen at the helm of affairs in India. There was hardly any aspect of their policies which remained uninfluenced by this gigantic and terrible reality, though often very much magnified as an all-absorbing phobia, determining the attitude of a fear-stricken people. The very fact that the French still possessed important island stations on the high seas which could be used as dangerous bases for implementing their cherished ambition to gain ascendancy on the Eastern Continent, had created doubts and fears in the British minds. They watched the extension of French hegemony across Europe with growing alarm. Anxiety over the progress of events was not limited to the Continent, for Napoleon's successful invasion of Egyptian territory kindled speculation as to the possibility of a French attack on India.[2] The British mind was overtaken by a grave apprehension of a probable combination of their Indian adversaries with their European rivals on their successful entry into the Indian subcontinent. Consequently, during the first decade of the nineteenth century, virtually all British diplomatic, commercial and military machinations in the countries to the west and north-west of India were directed towards the repulse of these horrible and dangerous anticipated threats.[3]

Lord Wellesley, the Governor-General of India from May 1798 to July 1805, found himself very much preoccupied with Francophobia. He took over his office in a state peculiarly apt to be seized both with dread and with hatred for any power that was France. About three months after his arrival in India, he received intelligence about the plan of General Malartic, the French Governor at the Island of Mauritius, to render military assistance to Tipu Sultan, the sworn enemy of the East India Company, in response to an appeal made by him through his two emissaries. To encourage the anti-

British designs of Tipu, a large body of French troops arrived at Mauritius and waited for an opportunity to cripple the British in India in alliance with the Sultan of Mysore. These dangerous proceedings at the French rendezvous on the Arabian Sea Island prompted Lord Wellesley and General Harris to take speedy measures with the sanction of the Home Government to meet any intending crisis and to eliminate the French influence from India for good. In pursuit of his vigorous policy, he enjoyed the confidence and support of the British Cabinet. As a first step, he planned to organize a formidable combination with the Nizam and the Marathas against the anti-British nursery in Mysore, and successfully destroyed Tipu and his independent kingdom. The Nizam was made the most subservient ally and was obliged to disarm and disband his French forces. He removed from service all French military adventurers, and pledged never to employ any European national hostile to the British.

This was not, however, the end of his anti-French endeavours in India. Fearing the probability of a French alliance, with the Marathas, the other most formidable power in India, he crippled their power by war and compelled all its confederates to sign humiliating subsidiary alliances, which were principally aimed at strengthening the British hold over the contracting powers and eliminating the French military adventurers from their territories. This scheme of subsidiary alliances ably devised by him served as a powerful instrument in his hands to accomplish the ends of his forward policy. Several other States of India were entrapped into it, and his grand project was brilliantly achieved.[4]

In spite of these successful anti-French activities in India, Napoleon did not abate his anti-British designs in the East. He found a powerful ally in the person of Paul I, the Czar of Russia, who felt alienated from Britain and welcomed his terms. This scheme, however, could not materialize due to the sudden death of the Czar on March 24, 1801.[5] Had their scheme taken a practical shape, it would have created a difficult situation for the British and endangered their interests in India. The knowledge of this Franco-Russian collaboration naturally obsessed the British mind with an acute sense of danger to their imperial and commercial interests in the Indian sub-continent through Persia. To meet the situation and to counteract the fear of French advance in Asia, with a sinister plan to destroy the British interests in the East, Lord Wellesley, known for his anti-Gallic tendencies, planned to woo the Shah of Persia to a friendly alliance. A mission to his Court under Malcolm established good understanding with his Government and signed a political and commercial Treaty on June 28, 1801.[6] Besides this, the Indian waters were fully guarded by the British navy, and the French movements from their island bases in the Arabian Sea were closely watched. By these means, the French nightmare of invasion of India through Persia was removed for the time being.

This state of the British mind, however, did not last long. On February 15, 1803, Decaen, the French General at Pondicherry, received instructions from Napoleon advising him to establish secret contacts with the Indian Princes to secure a strong base in India; and to devise plans for any future eventuality of a war with the British without arousing their suspicions.[7] Unfortunately for Decaen, events moved very fast in India and the British position had already been considerably strengthened on the eve of his arrival at Pondicherry. The French army under General Perron in Sindhia's service on which he banked so much had been removed from Gwalior territories by the Treaty of Surji Arjan Gaon prior to his despatch of an emissary to him from Port Louis. The French secret Agents in Indian States had been arrested as a measure of extraordinary precaution.[8] Their letters, frequently intercepted by the British, enabled them to know which of the Indian powers had to be kept under close observation. Decaen and his colleagues were confident of large help from them, not fully aware of the precarious position to which they were reduced by the vigorous policy of Lord Wellesley. Under these circumstances in India, it was quite certain that the French intrigues could not have caused any harm to the British, and any French attempt at invasion of India with a few thousand troops, would have ended in disaster. Notwithstanding these developments in India in favour of the British, Napolean suggested in his letter to Decres, the Minister of Marine, on January 16, 1805, a plan of sending an expedition to India. This, however, was soon abandoned, when Napoleon got the full appraisal of the situation in India from him.[9]

But soon international events took such a turn that Persia began to show more interest and leaning towards France than England. The reason for this change of relations was the refusal of England to help Persia in the restitution of her territories[10] from Russia on the unconvincing plea that she could not afford to spoil her good relations with that country in conformity with the Treaty of 1801. This unexpected refusal from friendly England at this hour of need disillusioned Persia and made her seek an ally elsewhere at any cost in order to safeguard its own integrity.[11] At this hour of turmoil in the Persian foreign policy, two French representatives, Romieu and Jaubert reached Teheran in 1805 and 1806 to collect the requisite information. Of these, the former died of illness without completing his mission, and the latter returned to the Imperial camp at Warsaw on February 8, 1807 to report his findings to Napoleon. He was preceded by Mirza Reza Khan, with whom Napoleon entered into a friendly political Treaty at Finkenstein on May 14, 1807 as a consequence of which General Gardanne was sent to Teheran as head of a military mission. He concluded a military and commercial convention.

This was not the end of Napoleon's political and military alliances. On June 14, 1807, he brought to knees the combined armies of Prussia and Russia at Friedland, and, compelled Czar Alexander I to sign a humiliating Treaty at Tilsit on July 9, 1807.[12] By this Treaty, the two great military powers of Europe lay prostrate before the military might of France; and it appeared that the foundations of the Napoleonic

Empire in Europe were firmly laid, and great hero had reached the meridian of his glory, ready to embark on an Eastern adventure. It enabled the French Emperor to secure the active collaboration of Russia in completing and enforcing rigidly the continental system, the greatest weapon in his hands to strike a disastrous blow on the prosperity and greatness of England without waging a war against it. Besides this, he was determined to annihilate the British Empire by a drive into her Asian possessions with the help of the Russian cossacks. He felt that it would be easier for him to transport an army from Paris to Delhi than from Boulogne to Falkestone.[13] At Tilsit, he had only one object in view, namely, to engage Europe at large in his contest a *outrance* against Great Britain. In the words of J. A. R. Marriott in this context, Alexander was an important asset in his diplomatic balance-sheet. The news of the Treaty of Tilsit had a very depressing effect upon the British statesmen, and raised their alarm to their finger tips.[14] The nightmare of Francophobia was found to be at its worst. The French peril to the British interests appeared to be most acute and psychologically very much magnified. The effect of this sate of mind had powerful influence upon the anti-French British decisions of that time.[15]

When Lord Minto took over office as the Governor-General of India in July 1807, he was very much overtaken by the dreadful Francophobia. A couple of months after his arrival, he received an intelligence of General Gardanne's anti-British activities in Persia, resulting in the establishment of French predominance in the councils of Teheran. This was highly prejudicial to the British interests in the East. The arrival of 300 French troops and 24 officers at Tabrez on the Western side of the Caspian Sea left no room for doubts in his mind that the ruler of France actively meditated the execution of his cherished plan of invading India through Persia; and that he had already made considerable progress in the furtherance of that project.[16] It feasibility, however, depended upon the nature of the assistance the French would receive from the Governments of Persia and Turkey. He believed that so long as France would remain engaged in the Continental War, she would not be in a position to implement her intended project.[17] But in the event of the continued submission of the subjugated powers of Europe, the French troops would be free for a military venture in the East which might not be beyond the 'scope, energy, ability and perseverance' of the French Emperor. He feared that if once Fench troops succeeded in penetrating into the Persian Dominions, the way would be opened for their other waves to traverse them and carry on further military incursions unchecked.[18]

It appeared to Lord Minto that the primary object of the French advance into Persia was to occupy the Port of Gombroon and the Islands of Armuz and Karrack in the Persian Gulf; and to use these acquisitions as bases for further infiltration in the East. The ascendancy of France, once established in the territories of Persia and the Persian waters, would enable her gradually to extend her influence by conciliation or by conquest towards India, and ultimately open a passage into the Dominions of the East India Company. In this situation, he felt convinced that the Persian opposition to France would alone frustrate their designs; and this could be brought about by convincing the Shah of Persia of the illusive benefits he hoped to acquire from the French alliance; and the positive harm that it might bring to him and his country. Therefore, with a view to alienating Persia from the influence of France, he decided to despatch an officer, in whose talents, zeal and ability, he could repose confidence, with full powers to negotiate with Persia.[19]

Subsequently, an intelligence was received by the Government of India about the disputes between the Ameers of Sind and the Shah of Afghanistan; and despatch of vakeels by the former to the Shah of Persia, seeking his help against the Shah of Kabul and promising to pay tributes to him on attainment of freedom from the Afghan yoke.[20] The Shah of Persia accepted the proposals of the Government of Sind and appointed an Agent to proceed to that country with his vakeels as a token of his friendly gesture.[21] The French emissaries in Persia took advantage of the presence of the vakeels of Sind and endeavoured to obtain the consent of their Government for the admission of French ships into its ports. It was alleged by the Government of India that these negotiations led to a satisfactory conclusion.[22]

These diplomatic conclusions in Persia magnified the danger of French invasion on India and transformed the fear in the Francophob minds of the British statesmen into an alarm of very serious magnitude. To them, the idea of the French ships using the ports of Sind appeared to be an anathema and potential and perpetual source of danger to the prized British interests in India. Greatly perturbed by this probability which appeared to be more in imagination than in reality, Lord Minto immediately resolved to have a firm grip over the critical situation and attempt the renewal of friendly relations already subsisting with Sind, with a view to preventing the French from taking the alleged concession which might give a foot-hold to them on the South-West extremity of India and a jumping ground for implementing their projected invasion of British India. The chain of French allianced from Persia, to Sind was the most disquieting phenomenon, pregnant with most serious consequences to the British shipping and commerce and their growing political hegemony in India. To give effect to his resolve, he decided to despatch a confidential envoy to the Ameers of Sind with definite instructions to ascertain the real nature and extent of the negotiations between the French and the Government of Sind; and also between the Government of Persia and Sind.[23]

This, he thought, would be an effective means of obtaining authentic information of the nature, extent and progress of the French designs, not only in that country, but also in the countries North of it as far as Kashmir and Kabul; and might prove an additional source of intelligence respecting anti-British intrigues of the French in Persia. No speculative opinions about the unreality or improbability of this danger were allowed to thwart the preparatory measures of defence which might be adopted promptly to meet any dangerous emergency. His acts were promoted by the supposition of the 'early approach' of a French force towards the confines of Persia and the expediency of meeting the impending danger as a first principle of prudence and precautions.[24]

The territories of Afghanistan and Punjab were also most vulnerable. Any Franco-Persian advance could be expected via this region. The Governor-General wanted to use these two states as buffers in order to safeguard the frontiers of the East India Company. The despatch of two emissaries, one to the Shah of Kabul and the other to Maharaja Ranjit Singh, was thought to be equally necessary. These two powers in alliance with France would have proved very dangerous to the interests of the Company. At any rate, the Governor-General did not want to leave anything to chance. By all possible means and with all-pronged diplomatic drives, he wished to keep the danger away from the British territories and to meet it outside their borders, if necessary. The rigid neutrality of his two predecessors and a purely defensive attitude appeared to him ineffective, meaningless and unnecessarily risky, destined to lead the British into a vortex from where escape without positive damage to British interests was improbable. Hence in the fit of Franco-phobia, but with a spirit of realism, the despatch of mission to various princes on and beyond the North-Western borders of British India; and the creation of an effective barrier against the French inroads in the form of inner and outer layers of states the inner layer being Lahore and Sind and the outer layer Kabul and Persia,—became his well-thought-out project.

The Court of Directors and the Foreign Office of England also realized the seriousness of the altered situation and concurred with Lord Minto in the adoption of his policy of counteracting the French danger to India by taking the border states into greater confidence and bringing them into a chain of definite defensive alliances.[25] At this juncture, the Francophobia in the British mind was at its height and it worked as the most powerful factor in determining the foreign relations of the Government of India.

IV

Rumours of Foreign Invasion

In the meanwhile, although the French had at last been effectively barred out from approaching India by sea, and although every native State accessible to hostile intrigues by the sea-coast had been bound over under heavy recognizances to the English alliance, yet the signs and warnings of danger now began to reappear in a different quarter of the stormy political horizon.

The Persian king, who had suffered heavily from a war with Russia in 1804-5 appealed for succour to Napoleon in Europe, and also sent a similar application to Calcutta. From India, where the policy of retrenchment and retraction at that moment prevailed, no encouragement was forthcoming. The French, however, who were just then in the midst of a desperate war with Russia, readily responded to the advances of Persia by sending an embassy for the conclusion of an offensive alliance against the common foe. Napoleon, who had just fought with heavy loss the drawn battle of Eylau, eagerly welcomed an opportunity of harassing the Russians in Asia, and also of resuscitating his favourite schemes of Asiatic conquest. His envoy to Teheran was instructed that his chief aim should be to form a triple alliance between France, Turkey, and Persia for the purpose of opening out a road to India. He was also directed to ascertain what co-operation might be expected within the country, particularly from the Marathas, if India could be reached by a French army.

Then came, in 1807, the battle of Friedland, when Napoleon used his victory to convert the Russian Emperor from an enemy into an ally of France. The offensive league with Persia was quietly transformed into an offer of mediation between that kingdom and Russia; and Napoleon set about organizing with Alexander I a fresh and much more formidable confederation against the English in India. Russia was already an Asiatic power, with a distinct inclination and momentum eastward. It is therefore no wonder that his ominous conjunction of France, at that moment supreme in western Europe, with the only European State that could further her designs upon India, should have roused and substantiated the alarms of an invasion by land; alarms that have never since ceased to recur periodically, gaining strength in proportion as their fulfilments has become by degrees less manifestly impracticable. The inevitable effect of this chronic disquietude has been, from the beginning, to fix the attention of the Anglo-Indian governments more and more, in the course of the present century, upon the north-west angle of India. And the concentration of our whole foreign policy upon that point has undoubtedly accelerated the expansion of our dominion in that direction, because in our anxiety about the only vulnerable side of our land frontier we have naturally pushed forward to secure it. No sooner, in fact, had the spectre of French troopships hovering about our sea-coast been finally laid under the waters of Trafalgar, than the apparition of European armies marching from the Caspian to the Oxus began to trouble the prophetic imagination of English statesmen.[26]

From the day when the Emperors of France and Russia exchanged pledges of unchangeable personal friendship at Tilsit, Napoleon incessantly pressed upon Alexander his grand scheme of a joint expedition through Turkey and Persia against the English in India, with the object of subverting their dominion and destroying the sources of their commercial prosperity. In 1807 the pre-eminence of France on the European Continent had reached its climax. Napoleon had defeated every army that had successively met him in the field; he had dissolved every league that had been made against him; and he had forced every leading State to join in a coalition for the rigid exclusion of English commerce from all their seaports. When, however, it became clear that these roundabout methods of attacking England were futile, and that nothing short of a direct home thrust would disable his indefatigable enemy, the French Emperor naturally turned his eyes towards the only important English possession whose frontier was not absolutely inaccessible to invasion from Europe by land. His imagination was fired by the recollection that Asia had more than once been traversed by conquering armies. That Napoleon should have seriously contemplated marching across Europe and half Asia to invade the territory of an island within twenty miles of the French coast—that he should have thought in on the whole less impracticable to send a force from the Danube or Constantinople to Delhi than to transport his troops from Calais to Dover—is certainly a remarkable illustration of the impregnability of effective naval defence. But his proposals obtained very half-hearted encouragement from the Russians, who had some useful acquaintance with the difficulties of Asiatic campaigning, and a wholesome distrust of the associate in whose company they were invited to set out. They were by no means eager to embark on distant eastern adventures, or to lock up their troops in the heart of Asia, upon the advice and for the advantage of the restless and powerful autocrat whose armies still hovered about their western frontier. They stipulated for a partition of the Turkish Empire as a preliminary dividend upon the joint-stock enterprise, and as a strategic base for any further advance eastward. To this condition, however, Napoleon refused his assent, alleging reasonably enough that it would be playing into the hands of England, since if the Russians were to take Constantinople the English would at once retaliate by seizing Egypt.[27] An imposing French mission was nevertheless sent to Persia, and the Anglo-Indian governments were much startled by the activity of the French agents at Teheran and other Asiatic courts.

Section III. Extension of Foreign Relations

It is from this period that we must date the embarkation of Anglo-Indian diplomacy upon a much wider sphere of action than heretofore. The English ministers soon discovered Napoleon's plan of an Asiatic campaign, and all his secret negotiations were thoroughly known to them. They regarded as a grave danger the project of a combined French and Russian expedition toward the frontiers of India; and it was at any rate plain that the Cornwallis policy of neutrality and a defensive attitude could not be sustained when these rumours were abroad. For the purpose of counteracting the French demonstrations, and of throwing up barrier after barrier against the threatened expedition from the Black Sea and the Caspian, the Indian Governor-General, Lord Minto, sent missions to all the rulers of States on and beyond his north-western border—to Ranjit Singh at Lahore, to the Afghan Amir, to Sinde, and to the Shah of Persia, who was just then overawed by the combined preponderance of France and Russia. Now that Napoleon had become Alexander's intimate friend and ally, the Persian king knew what to expect from French mediation, so he turned for protection to the English. At Teheran a treaty was settled, after much dispute and various misunderstandings (for the English envoy from Calcutta was superseded by another envoy from London), engaging England to subsidize Persia in the event of unprovoked aggression upon her. From Lahore the mission withdrew when, after some negotiations, it was discovered that Ranjit Singh claimed recognition of his sovereignty over territory south of the Sutlej river. At Peshawar the envoy to Afghanistan (Mountstuart Elphinstone) found the whole country distracted by civil war. The Afghan king, Shah Soojah, was barely holding on to the skirts of his kingdom; the Durani monarchy attacked on the west by Persia and pushed hard on the east by Sikhs, was already breaking up again into separate chiefships. Elphinstone's negotiations were cut short by the defeat of Shah Soojah, who fled into exile, to be restored thirty years later by an ill-fated expedition that eventually cost the English an army and the king his life.

But all these schemes for establishing close alliances and barrier treaties with Afghanistan, the Punjab, and Sinde were dropped or postponed as the tide of events began to turn again westward. The Spanish insurrection, and the preparations for invading Russia, soon provided Napoleon with such ample occupation in Europe that he abandoned his schemes of Asiatic adventure. Russia was now England's ally in a grand coalition against France; she made peace with Persia and with Turkey; and our apprehensions of danger from armies marching across Asia disappeared, for the time, when the long war which ended with Napoleon's overthrow left us in undisturbed possession of India. The searoads were guarded by an irresistible navy; the total collapse of the French Empire, the exhaustion of all the great European States, the manifest decay and immobility that were spreading through central Asia—all these circumstances united to secure us fourteen[28] years of comparative freedom from movements or demonstrations affecting our immunity from molestation by land. The only result of all the missions sent from India was, indirectly, the ratification in 1809, of a substantial frontier settlement with Ranjit Singh, who renounced, under pressure, his pretensions to sovereignty over certain Sikh chiefships south of the Sutlej. From that time forward his friendly relations with the English on his south-eastern frontier, and the civil strife within Afghanistan on the north-west, afforded him the means and opportunity of extending his territory across the Indus, of annexing Kashmir, and of building up the Sikh power with a solidity that kept it standing in alliance with the English for nearly forty years.

On the other hand, the eventual consequences of all this premature diplomatic agitation were by no means unimportant or transitory. We have seen how French rivalry accelerated our earlier conquests; and how at a later time the correspondence of native princes with France, or the presence of French officers in the Indian armies, aroused English susceptibility. It has been shown how this furnished Lord Wellesley with the necessary leverage for driving onward his policy of bringing into subjection or subordinate alliance every Mahomedan or Maratha State that might cross our path toward undisputed predominance in the interior of India. In the same manner the intelligence of Napoleon's projects first diverted our attention from the seaboard to our land frontiers, and first launched the British government upon that much larger expanse of Asiatic war and diplomacy in which it has every since been, with intervals, engaged. Up to the end of the last century the field of Anglo-Indian politics had been circumscribed within the limits of India, being confined to our relations with the Indian States over which England was asserting an easy mastery, by the natural and necessary growth of her ascendancy. Now for the first time we entered upon that range of diplomatic observation in which all the countries of western Asia, from Kabul to Constantinople, are surveyed as interposing barriers between Europe and our Indian possessions. The independence and integrity of these foreign and comparatively distant States are henceforward essential for the balance of Asiatic powers and for the security of our Indian frontiers. Before this epoch the jar and collision of European contests had been felt only in our dealings with the inland powers of India; we struck down or disarmed every native ruler who attempted to communicate with our European enemies. But from the beginning of the nineteenth century we have had little or nothing to fear from Indian rivals, and we have gradually taken rank as a first-class Asiatic sovereignty. The vast weight of our Indian interests has ever since weighed decisively in the balance of our relations, not only with all Asia, but with any European State whose views or dispositions might in any degree affect our position in the East. We have thus become intimately concerned in the political vicissitudes of every important State on the Asiatic continent. The chronic disquietude which began at this period has been the source of some hazardous military projects and premature diplomatic schemes, of two expeditions into Afghanistant, of a war with Persia, and of a policy that is constantly extending our protectorate far beyond the natural limits of India.

From the opening of the nineteenth century, then, may be dated the establishment of our undisputed ascendancy within India. From the same period also may be reckoned the reappearance of that susceptibility regarding the possible approach of European rivals by land, which led first to negotiations and treaties, and eventually to wars, between England and the foreign States adjoining or approaching her Indian dominion.

Section IV Internal Consolidation

So long as the European conflict lasted, the Anglo-Indian government had continued to survey watchfully all western Asia, and to stand on its guard against any movement by land that might seem to affect or endanger our position. In the meantime, our naval superiority enabled us to sweep all enemies out of the Eastern waters, and to occupy any point from which the coasts or commerce of India might be exposed to molestation. The connexion and constant interaction between political affairs in Europe and in Asia, which has exercised so important an influence on the expansion of our Asiatic dominions, is again illustrated by the events of this period. By 1806 Napoleon's supremacy had been established in European lands (outside Russia), but in 1805 the battle of Trafalgar had given England irresistible command of the seas. This sharp-cut division of land power and sea power-unprecedented, on so vast a scale, in history—operated materially to strengthen and enlarge the English position in the East. For whenever a European State was annexed to the French Empire or forced into alliance with it, its transmarine possessions were immediately seized by Great Britain. The Cape of Good Hope that important naval station half-way to India, had been finally occupied in 1806; and in 1810 Lord

Minto's expedition ejected the French from Java and the Moluccas—all Dutch Colonies; Abercrombie captured Mauritius and Bourbon, French islands; while of course all the Dutch and French settlements on the Indian coasts fell easily into our power. In this manner Napoleon's success in closing the European continent against England had the remarkable consequence that he was involuntarily building up and fortifying, instead of destroying, the British dominion in Asia. Moreover, when the French emperor promulgated in 1807 the Berlin decrees closing all the European ports against British goods, we retaliated by the Orders in Council which prohibited neutrals from trading with these ports, and the effect was to provide England with a temporary monopoly of all sea-borne commerce, especially of the invaluable trade with Asia. The sea-routes, the ports of shelter and supply, and the harbours, were all in our hands.

At the beginning of the long peace which followed the termination of the great war in 1815 England had secured undisturbed possession of her enormously valuable conquests in the southern seas—of the Cape, of Ceylon, and Mauritius. All the foreign settlements on the Indian seaboard were disarmed; and of the States within India not one could now measure its strength against our power and resources. Six of the chief principalities were now bound to our system by the subsidiary treaties. In western and central India, Baroda, Poona, and Hyderabad, in south India, Mysore and Travancore, and towards the north-west, Oudh with a large number of minor chieftainships—were all under our suzerainty and protection. Beyond our frontiers were the growing kingdom of Ranjit Singh in the Punjab, and the Gurkha State of Nepal along the southern slopes of the Himalayas. Only in central India there remained three principalities, surrounded by British territory, that had not yet come formally within the circle of our dominion. They belonged to the three families who still represented the fighting and predatory traditions of the Maratha confederacy, Sindia at Gwalior, Holkar at Indore, and the Bhonsla at

Nagpore. To these may be added, though the status was different, the ruling house of the Gaekwar at Baroda.

From the cessation of the great war that determined in our favour the contest with the native States for ascendancy in India we may also reckon the introduction of orderly administration within our territories, and of a systematic policy in regard to our neighbours, the recognition, in fact, of our imperial duties and obligations. The Mahomedan States of Hyderabad and Oudh were indebted for their survival to our protection; they would have been destroyed, but for our intervention, by fiercer and more vigorous rivals in the general scramble for dominion. Nevertheless it must be admitted that at times they had paid heavy salvage to us for their rescue. In some of our earlier transactions with them we had used the rough thoroughgoing methods of a stormy and dissolute period; and on emergencies their lands and revenues had been laid under severe contributions to our military expenditure. The time had now come when the British government, no longer driven to these summary expedients by the struggle for existence, but drawing from its own possessions an ample and secure revenue, could regulate its dealings in civilized fashion by settled treaties, and could begin to adjust all its dealings with native States on the fair and equitable basis of their subordinate relationship.

So also we had now some leisure for looking into the condition of our domestic administration, and bringing into some kind of order the great provinces which had been recently acquired. The investigation of land-tenures, the institution of an elementary police, the first serious attempts to check the brigandage prevailing in our districts, the arrangement and supervision of the local courts of justice, took substantial form at the beginning of this century; the roots of that immense system of organized government which has since spread over all India were planted at this season of comparative tranquillity. The first five years of the nineteenth century were occupied with continuous wars, with great territorial changes, with the removel landmarks, and the rearrangement of rulerships. But from that time forward the country under British jurisdiction has experienced immunity from foreign invasion or serious violation of its frontier, and even (except in 1857) from internal commotions. It may be questioned whether any State in Asia or even in Europe has enjoyed during the same period such complete political tranquillity.

Police

The progress of political transition in India, caused by the replacement of the hold of the Indian Princes by the introduction of the East India Company's rule, was not altogether peaceful. In the Bengal Presidency and Ceded and Conquered territories of the Upper Provinces, the scourge of dacoity and gang-robbery became rampant, causing widespread lawlessness and insecurity of life and property. The existing police force and the methods used by it were inadequate and ineffective safeguards against the unlawful activities and could not cope with the prevailing menace. Neither could the haunts of dacoits be discovered nor could they be apprehended and prevented from causing damage to the innocent subjects and also to the reputation of the Government.[29] The gang-robbers did not confine their depredations to particular parts of the country. They wandered from district to district taking advantage of the local circumstances. Very often, they defeated the nearly matured plans of a Magistrate for their apprehension, by their emigration to another district, outside their jurisdiction, where the daroghas, zamindars and others, whose aid he required, were not subject to his orders.[30] Consequently, gang-robbery, murder, arson and wounding created the greatest terror to the inhabitants of the Company's territory.[31] The Fifth Report from the Select Committee on the Affairs of the East India Company volume II gives an exhaustive account of the nature of lawlessness in Bengal and the Upper

Provinces. In the interest of sound administration and public tranquillity, Lord Minto's attention was drawn to the suppression of lawless elements by overhauling the police machinery.

A special provision was made under Regulation IX of 1808 to secure the apprehension of notorious robber chiefs with the assistances of the landholders and other respectable men. To enforce this cooperation, the Magistrates were empowered to publish any neglect or connivance either by fine or imprisonment upto one year.[32] Subject to confirmation by the Nizamat Adawlat, they could even attach their estates on suspicion.[33] With the operation of this Regulation, aided by the activity and vigilance of the Magistrates, the crimes of dacoity and highway robbery from Nadia, Rajshani, Dacca and Twenty-four Parganas were nearly suppressed.[34]

For the elimination of lawless elements form other districts, two Superintendents of Police were appointed; one for the division of Patna, Banaras and Bareilly, with powers to execute the warrants against principal offenders, guilty of the commission of robberies and other crimes by open violence, either by means of their own officers or through the local authorities as they might judge proper.[35] In the execution of this work, considerable discretion was allowed to them. They were required to have full knowledge about the actual strength of the police force in the different parts of their jurisdictions and to keep the Government regularly informed of fresh developments regarding the state of public offences and to seek its orders to meet new situations. They were authorized to correspond with the officials of the other departments to elicit information upon subjects connected with the discharge of their duties.[36] They were to keep themselves in touch with the Governor-General-in-Council through the Secretary in the Judicial Department upon all matters connected with their office.[37] To facilitate their work, orders were issued to the District Magistrates to transmit expeditiously all information obtained by them from time to time regarding the commission of any dacoity, murder, arson or highway robbery.[38] The District and Provincial officers of all ranks and also the law-courts were enjoined to affort every 'aid and cooperation' to them in the dishcarge of duties entrusted to them.[39] Resistance to the police in the execution of the warrants was declared punishable.[40]

This arrangement was successful in discovering and apprehending several gangs of dacoits and their leaders. But the gang-robbery was not wholly suppressed and crimes were not completely eradicated. However, on the retirement of Lord Minto they became less frequent and were less marked with cruelty and bloodshed. For the discovery of crimes and apprehension of public offenders, handsome rewards were paid to the police personnel.

Customs

The land and sea customs were one of the important sources of revenue to the East India Company. The land customs were the inland duties and the sea customs were the import and export duties. Prior to the arrival of Lord Minto, the rules and regulations governing the collection of both these duties were not donducive to the trade and commerce of the country. The merchants were frequently harassed and hampered in their trade by the vexatious practices on the part of the customs officers. Often their goods were confiscated on the ground of nonpayment of duties. Attempts on the part of merchants to evade duties were not infrequent. Most often they carried goods which did not fully conform to those mentioned in the rowannahs in their possession. But the most pronounced feature was the misapplication of the regulations.[41]

From the researches already done on the subject, it is known that a merchant going from Fatehgarh to Calcutta met a search-house every ten miles besides the regular inland custom-houses. In most cases, the merchants got relief by paying something to the petty customs officers which together with the Government duty 'became almost prohibitive to the merchant who did business on a small scale'. These practices led to disputes between the two and numerous petitions were received by the Government complaining against the vexatious delay and detention to which the goods of the merchants were subjected.[42] To remove these evils, Lord Minto reorganized the customs collection by promulgating his famous Regulation IX of 1810. By it, a chain of inland custom-houses was established in Meerut, Murshidabad, Dacca, Chittagong. Balasore, Hooghly and Calcutta.[43] For administrative convenience and efficiency, the inland customs-houses west of Bihar were grouped together into three zones, viz. Agra, Kanpur and Banaras which controlled and operated the customs houses situated at Meerut, Allahabad and Farrukhabad and Mirzapore respectively with the assistance of their Deputies. In Banaras and the Ceded and Conquered territories, these customs-officials were placed under the authority and jurisdiction of the Board of Commissioners. In Bengal, Bihar and Orissa, they functioned under the Board of Revenue.[44]

To prevent evasion of duties and ensure their effective collection, the customs-houses were linked up with a number of customs-chowkies established on the principal routes at a regular gap of four miles. These chowkies were impowered to detain goods liable to duty, passing through their jurisdiction, unaccompanied by rowannahs till the receipt of orders from the Collector of Customs regarding the disposal of the case. Duties were paid at the office of the Customs-Collector or his Deputy.[45] Goods for which the duty was paid once, were not liable to any further duty while passing through the Company's territories. The articles already in domestic use were not subjected to any duty. In cases where goods were damaged in transit, duty levied on them was based on depreciated value. To prevent the misapplication of rules by the customs officials, a book of rates of customs, certified by the Board of Revenue and Board of Commissioners was kept in the customs houses and subordinate chowkies for public verification.[46]

The inland customs-collectors and their Deputies were authorized to grant towannahs on an application given by the proprietors of goods or their authorized agents. To discourage smuggling, they were empowered to confiscate the goods other than those mentioned in the rowannahs or subjected them to double duty.[47] A rowannah was considered to be in force for one year only. On the expiry of its period, the rowannah was to be renewed for another year on payment of a one-half per cent duty on goods in the possession of the merchant. The imported articles were furnished with rowannahs by collectors or customs at Calcutta, Chittagong and Balasore on the payment of the duty in accordance with their quality and quantity.[48]

This Regulation was an improvement on the existing system in the custom department. It proved helpout to the Government and the merchants in the realization and payment of the customs duties and freed the movement of goods from harassment.

Postal System

The rudimentary postal system operating under the East India Company was also not free from defects. The system of conveyance of heavy despatches, packets and parcels by the bahangi post as introduced during the time of Lord Wellesley was not well defined. The Government of Lord Minto attended to these problems and removed the prevailing defects in the postal administration. By a notification of the Postmaster General on July 10, 1809, the scope and charges of the mail and bahangi posts were clearly defined. All overseas letters above eight sicca rupee weight[49] were to be forwarded by bahangi and charged as bahangi parcels.[50] This rule was also made applicable to the inland letters of 25 sicca rupee weight or above. Parcels and packages, in all cases, were charged at bahangi-rates which were lower than those of the mail.[51] Overseas parcels containing news papers and pamphlets were to be forwarded only by dak bahangi. One rupee was charged for 25 sicca rupee weight and six rupees for 250 and above sicca rupee weight.[52] The sum of six rupees was fixed as the maximum postage for such parcels. No change was made in the charges of the mail post. Better facilities were provided for the expeditious despatch of overland private mails to Madras and Bombay. This pacified the European population in the Presidencies.

Education

The East India Company's apathy towards Indian education continued till the time of Lord Minto. Primarily concerned with commercial ends and administration of territories under its direct control, it evinced little interest in the public welfare. Consequently with the decay of Indian political powers, the indigenous educational institutions began to decline for want of patronage and financial assistance. Beyond some highly inadequate individual British interest in education practically nothing substantial was accomplished.

Lord Minto evinced some interest in the promotion of education amongst the British Indian subjects. In his famous Minute of March 6, 1811 on education, he reviewed the decadent position of science and literature in India, and attributed it to the want of that encouragement which was formerly afforded to it by princes, chieftains and opulent individuals under the native Governments.[53] In his views, the immediate consequence of this state of affairs was the growing neglect of the study of useful and valuable books in Indian literature.[54] Visualizing the harmful effects of this tendency, he apprehended the extinction of Indian learning and scholarship by the neglectful attitude of the governing authorities. He felt that ignorance of the Indians was not only depriving the Government of the benefits which the spread of education could afford to it, but also obstructing its measures for better administration.[55] The prevalence of the crimes of perjury and forgery amongst Indians was attributed to the want of instructions in the moral and religious tenets of their faith. He further submitted proposals for reforming the Calcutta Madrassa and the Banaras Sanskrit College; and approached the Court of Directors for the sanction of an additional grant for starting two Sanskrit College—one at Nuddea and the other at Bhour and some new Madrassas at Bhagalpur and Jaunpur.[56] His aim, thus, was to preserve a high standard of Hindu and Islamic culture through the establishment of these institutions. He regretted that the British nation 'particularly distinguished for its love and successful cultivation of letters in other parts of the Empire, should have failed to extend its fostering care to the literature of the Hindus and to aid in opening to the learned in Europe and repositories of that literature', and had fears that if the Government did not come forward with financial help and encouragement to education, the damage so caused would be irreparable.[57] This powerful and convincing advocacy for the cause of Indian education and untiring efforts of the protagonists of Indian education in England had a significant impact on the decisions of the Parliament in 1813.

The day-to-day educational needs of the College of Fort William could also not escape the attention of Lord Minto. To this training institution, he lent his full support and recognized in it the two-fold object of promoting knowledge among the Anglo-Indian public servants and the restoration of Oriental literature to its due positions. The College library was enriched with a new stock of Persian and Arabic books worth five thousand rupees.[58] Foreign languages like Burmese and Malay received patronage. Dr. Leyden, an erudite scholar of the time, was encouraged to prepare vocabularies in the Burmese and Malaya languages which enabled the authorities of the East Indian Company to take greater interest in the affairs of the countries on the South-East frontier of India, particularly in the Eastern Archipelago, for promoting their Imperial interests.[59] The Government also helped in the publication of an edition of the Sanskrit dictionary and compilation of Sanskrit rules of Grammar.[60]

The interest taken by Lord Minto in the field of education was not officially sponsored by the Home Government. It indicates his approach to Indian education as an administrator. In unfolding his views, he did not chalk out either a comprehensive scheme of Oriental education or a new plan of intellectual development of Indian subjects. He only laid stress on the need to prevent decadence of learning in India in the interest of his administration and indicated the directions in which the Company should move. Grant of patronage to indigenous education and nothing more was intended by him in his Minute. Among the British officers in India who took interest in education, he can be termed as an Orientalist.

The non-existence of a separately ear-marked educational fund and the lack of interest and sympathy towards the educational needs of Indians on the part of the East Indian Company were the main hurdles operating against any sincere endeavour in this connection. By 1813 the enlightened British public opinion in England drifted in favour of assumption of responsibility to promote intellectual advancement in India as a necessary corollary to the missionary clause, for the inclusion of which in the Charter Act of 1813, the Clapham Sect, the British Missionary Societies, Wilberforce, Charles Grant and their associates had been persistently lobbying. Consequently, a sum upto £ 10,000 a year was earmarked for public education and the Company accepted it reluctantly. Considering the size of the British territory in India and its population, this amount was insignificant and appeared almost as a mockery to an enthusiast for Indian education. It was only a half-hearted measure by which nothing substantial could be expected. Even this little amount was not spent in its entirety. For several years, savings were made out of it at the cost of perpetual ignorance in India. There existed a great gulf between the policy announced and the policy actually pursued. The indigenous educational institutions continued to decline without any effort on the part of the Government to replace them by new ones. Only the missionaries showed some interest in this direction with their limited end in view. However, introduction of a clause for education in the Charter Act of 1813 indicated a change in the British policy and it was a good gesture. Official interest in education awaited the efforts of Lord William Bentinck, Thompson, Elphinstone, Lord Macaulary and Lord Dalhousie.

Missionaries

Lord Minto found that the missionaries had commenced a 'pious war' against the doctrines of Muhammedan and Hindu religions with unrelaxed vigour and decided to avoid the natural apprehensions aroused in India by their unrestrained expressions in speeches and writings. They published certain tracts called 'Addresses to Hindus and Muhammedans'. The ideas contained in them offended the religious sentiments of the Indian people.[61] Their other publications like Rise of Wisdom,' The Forerunner of the Holy Bible' and Distinction were abusive of the religions of the Hindus. In these publications, they showed Christ superior to Lord Krishna and claimed superiority of Christianity over Hinduism.[62] As a guardian of the public safety, Lord Minto apprehended that the issue and diffusion of such publications might antagonize Hindus and Muslims and constitute a danger to the Company's political position. He, therefore, requested the Danish Governor of Serampore to suppress further diffusion of such inflammatory pamphlets and imposed a strict censorship on their preaching and publishing activities which Charles Buchanan criticized as anti-Christian.[63] In reply, the Governor assured him to comply with the request.[64]

The Governor's assurance, however, did not serve the purpose. The activities of Baptist missionaries of Serampore continued. Their preaching and propaganda against the Indian religions, conversion of Indians to Christianity and publication of pamphlets, prejudicial to the local religions, remained unabated. The Governor-General felt alarmed by their activities and as a precautionary measure suggested the removal of their press from Serampore to Calcutta, where their publications were to be under the immediate control of the officers of the British Government.[65] The missionaries were reluctant to accept this proposal and sent a memorial to the Governor-General enumerating the hazards to which they would be exposed by their compliance to his wishes and promising to refrain from any activity prejudicial to law and order.[66] The Governor of Serampore also requested Lord Minto to allow the missionaries to stay at Serampore. At this assurance and cooperation of the missionary leaders and the Governor of Serampore, Lord Minto expressed satisfaction and revoked his demand for the transfer of their press to Calcutta.[67] On this, Willian Carey thanked the Governor-General for his goodness to allow the Baptist missionary press to function at Serampore.[68] The Court of Directors accorded santion to this measure.[69] But in 1811, when some missionaries arrived in Indian without licence, they were made to depart immediately.[70] The Governor-General, thus, did not encourage these missionaries who violated the law of the land.

Personally Lord Minto was not opposed to the progress of Christianity in India. In fact, his feelings ensured them his warmest encouragement. His softness for their work was evinced by the permission, he granted to the 'Baptist Missionary Society, to establish their centres at Agra and Delhi. He was of the view that the missionary work had a bright future in India only if its workers could concentrate their attention on convincing the Indian people of their faith by an amiable and persuasive approach rather than by their antagonizing ways. However, there was no change in the attitude of the Court of Directors towards the missionary activities in India and restrictions on their entry and residence in the British territories continued. But fully aware of the causes of the Vellore Mutiny and quite conscious of his duty to implement the Court of Director's policy of perfect religious toleration in their Dominion, he did not want that the religious freedom should be absurd and difficulty problems be created for the administration by the missionary enthusiasts. As the political head of the Company's affairs in India, he could not give countenance to any violation of the laws of the realm. The political expediency and the sense of public duty imposed upon him the obligation of checking their imprudence and overzealous haste.

The continuance of restrictions on the freedom of entry of the missionaries in British India, made Claudius Buchanan, a Chaplain of the Presidency of Bengal, highly critical of the policy of the East India Company in relation to the evangelicals. On his retirement of England in 1828, he started an agitation against the attitude of the Government of India and stressed the need for regular ecclesiastical establishment with a bishop and archdeacons qualified to advise Government on religious matters. His representations, the writings of Marshman and other missionaries and the zeal created in England for grant of freedom to missionary work in India, created climate in favour of the withdrawal of existing restrictions on their work and shaped the religious clause of the Charter Act of 1813.

Charter Act of 1813

Towards the end of the Governor-General of Lord Minto, the constitutional question relating to British India engaged the attention of the Parliament of England and the Home Government. The Charter Act of 1793 was to expire in 1813. Besides the normal matters effecting the administration of British India, several important issues cropped up during this period both in India as well as in England. The main consideration was that the Company's territory in India had expanded so much that fresh thought had to be given to the issues already discussed by the parliament several times in the past. Under the changed circumstances greater emphasis was laid on the inexpediency of combining both the commercial as well as political functions under a privately Chartered Company as originally thought in 1773. The industrial revolution in England was rapidly changing the commercial life of England and the economic thought of the period. The new economic theory of *laissez faire* was taking root in the British mind. By it the monopolistic system of trade was considered as incompatible with the British commercial prosperity. The British merchants keenly felt the loss of commercial advantages which the Company's monopoly had entailed to them. Napoleon's Continental System, though not fully successful, had adversely affected the economic fortunes of the British commercial class. Moreover, there was severe depression after 1810, effecting North England and the Midlands, the areas most dependent on foreign trade.[71] The situation worsened in 1811, when the American Non-Intercourse Act came into force for the value of exports fell from £ 1,12,17,685 in 1810 to £ 1,84. 7,9,17 in 1811.[72]

Under these circumstances it was not unnatural, if the British merchants, impelled by the new forces, claimed a share in their country's trade with India without any embarrassing commercial rules and regulations. This demand was strengthened on the plea that the commercial concession which simply allotted a certain quantity of tonnage annually for the accommodation of the private trade two decades ago in 1793, was very slight. Hence the limited quantity of the allotted tonnage to them, charged with a heavy freight and burdened with the inconvenient regulations, formed a subject of population complaint which could not be easily ignored in the age of economic liberalism.

The British Parliament had not abandoned its responsibility altogether. Long before the expiry of the previous Charter, the detailed investigation into Indian affairs was entrusted to a Select Committee of the House of Commons, appointed on March 11, 1808. Its enquiries running into five volumes, furnishing an exhaustive mass of information on various aspects, relating to the internal administration of British Indian came to light in 1812. These reports became the basis for the parliamentary Bill introduced by Lord Castlereagh for the renewal of the Charter.

During the course of debates the questions most hotly discussed was the need for change in the status and character of the East India Company from a commercio-political body to a purely political institution and the right of British public for free trade with the British Empire *vis-a-vis* those of the Company. Till then, the Company had enjoyed the monopoly of both the Indian and the China trade without any serious challenge. But now under the changed circumstances[73], the English merchants were vehemently critical of the exclusive commercial right of the East India Company, enjoyed since the last years of Queen Elizabeth I. Never before were the anti-monopolistic arguments of Adam Smith so strongly emphasized in the Parliament as on this occasion. The opposition was based on four pleas, advantageous to England, namely, the extension of British commerce and industry through private trade discouragement to the diversion of Indian trade to other countries of Europe and America, reduction in the cost of trade, especially transport and ware-housing changes due to free competition and cheapening of the Indian raw imports into Britain.[74]

Impressive and well-argumentative petitions and representations poured in from commercial towns like London, Bristol, Liverpool, Glasgow, Birmingham, Manchester, Shefield and Nottingham in support of the question at issue, requesting the parliament not to grant the renewal of the monopoly of the Indian trade to the Company, but to throw it open to all British subjects.[75] Delegates from the outports empowered to act for the mercantile communities to watch over their interests, reached London.[76] The unanimity of interest shown by the mercantile and industrial interests all over England on this occasion was remarkable and unique.

Acrimonious debate ensued on this momentous issue. The advocates of the Company's monopoly in India denounced the petitioners as looking only to their own self-interest. Charles Grant criticized the supporters of free trade principle of Adam Smith, based on prejudicial sources, as one-sided and incomplete and their attack on the Company as 'rash and crude'. We warned Sir Henry Dundas that free trade would lead to an 'unrestrained, unlimited intercourse and this would mean finally hazarding our power in the East'. Any relaxation in the basic fundamental of the Company's commercial monopoly would be a prelude to British colonization in India.[77] The unrestrained colossal influx of all sorts of Britons into India would undermine British practice and 'the days of the British rule in India would be numbered'.[78]

The Directors of the Company struggled hard for their privileges and characterized the advantages of free trade as illusory. They strained their nerves in support of their claims and predicted that consequences of change in the British commercial policy towards India would be more injurious to England and to British India than the advantages anticipated.[79] It would result in the entire subversion of their Company and the resultant competition would be injurious to the finances and industrial advancement of England and bring economic ruin to India.[80] The distinguished servants of the Company like Warren Hastings, Teignmouth, John Malcolm and Thomas Munro gave their evidence in the Parliament in favour of their arguments advanced by the advocates of the Company.

Equally strong were the arguments advanced by the opponents of the Fast India Company. Believing that the commercial monopolies were in their nature, inexpedient, impolitic and unjust, they pointed out the negligence, wasteful ways and prodigality of the Company as defects inherent in the system of joint stock companies which were not likely to be practiced by merchants. In their opinion, the monopolistic system had locked up national capital, retarded improvement and cooled the ardour of healthy competition. It was responsible for chilling down the commercial enthusiasm of the woollen manufacturers of Gloucester, Wiltshire, Exeter, Shrewsbury, and other places and was unconducive to the development of private wealth, and national revenue.[81] They held a conviction that the assertion of the Company that no extension of trade was possible with India was monstrous and untenable and treated the concept of exclusive privileges as 'humiliating to individuals, degrading to the national character and a national grievance.[82]

In face of formidable opposition, the Company's viewpoint could not prevail. The Parliament passed a resolution which conferred the right of trading into and from all parts and places within the limits of the East India Company's Charter on all His Majesty's subjects for 20 years. This resolution was incorporated in the new Charter Act of 1813 and became its first section.

Another issue that kept the Parliament engaged for some time was the China trade of the Company. As compared to the Indian trade, the trade with China was small in quantity. It was largely confined to a factory in the vicinity of the city of Canton where trade could be carried on only through a society of fourteen Hong merchants to whom the Chinese Government had entrusted its tea trade. The Company had no political hold over any part of China and its trade depended largely on the bounty and goodwill of the Government of that country.

In respect of this trade, therefore, Charles Grant's warning against free trade was heeded and his advice was accepted. While the monopoly of tea trade was vital for the Company, its land was not destined to be conducive to the commercial advantages of England. There was an apprehension that unrestricted tea trade would encourage smuggling, increase chances of conflict with the Chinese officials, increase the cause of annoyance to the Celestial Empire and put an end to the trade privileges altogether. This fear weakened the case of opposition and proved to be the most powerful motivating factor in the decision taken by the Parliament in this regard. Consequently, the Parliament passed another resolution which became Section two of the Charter Act by which the 'exclusive right of trading, trafficking and using the benefits of merchandise and tea from China and from all islands ports, coasts, cities, towns and places between the Cape of Good Hope and the Straits of Magellan, were conferred on the East India Company".[83]

The third important issue taken up by the British Parliament on June 22, 1813 was concerned with the removal of restrictions on the free entry of Christian missionaries into British India. Lord Castlereagh, the Foreign Secretary initiated the debate on this issue by a statement that unrestrained migration of Christian missionaries to India would not be inconsonant with the tranquillity and security of the British possessions in India and he did not see danger to British rule if they were allowed to proceed to India under the supervision of the Court of Directors. The resolution as contained in the Bill was however opposed by the advocates of the East India Company on the plea that it was fraught with the most fatal consequences to the British interests in India. It would not only defeat the object for which it was made, but would lead to universal fear and discontent all over the country. It was argued that in a caste and religion-ridden country like India, it would convert its timidity into desperation and subordination into defiance and would kindle a flame which would destroy not only the British interests in India, but all those who professed the faith. Even Lord Teignmouth who was connected with the religious party, admitted that considerable peril might be apprehended from indiscreet zeal and that any enactment for the conversion of the natives would be attended with grave danger.[84] William Wilberfore who defended the conduct of the Baptist missionaries in Bengal and claimed moderation for them for their piety and learning, denied that the only object of the resolution was to permit the missionaries to propagate Christianity in India, but their main object would be to enlighten the minds of Indians through education, the progress of science and the publications and circulation of the scriptures in the Indian languages.

In case of a refusal by them, the Board of Control was authorised to issue a licence. To meet the dangers pointed out by the Company in throwing open the gates of India to the Britons for religious or commercial purposes, it was decided to cancel the licence of such persons whose activities were found to be prejudicial to the interests of the company, and to ask them to leave India.[85]

Another section of the Bill related to the facilities to be provided for the promotion of learning in British India. Robert Smith proposed for the appropriation of a sum of money for the promotion of native literature and the establishment of colleges in British India. The Court of Directors opposed this proposal and showed reluctance to accept a responsibility of this kind on the plea that education should not be regarded as a responsibility of the state. It was not so even in their own country. They considered the resolution as extraordinary and extravagant. Influenced more by financial than by philanthropic motives, they resisted all attempts to increase obligations, affecting their dividends. The sponsors of the move, however, did not budge from their stand and wanted no compromise on what they considered to be an essential duty under the special circumstances in India. They were influenced largely by the British Orientalists in India and England who had been strong advocates of the revival and improvement of Indian literatures owing to the progressive decay of Indian learning with the establishment of the Company's rule and the ignorance of scientific knowledge amongst the Indian subjects. Against the wishes of the East India Company and much to the chagrin of its advocates, the move was carried and a sum of one lakh of rupees was earmarked annually for the revival and improvement of literature and promotion of knowledge of sciences in British India.[86]

An important point connected with the entry of English traders, teachers and missionaries into India as a result of the resolutions passed was to provide against the danger of an unlimited and unlicenced influx of British into India. A fear was entertained the British establishment in India might be a source of resentment in that country which might follow either the example of American colonies, or be subjected to British cruelties and oppressions which the Company's functionaries would be unable to present. Against both these tendencies, a counterpoise was considered necessary.

Quite an important section in the Parliament regarded these oppressions as 'exaggerated and visionary'. It was of the opinion that trade in India would be confined to the principal settlements, where persons engaged in it would be immediately under the eye of the most powerful and vigilant officials, and the persons proceeding to India would be engaged in peaceful callings. However, as a precautionary measure, it was decided that 'no persons, except those in the Company's employ, shall be allowed to go to India as residents without a licence either from the Company or the Board of Control and that the Indian Government shall retain authority to send out of the country any individual from whom they may think it advisable to withdraw the licence to reside in India'.

Persons entering Company's territories without licence were to be treated as interlopers and the Company's Government was empowered to restrain, by summary conviction, British subjects in India who overstated or were found without a licence or certificate. If such persons were sent home, they could not be prosecuted afterwards.[87] But where they were convicted and the case was found to be appealable to the Sadar Diwani Adawlat or the Courts of the local Governments, they were allowed to file the appeal to His Majesty's Courts.[88] In cases of trespass or assault committed by them on Indians and the cases concerning debts taken by them from Indians, they were placed under the jurisdiction of the Justices of Peace. As a measure of their safety, the Englishmen residing at a distance of more than ten miles from the Presidency towns, were required to register themselves with the District Magistrate and they were placed, for civil cases, under the jurisdiction of civil courts.[89]

Besides these important sections, the Charter incorporated several comparatively less important decisions relating to the Company's patronage, training writers, military establishment, Parliamentary control and judicial administration. The Company's power of patronage was continued for another twenty years. Under the supervision of the Board of Control, the civil servants of the Company continued to be tained in the College of Haileybury. The persons recruited as writers were to undergo successful training for four terms. For the training of the Company's militia, the military school at Adiscombe was maintained and controlled by the Board of Control.

Financial supervision and control of the Parliament over the Company's commercial accounts in India was increased. The Company was required to maintain its commercial and territorial accounts separately. Its accounts were to be scrutinized by the Court of Directors and they were to be presented annually to the Parliament. For the disbursement of revenue, priorities were laid down. The maintenance of troops and payment of dividends was made the first charge on the revenues of India, expenditure on the civil and commercial establishments was the second and the expenditure on other items was to be the last charge. The dividend to the Proprietors was fixed at 10½%.

In judicial matters, the Indian subjects of the Company were declared amenable to the Provincial Courts for all crimes. Special penalties were enacted for theft, forgery, perjury and coinage. Special judicial privileges were accorded to the British residents in India.[90]

The Charter Act of 1813 is a significant landmark in the constitutional history of India. It renewed the privileges of the East India Company for a further period of twenty years and preserved the indirect sovereignty of the crown over the Company's territorial acquisitions in India. The powers of the Board of Control were enlarged and Parliamentary supervision over the accounts of the Company was increased. Its control over the civil and military training of the Company's servants was significant.

The Charter abolished the Company's trade monopoly with India and allowed it to retain its hold over the China trade unimpaired. By throwing open the Indian trade to all British merchants, the first blow on the monopoly of the East India Company was inflicted. Now the Company became one of many competitors for the Indian trade without any special privilege. English capital and enterprise began to flow freely into India, resulting in keener commercial competition with the indigenous products and leading ultimately to the decline of Indian industrial handicrafts which could not compete with the machine-made goods. British trade with India increased in volume and became financially very lucrative. The British industrialists were benefited considerably. A fresh impetus was given to British industries while the industries in India tottered, tumbled and struggled for survival, without any hope of success. The economic drain from India increased in volume as the profits derived by British merchants from Indian trade did not remain within its borders but went to England. From this date began rapidly the economic decline of India due to the growing dependence upon agriculture and unemployment and poverty among the Indian people. Thus the economic effects of the British rule on India began to be increasingly felt even by the common man.

Although the East India Company lost its monopoly of Indian trade, it was not completely shorn of its commercial character. With China trade in its hands, its dual character still continued and required another agitation to end it.

The end of the Company's commercial monopoly of Indian trade, the insertion of the missionary clause and the earmarking of an educational fund for the benefit of the subject people against the wishes of the Company were symptomic of the triumph of liberal public opinion in

England which was interested in promoting British interests in India by all possible means, but was not, at the same time, completely negligent of the basic minimum duty to the governed.

REFERENCES

1. Gupta, H. L., *Francophobia and its Impact on British Activities in India* (Mss. unpublished).
2. Mariott, J. A. R., *The Eastern Question*, pp. 176-77.
3. Panikkar, K. M., *op. cit.*, p. 7.
4. A large force of Cossacks and Russian regulars were to march by way of Turkestan, Khiva and Bokharan to the Upper Indus valley, while 35,000 French troops under General Massena were to descend the Danube and going by way of the Black Sea and the Caspian, were to make an attack on Persia, take Herat and then Candhar and unite with the Russians on the Indus. (Shneidman, J. L. *The Proposed Invasion of India by Russia and France*, an article in Journal of Indian History; Vol. XXXV, pp. 168-75.
5. A large force of Cossacks and Russian regulars were to march by way of Turkestan, Khiva and Bokhara to the Upper Indus valley, while 35,000 French troops under General Massena were to descend the Danube and going by way of the Black Sea and the Caspian, were to make an attack on Persia, take Herat and then Candhar and unite with the Russian on the Iadus. (Shneidam, J. L. *The proposed Invasion of India by Russia and France*, an article in Journal of Indian History; Vol. XXXV, pp. 168-75.
6. Aitchison, C. U. *A Collection of Treaties, Engagements and Sanads*, Vol. XIII, pp. 49-53.
7. Sen, S. P., *The French in India*, p. 562.
8. Sen, S. P., *The French in India*, p. 574.
9. *Ibid.*, pp. 574-78.

10 Georgin. Armenia and North-Western Provinces of Persia were annexed by Russia.

11. British Resident at Bushire to Edmonstone, Secy. Pol. and Secret Deptt. July 16, 1807, For Deptt Secret Const Sept. 28, 1807, Cons. I.
12. Fischer, H. A. L., *Studies in napolenic Statesmanship Germany*, pp. 144-45.

13. Williams, Henry Smith, *The Historians's History of the World*, Vol. XIII, p. 562.
14. Marriott, J. A. R. *The Eastern Question*, p. 185.
15. *Ibid.* 'I detest the English,' said Alexander embracing Napoleon, 'as much as you do and I will uphold you in anything, you attempt them'. In that case,' Napoleon replied, 'peace is concluded'. Williams, Henry Smith, *op. cit.*,
16. Secret letter to the court of Directors, Feb. 9, 1808.
17. *Ibid.*
18. *Ibid.*
19. Minute of Lord Minto, Jan., 30, 1808, For Deptt. Secret and Seperate Jan. 30, 1808, Cons. 1.
20. Secret letter to the Court of Directors, March 31, 1808.
21. *Ibid.*
22. *Ibid.*
23. Secret letter to the Court of Directors, March 31, 1808.
24. *Ibid.*
25. Secret letter from the Court of Directors, Sept. 14, 1808.
26. Lecky mentions (*History of England,* vol. v, p. 850 a remarkable letter written from Berlin in 1786 by Mirabeau, on the possibility of Russian armies some day penetrating through central Asia into India. Mirabeau had heard that the Russians made an unsuccessful attempt in 1783 to seize Astrabad in Persia, with the object of ultimately pushing on to India, and he predicted that some day the Russians might in this manner so threaten the English power in India as to produce a complete change in the system of European politics. The prophecy is indeed remarkable, but the rumour was premature. All that the Russians had done was to send a small force to the south-eastern shore of the Caspian, for the protection of their commerce in that quarter. See Forster's *Journey (1798) vol. ii. p. 201.*
27. The whole correspondence, recently published, is worth careful study, seeing that diplomatic situations and national *rapprochements* have a certain tendency to recur.
28. 1812-1826. Russia attacked Persia in 1826, and made a long stride eastward in 1828, which revived our anxieties.
29. *Fifth Report from the Select Committee on the Affairs of the East India Company*, Vol. II, p. 607.

30. Fifth Report, *op. cit.*, Vol. II, p. 607.
31. *Ibid.*
32. Regulation IX of 1808.
33. *Ibid.*
34. Fifth Report, *op. cit.*, p. 616.
35. Regulation X of 1808.
36. *Ibid.*
37. *Ibid.*
38. Fifth Report, *op. cit.*, p. 608.
39. Regulation VIII of 1808.
40. Regulation X of 1808.
41. Ghosal, H. R. *Economic Transition in the Bengal Presidency*, p. 193.
42. Ghosal, H. R., *op. cit.*, p. 195.
43. Regulation IX of 1810.
44. *Ibid.*
45. *Ibid.*
46. *Ibid.*
47. *Ibid.*
48. Regulation IX of 1810.
49. One tola was equal to one sicca rupee weight.
50. Sandeman. H. D., *Selections from Calcutta Gazettes*, Vol., III, pp. 70-72.
51. *Ibid.*
52. *Ibid.*
53. Minute of Lord Minto, March 6, 1811, For. Misc., Cons. 3.
54. *Ibid.*
55. *Ibid.*
56. *Ibid.*
57. Minute of Lord Minto, March 6, 1811, For. Misc., Cons. 3.
58. Public Gen. letter to Court of Directors, Jan. 12, 1810.
59. Secretary, College of Fort William to Edmonstone, Feb. 4, 1811, Home Misc, Vol. 561.

60. *Ibid.*

61. Lord Minto to Governor of Serampore, Sept. 1, 1807, For. Deptt. Secret, Cons. Sept. 1, 1807, Cons. 2.

62. At a meeting of the Governor-General-in-Council, dated nil, For. Deptt. Secret, Cons. Nov. 2, 1807, Cons. 1-3.

63. Lord Minto Governor of Serampore, Sept. 1, 1807, For. Deptt. Secret, Cons. Sept. 1, 1807, Cons. 2.

64. Governor of Serampore to Lord Minto, Sept. 2, 1807, For. Deptt. Secret, Cons. Sept. 8, 1807, Cons. 3.

65. Lord Minto to Governor of Serampore, Sept. 5, 1807, For. Deptt. Secret, Cons. Sept. 15, 1807, Cons. 4.

66. Memorial of Missionaries to Lord Minto, Sept. 30, 1807, For. Deptt. Secret, Cons Oct. 5, 1807, Cons. 6.

67. Lord Minto to Governor of Serampore, Oct. 5, 1807, For. Deptt. Secret, Cons. Oct. 5, 1807, Cons. 9.

68. Carey to Edmonstone; Oct. 20, 1807, For. Deptt. Secret, Cons. Oct. 26, 1807, Cons. 3.

69. Secret letter from the Court of Directors, Sept. 17, 1808.

70. Countess of Minto, *op. cit.*, p. 82.

71. Darwall, F. O., *Papular Disturbances and Public Disorder in Regency England*, p. 53.

72. *Ibid.*

73. Parl. Debates, House of Commons, Many 6, 1812.

74. *Ibid.*

75. *Ibid.*

76. *Ibid.*

77. Embree, A. T. *Charles Grant and East India Company*; *pp*. 165-66.

78. Embree, A. T. *op. cit.*, pp. 166-67.

79. Chairman of Court of Directors to Robert Dundas, June 13, 1812, Parl. Papers H. C., pp.

80. *Ibid.*

81. Report from the Committee of Correspondence to Court of Directors, Feb. 9, 1813, parl. Papers H. C., p. 2.

82. *Ibid.*

83. The navigation and transporation of foreign goods were to be made in English-builtships. It was unlawful for any person,

except the East India Company and those who had obtained their licence for that purpose, to ship, carry or put on board any ship in the East Indies. Ships in private trade were not allowed to go within certain limits, without licence from the Court of Directors. (Section VII, VIII, IX).

84. *Ibid.*

85. Sections 36 and 37 of the Charter.

86. Section 43 of the Charter.

87. Section 104 of the Chapter.

88. Section 107 of the Charter.

89. Sections 110-11 of the Charter.

90. Sections 109-10 of the Charter.

5

Diplomatic Missions

(a) Mission to Lahore

Lord Minto sent a political mission to the Court of Lahore and his choice for it fell upon C.T Metcalfe who was the most promising of the younger civilians and one of the best among diplomats. He was required, firstly to counteract the alleged French designs of an attack on India by wooing Maharaja Ranjit Singh to an alliance; and, secondly, to secure for the Company political control over the Cis-Sutlej territory by preventing the Sikh chief from extending his territory to that region.

Metcalfe was received at Kasur by Ranjit Singh. He was however, apprehensive and suspicious regarding the motives of this mission. The British envoy stated that the friendship which subsisted between him and the British, had induced Lord Minto to depute him, in order to communicate some important intelligence with which the Maharaja's interests were materially concerned.[1] He told him that the British Government had received reliable and authentic reports that the French who were endeavouring to establish themselves in Persia, had planned the invasion and seizure of Kabul and the Punjab.[2] Therefore, treating the British interest and that of the Maharaja to be identical, the Governor-General of India had commissioned him to negotiate with him some arrangements, for the extirpation of the common enemy, and appointed Mountstuart Elphinstone as envoy to the court of the King of Kabul for a similar purpose, who would, in a short time, pass through his State with his permission.[3]

Several meetings took place; some between the envoy and the Maharaja and others between him and the Maharaja's principal minister.[4] But instead of any substantial outcome of an agreed nature, serious differences of opinion ensued between the two parties. In one of these meetings, the Maharaja's ministers put forward three proposals for an agreement, *viz,* (a) a close alliance between the Maharaja and the British Government declaring the friends and the enemies of the one as the friends and the enemies of the other; (b) recognition of the Maharaja's claim to sovereignty over the entire Sikh country; and (c) assurances by the British Government that the proposed mission to Kabul would not interfere with the Maharaja's claims upon the territories of the king of Kabul.[5]

To Metcalfe, these proposals appeared to be merely a cloak to conceal the Maharaja's real design. He, therefore, did not appreciate the humour of this farce and instead of conceding to them, he preferred simply to impress his views on them. With regard to the first one, he expressed the wish of his Government to form an alliance with the Maharaja only for defensive purposes. Regarding the second proposal, he proposed to defer discussion on it till the receipt of the letter of the Governor-General containing his views on the Cis-Sutlej region. On the third proposal, he assured the Maharaja's counselors that the British mission to the Court of the king of Kabul was calculated to promote the interests of the Lahore Durbar and it was primarily intended to bring the Maharaja and the Shah of Kabul together against the common enemy.[6]

These explanations of Metcalfe did not satisfy the Maharaja, because his intended object was not achieved and his main proposal was not categorically conceded. The evasive replies of the British envoy appeared to him entirely unconvincing.

Meanwhile, the Sikh chief crossed the Sutlej and encamped at Khai, a village about 12 miles inland. Metcalfe followed him and had a meeting with him, in which the negotiations did not show any appreciable advance. On October 4,1808, the Sikh Chief advanced from Khai to Faridkot, disregarding the protests of the British envoy who stated that the aim of his mission was to negotiate a settlement, not to accompany him on his military campaigns.[7]

Now Metcalfe submitted the draft proposals of the Treaty consisting of three clauses. Firstly, a defensive alliance between the two States against France in the event of an invasion; secondly, free passage and assistance to the British army, should it be necessary to meet the enemy beyond the Indus or in Afghanistan, and thirdly, the maintenance of a British line of communication with Kabul and protection to its messengers and runners by the Maharaja.[8]

The Draft Treaty contemplated an alliance only against the dread of French invasion which rattled in the Governor-General's mind. But to the Maharaja, France was merely a name and nothing more. Having no connection with it, he neither loved it nor hated it. He rather feared the Company, a formidable power on his borders. He felt the absurdity of Metcalfe's assurances that the proposed defensive alliance against France was the outcome of the Governor-General's sincere regard for him; and that the Punjab and not British India would benefit this alliance. He believed that it was England and not Lahore which was the enemy of France.[9] He, therefore, felt convinced that if the British desired him to join them, they must pay for it ans concede to his proposals. Swayed by these convictions, he pressed on the British envoy to accept his point of view and endeavoured to capture as much of the Cis-Sutlej territory as he could, while the negotiations were pending.[10] Under these circumstances, the 'big words' which Metcalfe had spoken in connection with the aim of his mission, began to shrivel into insignificance.

Considering it as the most appropriate moment to obtain concessions from the British Government, the Lahore Chief submitted his own draft of a Treaty[11] on October 8,1808, consisting of three propositions; the first asking for British non-interference in his disputes with the sovereign of Kabul; the second, proposing a perpetual alliance between him and the British; and the third, declaring his right of sovereignty over the whole Sikh territory. In reply to these proposals, Metcalfe stated that he had no authority from his Government to make any promise or sign any Treaty regarding Ranjit Singh's connections with Kabul or the Cis-Sutlej States.[12] Ultimately, after due deliberations, it was decided that the draft proposals for a Treaty submitted by the two parties should be despatched to Calcutta for the consideration of the Governor-General.[13]

In the meantime, the Sikh Chief continued his career of conquest in the Cis-Sutlej region with full zest and vigour ignoring the complaints and remonstrances of the British envoy. He marched from Faridkot to Malerkotla, a town about 60 miles eastward. Its Chief, Ata-ulla-Khan, submitted almost without resistance.[14] By persuasion, the Maharaja again dragged the British envoy to Malerkotal.[15] Now the feeling of his being used as a tool to work out the Maharaja's ends became firm in his mind. He therefore, refused to accompany him further and felt so much disgusted that he desired some place to be assigned, where the mission might stay, till the Maharaja was free from his campaign and instructions were received from Calcutta.[16]

Thereafter, Metacalfe was asked to proceed to Amritsar; and the Maharaja hastened to complete his work.[17] Soon he annexed Ambala and brought Mehtab Singh, the Chief of Thanesar, to submission,[18] The Raja of Patiala exchanged turbans with the Maharaja, and thus agreed to be friendly with him.[19] At Shahabad, which was also captured, the Chiefs of Jagadhari, Burea and Radawar attended the Maharaja and offered *nazars* to him according to their means.[20]

Under these circumstances, Lord Minto sent a strong note of protest to the Maharaja in which he reminded him of the existing engagement of amity between him and the Calcutta Government and expressed great surprize and concern at his measures to subjugate the Cis-Sutlej territories.[21] He vehemently criticized the Maharaja's policy of aggrandizement and put forward British claims on the States of that region. He made it clear to the Maharaja that by the issue of a war with the Marathas during Lord Wellesley's time, the British Government became possessed of the power and rights in the north of Hindustan.[22] At that time, the Maharaja had no claims on that region. It was also made clear that even in the early period of the British contact with the Maharaja, a communication was received from him by Lord Lake proposing to fix the Sutlej as the eastern boundary of the Lahore territories.[23] This was treated by Lord Minto as a clear proof of the Maharaja's awareness at that time that the Cis-Sutlej region was dependent on the power paramount, North of Hindustan. He adopted, therefore, a firm attitude, and stated that the British Government would not consent to the establishment of his or anybody else's overlord ship over the Chiefs of that region. His contention was that in accordance with the established custom those Chiefs were and would remain under the protection of the British who were the successors of the Marathas in that region.[24] This *claim* appeared to be a very far-fetched one lacking any sanction-legal customary or otherwise.

Having thus refused to acknowledge the Maharaja's rights over any Cis-Sutlej territory. Lord Minto advised him to restore all the places, subjugated by him, to their former possessors, and confine his army to the right bank of the river Sutlej.[25]

The Governor-General's suggestions contained in his note were not liked by Maharaja Ranjit Singh, and he was least inclined to accept them.[26] For some time, therefore, he felt greatly agitated and was in a state of indecision.

At last, on December 21, 1808, a meeting took place between the Maharaja and the British envoy. The British envoy demanded cession of the territories, annexed by the Maharaja, such as Ambala, Sahnewal, Faridkot and all other places annexed since his arrival in the Maharaja's camp.[27] Shuffling explanations were made by the Maharaja of the reasons for their capture. But any declaration that they would be ceded was cautiously avoided. He brought the negotiation to an end without giving any decisive reply.[28]

Soon after this, the British Government became firm in its stand. This was mainly on account of the momentous changes in European politics. Napoleon Bonaparte because entangled in the Peninsular War. The British were now no longer apprehensive of Napoleon Bonaparte reaching within striking distance of India, and his menace was a wearing sway. Thus encouraged by the indefinite suspension of Napoleon's plan of invading the eastern countries, the British Government was not, at any rate, disposed to allow its western frontier to be in a chronic state of invasion or disturbance. The Governor-General, therefore, abandoned the idea of coaxing the Lahore Chieftain to an immediate alliance, and decided to have a different approach to this problem.

Having come to the determination that Sutlej should be the limit of Maharaja Ranjit Singh's acquisitions in that direction, the British Government, in order to uphold its resolution, immediately commanded the advance of a sufficient body of troops under the command of Lieutenant Colonel Ochterlony, who was instructed to establish a military post at the river Sutlej and to support Metcalfe in his negotiations with Ranjit Singh.[29] In fact, it was done so to overawe the Sikh Chief and compel him to give up his claims on the Cis-Sutlej region. Ochterlony reached Ludhiana on January 19, 1809.

This firm attitude of the British Government alarmed Ranjit Singh Doubting British motives, he began to make secret military preparations to meet the eventuality of a war with them. A major part of his army, under Dewan Mohkam Chand, the best of the Sikh Generals, famous for his conspicuous valour and equally well-known for his anti-British feelings, who was then assisting Raja Sansar Chand of Kangra in driving away the Gorkhas from his territory, was called back and ordered to march to the Phillaur Ghat, on the river Sutlej, opposite to the town of Ludhiana.[30] The Maharaja also summoned back all those Chiefs who had retired to their homes on leave.[31] He also accelerated the production of war material, including equipment, weapons and ammunition.[32] These military preparations of the Maharaja and his frequent consultations with his chiefs bespeak of his determination to put up a stiff resistance to the British in case his territory was attacked.

At this time, a military incident occurred at Amritsar, in which an attack was made by the Akalis[33] of the Golden Temple on the Muhammedan soldiers of Metcalfe's escort, who had gathered for the Muharram[34] celebration. In this clash, the Akalis, under their renowned leader, Jathedar Phula Singh, were completely routed by the few British sepoys.[35] This defeat, though minor, appeared to have created a great impression on the Maharaja's mind. After this traumatic experience, it appears that the Lahore Chief realized the inadequacy of his resources compared to the British, and perceived that it would be a suicidal step to persist with fetish obstinacy for coping with the fast moving challenge of war. This explains why he gradually became eager for a Treaty of Alliance. He agreed to the demand for withdrawal of his troops from Ambala and its restoration to Rani Dya Kaur.[36] But he evaded the demand for the restoration of other territories.[37]

At the next meeting, therefore, the question of the restitution of other places, such as, Faridkot, Khur, Khanpur, Sahnewal and Kot Kapura, was reopened by the envoy.[38] But the Maharaja was reluctant to agree to these terms at Sahnewal was not a new conquest, and Faridkot was a place dependent on Kot Kapura which was one of his earlier conquests.[39] The two parties, therefore, parted without being nearer to an agreed settlement.

Thereafter, the British Government adopted a firm attitude. It decided to force Ranjit Singh to relinquish the territories under dispute. To bring this about, as a preliminary step, Sir David Ochterlony issued a Proclamation on February 9, 1809, declaring that all the Cis-Sutlej states were under British protection and that any aggression by the Chief of Lahore would be resisted with arms.[40] The peremptory demands for the restoration of the fortresses occupied by Maharaja Ranjit Singh in the Cis-Sutlej region to their original possessors and the withdrawal of his troops from the eastern bank of the river, coupled with the threat of taking military steps against him in case of non-compliance, created further alarm and suspicion in his mind regarding British intentions.

This stiff attitude and successful stroke of diplomacy of the British Government greatly upset Maharaja Ranjit Singh. Realizing that circumstances were going against him, he was constrained to prolong negotiations without risking a war which might prove disastrous to him. The rulers of the Cis-Sutlej to whom British protection was accorded, were destined to support the British more to weaken his ascendancy in that region. This opened his eyes to the gravity of the situation and the unwisdom of risking a military clash with the British supported by his own kith and kin.

At last at a meeting attended by the Maharaja, his Council of ministers and the British envoy, he found no other way out but to abandon his pretensions. Although his stand in the dispute was not altogether baseless nor was the British demand justified, he reluctantly agreed to restore Faridkot, Khur and Khanpur to the original possessors under the pressures of circumstances which he could not control.[41] Consequently, he issued order for the withdrawal of the principal part of his army from the left bank of the river, and his army evacuated Faridkot on April 2, 1809.[42]

An able administrator, imbued with driver, energy, imagination and far-sightedness, Maharaja Ranjit Singh felt that his own position in the Punjab was hardly established, because only a portion of it had so far come under his control, which, too, had not yet been fully consolidated. He feared that the pro-British faction consisting of some of the Sikh Chieftains of the Cis-Sutlej region, might shake off its allegiance to him at the time of emergency, and rise in rebellion against him with the help of the British, and thus topple his hard-earned ascendancy. He was also well aware of the inexhaustible resources of the British, and considered it a folly to strike his head against the stone wall, and thereby expose his kingdom to imminent hazards.

Having been fully convinced that the decision of the British Government was irrevocable and the amity of the mighty strangers was less formidable than their enmity, the Maharaja realized the utter helplessness of his cause and submitted to the inevitable, more out of a motive of self-interest than in a spirit of resignation, by pruning his scheme of conquest of the Cis-Sutlej states. In fact, he made the best of the bargain by withdrawing his forces from the south of the Sutlej, and entering into a Treaty with the British on April 25,1809.[43] This decision of Maharaja Ranjit Singh indicates his realistic approach to the complicated issues involved in his disputes with the infinitely superior British military power.

The Treaty of Amritsar consisted of there clauses. It was agreed that perpetual friendship would subsist between the two Governments; the British would not interfere in the Trans-Sutlej region, and the Maharaja would not encroach upon the Cis-Sutlej territory. The Treaty was to be considered null and void if either of the parties violated any of these articles.

This Treaty is considered a most significant landmark in the history of British relations with Maharaja Ranjit Singh. While it afforded security to the British interests in the Cis-

Sutlej region against the constant aggressive designs of the Lahore Chief; it compelled Maharaja Ranjit Singh to abandon his eastward ambition. It also paved the way for the British to bring the Cis-Sutlej Sikh Chiefs under their protection and enabled them to divert their resources successfully against the Gorkhas, pindaris and Marathas during the Governor-General-ship of Lord Hastings.

Besides, this Treaty marked the beginning of the westward drive of British influence and military power beyond the river Jamuna, which could not be finally completed till the death of Maharaja Ranjit Singh and two trials of military strength with the Sikhs. This transaction gave them a good deal of confidence in the success of their astute diplomacy, marked with clear perception of realism. They realized that the turbulent Maharaja was tamed and, with his amity, friendship and co-operation they would be able to face any foreign invasion from the western frontier. These were the important achievements, pregnant with deepest significance for the British, brought about by the fear of a probable French drive towards India by the overland route. Henceforth, Punjab under Maharaja Ranjit Singh remained a buffer state between British India and territories beyond the geographical frontier of western India throughout the period of British involvements for establishing their ascendancy in other parts of the country and becoming an unchallenged power paramount in the vast sub-continent.

This Treaty struck a serious blow at Maharaja Ranjit Singh's ambition of bringing the Cis-Sutlej Chiefs under his banner. It sealed once for all his military manoeuvres across the Sutlej, and ended for ever his highly cherished dream of becoming the overlord of all the Sikh Chieftains and realizing the unfulfilled aspirations of Guru Gobind Singh to unite the Sikh community into a solid, compact and homogeneous socio-political unit. From this time onward, it was not improbable if Maharaja Ranjit Singh began to feel the British ascendancy in the East as a hard reality. Though, he had signed the Treaty under the pressure of highly compelling circumstances, he was not happy in his heart. Considerably overcome by an intermixture of frustration, disappointment, resentment, alarm as well as suspicion, he could not decide for a while what subtle policy he should, follow. However, he remained fully vigilant on the right bank of the river Sutlej and maintained his military forces all along it as a measure of security of his hard-built and small kingdom till he was convinced that the British would not cast a covetous eye on the Trans-Sutlej region. Soon after, when the East India Company got itself involved into innumerable political complications and engaged itself in the struggle for political ascendancy, territorial and administrative consolidation, he reconciled himself to his fate and began to look to the North, West and South for satisfying his lust for territories.

It is difficult to state how far these achievements were a compensation for the diplomatic defeat and great loss of prestige, sustained by him in 1809, and the permanent blockage of his road to the East. Nevertheless, the diversion of his attention which might be regarded as a logical inevitably of the Treaty of Amritsar, was undoubtedly a new field of operation. But it cannot be treated as a gain to Maharaja Ranjit Singh directly emanation from the Treaty and hence it is difficult to admit that in this respect the Treaty was useful to him. The only point worth considering is that the Treaty secured his western border from any future British encroachments and thus prevented the possibilities of a clash of the ambitions of the Lahore Chief and the British Government no the eastern bank of the river Sutlej. In fact, the Treaty post-poned that eventuality for about thirty-five, years and thus afforded an opportunity to the Sikh Chief to strengthen his hold on the Trans-Sutlej region. However, the Treaty of Amritsar led to the development of cordial and friendly relations between the Maharaja and the British Government, though it never became a source of positive gain to him. On the contrary his southward drive too was discouraged by Lord William Bentinck.

(b) Mission to Sind

After Lahore Lord Minto made Sind the target in his inner layer of the scheme of political mission sent abroad. He realized the importance of having close friendly relations with the Ameers of Sind, whose territories lay at a place of immense strategic importance for British India. Sind was maritime state with a vast harbour on the Arabian Sea Coast and a large water channel connecting its northern end with the southern seaport. Geographically, it was the nearest port of India to Europe. Its land frontier was contiguous to the tribal belt of Baluchistan, across which existed two independent kingdoms of Afghanistan and Persia, ruled over by the same religious fraternity. One of them, the Ameer of Kabul, was their political superior, while the other one, Persia, was a traditional enemy of Afghanistan and was gradually coming under the French influence. Under instructions from Napoleon Bonaparte, his representative, General Gardanne, was actively engaged in his diplomatic manoeuvers to supplant British influence from Persia and bringing it under the French orbit. These geo-political considerations and the determination to ward off even the remostest possibility of a danger to the British Empire in the East and its over-sea trade on which depended the prosperity and power of the British nation, made it imperative for the East India Company to court the friendship of the Ameers of Sind and to establish a strong barrier against the threat of a French invasion on the south-western part of India, which was exposed to danger from two ends.

With this end in view, Captain Seton was deputed as the British envoy to the Court of Sind,[44] with definite instructions; viz, (a) establish friendly and cordial relations with the Ameers of sind; (b) to seek their cooperation against the French advance towards the East, and, (c) to demand the establishment of a British Residency and a commercial factory in their territory.

But Captain Seton departed from the instructions of his Government. He made an offer of the closest cooperation of British political interest with the State of Sind; and soon entered into a defensive engagement; which consequently terminated in the execution of a Treaty on July 18, 1808.[45] Treaty imposed on each party an obligation to furnish military aid at the requisition of the other without any limitation or condition. Captain Seton signed this Treaty on the understanding that the Ameers of Sind would ask for the assistance of British troops only for repelling the advance of a French army towards their country and for no other purpose. But no specific mention of it was made in the Treaty. In doing so, he acted hurriedly, ignoring the obligations that the Treaty imposed upon the British Government to furnish its troops to Sind even for other purposes also, such as the attempt of the Ameers to resist the claims of the Court of Kabul to tribute.

The British Government feared lest the Court of Kabul should misunderstand British motives in Sind and thus develop hostile relations with it.[46] On account of the probable French advance towards the East, the British Government, at this moment, could not afford to spoil its relations with Kabul which occupied an equally important strategic position. When Lord Minto was planning to woo the Afghan monarch to an alliance against the French, the engagement with Sind as signed by Captain Seton, might have brought imminent hazards to the British diplomatic agent, engaged in negotiation a treaty of friendship and amity with the Kabul monarchy. The calcutta Government, therefore, disapproved of the conduct of Captain Seton and refused to ratify the engagement as it was likely to land the East India Company into serious political complications on the western frontier.[47]

The refusal of the Calcutta Government to sign this engagement was views with considerable misgivings by the Ameers who did not even evince their inclination to establish friendly relations with the British Government. They doubled British motives and their minds were filled with jealousy and suspicion. Instead of forming a common cause with the British, they sprang a surprise on them by demanding the recall of Captain Seton.[48]

To recover the ground lost by the unauthorised conduct of Captain Seton in Sind and to accomplish the objects originally proposed to him, Lord Minto deputed Nicholas Hankey Smith as the British envoy to Sind.[49] The mission was fitted magnificently. A sum of five thousand rupees was advanced for its expenses. The British mission was received well on its reaching Sind. After the exchange of formal courtesies in which the British envoy gave an appraisal of friendly relations between East India Company and Sind, he set down to the real business of his mission.

Behind the profession of apparent amity and friendship, it appeared that there lurked an element of suspicion on both the sides. During his stay in Sind, the British envoy made use of the services of Haji Amar, a respectable merchant of Sind, who had been in the confidence of Nathan Crow during his last commercial mission in 1800.[50] This merchant was used as an instrument for collecting and furnishing day-to-day intelligence regarding the sentiments of the Government and people of Sind towards the British mission.[51] Haji Amar's accounts stated that the military operations of the British detachment under Colonel Walker in Cutch, just on the border of Sind, had produced great alarm in the minds of the Ameers, who began to entertain the fear of a probable British invasion of their territory after the successful subjugation of Cutch by him.[52] They also developed an impression in their minds that the British mission was connected with designs hostile to the interest of their country. Besides, the emissaries of the Raja of Jodhpur and Bahawal Khan urged Ghulam Ali to dismiss the British envoy as he was in Sind only to obtain geographical information as a prelude to domination.[53] They pointed out that Sind was the only country bordering India that had not yet fallen under British sway. These arguments impressed the ministers of the Court who were divided in their opinions as to the nature of the treatment to be accorded to the British enviroy; whether they should deprive him of his belongings and order his dismissal or allow him to stay on in Sind so that he could be detained as a hostage in the event of an invasion of their country by Colonel Walker.[54]

In strict conformity with the instructions of the Governor-General, the British envoy showed his keenness to befriend the Ameers of Sind. Compared to the sentiments of the Ameers of Sind and their ministers, he adopted the least offensive attitude towards his hosts. He apprized them of the views of the British Government and the aims of his mission.[55] He thus tried his best to dispel from the minds of the Ameers the fear that his Government had hostile designs in Cutch and to assure them of the best of British intentions to perpetuate friendly relations with their country.[56]

There reassuring sentiments of Smith, however, did not go for towards creating a conviction in the Ameers' minds that the British activities on the borders of their country and the despatch of the mission to their Court, were not motivated by any sinister design. Swayed by self-interest and keen to extend their sphere of influence in Cutch, they reiterated their old proposal with a slight modification, contained in a new explanatory clause, added to the original proposal.[57] In that they proposed to retain five-eights of the annual reveneus of Cutch with them and to offer three-eights of it to the British Government, should it cooperate with them in the subjugation of Cutch.[58] In the event of British disinclination to accede to their proposal, they expected that the British Government would not oppose them in their efforts to establish their ascendancy in Cutch. In this contingency alone, they expressed their willingness to conclude an agreement of offensive and defensive nature against the French as proposed by the British envoy.[59] Moreover, in return for British cooperation in the subjugation of Cutch, they promised to allow the re-establishment of a British factory in their country.[60] Their second concession was not to be valid under any other circumstance.[61]

These friendly proposals received due appreciation from the British envoy, who, however, could not see wisdom and justice in offering British military help to the Ameers of Sind in the fulfilment of their political ambition to subjugate Cutch.[62] He considered British consent to their proposal as an act of unprovoked aggression against a friendly State and a gross violation of public faith which was destined to create doubts and suspicions even in the minds of the Ameer of Sind. He was sure that instead of leading to any fruitful relations with Sind, this wrong step would only tend to stake the honour and integrity of the British and destroy whatever little confidence their name had in the Ameers' minds.[63]

With these ideas in his mind, the British envoy expressed inability of his Government to accede to the demand for military help against Cutch, resisting the lure of a reward to re-establish a British factory in Sind. Instead, he proposed the substitution of a British Agent in Sind.[64] This new proposal was not received with categorical acceptance by the Ameers who shelved the issue by a reply that they would deliberate upon his proposal and intimate to him their reaction in due course. Having thus realized that no useful purpose would be served by continuing further discussions on their proposal with Smith, they expressed their desire to despatch their Vakeel to Calcutta as a mark of confirmation of the friendly relations subsisting between the two Governments and to explain their view-point to the Governor-General in order to obtain his help against Cutch.[65]

Gauging little possibility of convincing the Ameers to agree to his proposal to conclude an unconditional friendly alliance, the British envoy acceded to their proposal to despatch a Vakeel to Calcutta and expressed his desire to accompany him at the end of his mission.[66]

This did not bring about an abrupt termination of negotiations for a friendly alliance with Sind. As a result of protracted negotiations, the Ameers expressed their determination to agree to the restoration of British commercial relations with their country only on the condition of British help to them against Cutch. However, with regard to the proposal for a permanent British residency in Sind, they stated that they would accept only a yearly despatch of a British envoy to their country provided the British Government also agreed to admit their Vakeel to Bombay on similar terms.[67]

At last, the discussion brought the two parties nearer to an agreed settlement. On August 22, 1809, the Ameers deputed Akhund Muhammad Bucca Khan to propose to the British envoy their decision to conclude a Treaty having for its basis the principle that the friends and enemies of one State should be the friends and enemies of the other.[68] The British envoy accepted the principle underlying the proposed Treaty and accompanied the Ameer's representative the same evening to their Durbar, where they offered a Promissory Engagement for Smith's concurrence, which was agreed to by him.[69] Consequently, a Treaty of friendly alliance consisting of four clauses was signed on the same date.

This Treaty of Hyderabad stipulated, firstly, 'eternal friendship' between the British Government and the three Ameers of Sind, viz., Meer Ghulam Ali, Meer Kureem Ali and Meer Murad Ali; secondly, demonstration of no signs of enmity on either side against each other; thirdly, mutual despatch of vakeels to each other's capital, whenever necessary, without any obstruction from any side and fourthly, prevention of 'the establishment of the tribe of French in Sind'. The first two clauses of this Treaty were mere expressions of general friendship; the third opened the door for future consultations, discussions and negotiations between the two Governments through accredited Agents and the last one prevented the admission of any French man into Sind.[70]

This Treaty is considered a significant political event in the East India Company's relations with the Ameers of Sind. It led to the development of friendly and cordial relations between the two Governments which became a basis for fostering their commercial relations after 1834. It provided a barrier against the apprehended French invasion of India from the Western side, and prevented the possibilities of an anti-British alliance between the French and Sind. All the fears of the Francophob British mind that Sind might become a centre of French intrigues and conspiracies or a spring-board for their encroachments into the British territories, disappeared for ever. This provided security to the British to the Southern-half of the Western frontier of British India and enabled them to deal freely with the problems of the internal consolidation and relations with the Indian States. The friendship with Sind encouraged Lord Minto to concentrate on negotiations for friendly anti-French alliances with Afghanistan and Persia, the two possible centres of French advance towards India. An an indirect effect of it, it prevented their newly established friendly relations with the British.

Thus judging the importance of the Treaty from the two standpoints, it can be safely assumed that it placed the British Government in an advantageous position and much of the gain was on its side. In fact, in the whole transaction, the British Government had the upper hand, as the Ameers of Sind, who were formally dependent on Afghanistan, were inclined to have friendly relations with the British as a counterpoise against the overbearing conduct of their Afghan overlords. It is quite surprising that the direct and indirect advantages to the British were gained without ample compensation to Sind, possibly because its Ameers considered it a privilege to have friendly relations with the British as they were not fully sovereign princes. It is equally surprising that no objection was raised to this Treaty by the Government of Kabul, possibly because it was contented with the receipt of the annual tribute from them.

The Treaty of Hyderabad, however, did not prove very beneficial to the interests of Sind. The only gains to them from it were the establishment of friendly relations with the mighty British power in India and their satisfaction that they might be freed in future from any unduly aggressive dealings of the Afghan monarch. Although nothing was stipulated in the Treaty about Cutch, it became evident to the Ameers of Sind that their ambition to expand South-eastward was virtually crippled as the British Government would look upon it with positive disfavour. This undoubted disadvantage to them was the indirect effect of the Treaty which probably the Ameers had not contemplated while putting their signatures to it. For want of conclusive evidence, it is difficult to surmise if they also felt shocked by this indirect effect of the Treaty as was Maharaja Ranjit Singh by the prevention of his eastward drive by the Treaty of Amritsar.

The relations between the British Government and Sind did not develop during the later years of Lord Minto's administration in India. The realization, that Napoleon, enmeshed in dynastic intrigues and unable to extricate himself from the Iberian Peninsula, posed no threat to India soon returned the affairs of Sind to their original obscurity.

(c) Mission to Kabul

The third mission was send to Kabul on October 13, 1808. Situated beyond the North-Western frontier of India which was the expected route of Napoleon Bonaparte's advance towards the East. Lord Minto realized is strategic importance and did not think it feasible to leave it out of the chain of his political missions send abroad. To achieve this objective, he decided to despatch a mission to Kabul in order to negotiate a defensive treaty of alliance with the Afghan monarch.[71] The choice for this guber national post fell upon Mountstuart Elphinstone, a young talented member of the civil service who had risen rapidly in the East India Company's service by giving proofs of his great ability and resources as British Resident at the Maratha Court of Poona.

Duly instructed by his Government and accompanied by his retinue, Mountstuart Elphinstone embarked on his mission on October 13, 1808 in the capacity of Envoy Plenipotentiary to Kabul.[72] The king accorded the British envoy a cordial reception. Elphinstone appraised the Afghan monarch of the intelligence his Government had secured regarding Napoleon Bonaparte's alleged programme of expansion towards India through his territory and his diplomatic manoeuvres to seek the military cooperation of the Government of Persia in this adventure on the basis of the previous alliance[73] with it. Napoleon was said to have promised Persia the whole of the Afghan monarch's territory and a part of India as the price of its co-operation with him in the conquest of the East. The envoy suggested to the kind that in the face of a strong combination of this kind, endangering both Afghanistan and India, he and the British Government should unite against the common danger, and thus put up a stiff resistance to the sinister design of the French Pro-consul.[74]

Shah Shujah envinced interest in the British envoy's disclosure of the French design in the East; and frightened by new impending danger to the integrity of his State, he responded favourably to Elphinstone's proposal for checkmating the French menace. But notwithstanding these outward appearances of an apparent desire of the king to agree to Elphinstone's proposals, the Court of Kabul entertained doubt and district in regard to the British plea and apprehended British designs in Afghanistan.[75]

After meeting Shah Shujah, Elphinstone began negotiations with the entire Court with a view to allaying doubts and suspicious in the minds of the ministers, thus furthering the cause of his mission. In one of these meetings, Abul Hasan Khan and Mulla Jaffar, the two prominent ministers, endeavoured to persuade the envory to supply some pecuniary assistance to Shah Shujah to enable him to suppress the internal rebellion of Shah Mahmud, one of the contestants to the throne of Kabul who had shown strongly defiant attitude against the authority of the reigning monarch by raising the banner of revolt against him.[76] In support of this proposal, they impressed upon the British envoy that the Afghans wee a powerful people able to cope with all foreign invaders; and in the event of a Franco-Persian attack on Afghanistan, they would not require British assistance.

They tried to convince him that if Shah Shujah was replaced by another rebellious Afghan Chief before the probable Franco-Persian interference, British assistance to him 'would cost the British millions, what might now be done for thousands.[77]

Mountstuart Elphinstone had definite instructions from the Governor-General to confine his activities strictly to a Defensive Alliance with the Afghan King against the Franco-Persian move. He, therefore, did not show any inclination to deviate from the policy laid down for him and refused to take any part in the fratricidal conflicts of the Afghans.[78]

During the course of negotiations at Peshwar, virtually entire Afghanistan became ablaze with internal rebellions, causing disorder and confusion everywhere.[79] Shah Mahmud, his son, prince Kamran and a number of other princes of the royal family made common cause with Fateh Khan, the Chief of a 'very considerable tribe'; and raised the standard of revolt against Shah Shujah at a time when more than half of his army had gone on an expedition to Kashmir.[80] Therefore, the fate of Afghanistan and turn of events in Shah Shujah's favour depended upon the timely return of his troops from Kashmir about which he was very optimistic. The remnants of the army at his disposal could hardly be a match against the rebels. Under these circumstances, Shah Shujah's fate hung to the balance if the rebel Chiefs mobilized their forces and launched a massive attack on him prior to the return of his forces from Kashmir. The hope of his gaining the upper hand over his rebellious adversaries, therefore, appeared to be almost remote and doubtful.[81]

Another cause of Shah Shujah's weak position was that the major revenue-yielding areas of the Afghan Kingdom which were the conquered parts outside the tribal land, had nearly thrown off his yoke and had gone out of his control, making the King financially resourceless. Certain other conquered parts which were assigned in *Jagir* in the past to the Afghan *sirdars* as a reward for their services to the ruling Afghan family, were hardly of any financial advantage to him. Thus at this juncture of serious internal political disturbances, Shah Shujah found his position militarily and financially weak, the only ray of his hope being the possibility of the return of his main troops from Kashmir.[82]

On March 16, 1809, Mulla Jaffar invited Elphinstone to spend the day with him in the tent, pitched in one of the King's gardens. The British envoy was accompanied by his advisers, Alexander and Strachey; and Mulla Jaffar by his colleagues, *Kazi* Sher Muhammad Khan, Sheikh-ul-Islam and Mir Abul Hasan Khan.[83] At his meeting, the British envoy explained to the Afghan party about the feasibility of a Treaty of defensive alliance between the two Governments, which would, in fact, checkmate the probable French advance towards the East and remove, with British assistance, the danger to which Afghanistan was exposed. But the Afghan diplomats insisted on an alliance of offensive and defensive nature not only against France, but also against all their enemies. This proposal did not find favour with the British envoy who expressed he inability of his Government to enter into such a league as the British Government did not want to embroil itself in internal squabbles of Afghan monarchy to afford its military assistance to the British in their wars in various parts of the world.[84]

Having gauged the moods and sentiments of the King and his ministers, the British envoy prepared the draft of a Treaty,[85] in which he stated, firstly, that friendship would subsist between the two Governments; secondly, the Government of Kabul would not allow passage to the French army through its territory, and, thirdly, the British Government would help the Government of Kabul in case of an attack on it by the French. When these proposals were presented to Shah Shujah, they did not meet with his full concurrence.[86] He, therefore, advised Mullah Jaffar to inform the British envoy that his draft could not be accepted as the basis of a treaty, because it was one sided and afforded all the advantages to the British and none to him.[87] While the

King of Kabul was required to renounce his connections and communications with the enemies of the British and was to oppose them with his whole force, they were not to offer him any assistance in the suppression of the existing internal disorders and maintenance of peace in his country.[88]

Consequently, Mulla Jaffar informed the British envoy that his proposals would not serve the purpose of his Government and asked him to introduce 'something more enticing' to his monarch than what he had offered. After the exchange of these view, Mulla Jaffar presented the draft of a treaty to Elphinstone in which he expressed his King's willingness to establish friendly relations with the British; and his assurance not to allow passage to the French through his territory.[89] With this preamble, he solicited British help both in men and money to quell the internal disturbances in Afghanistan. But the British envoy objected to the last proposal and made it clear to Mulla Jaffar that it would be inconvenient, perhaps impossible, for his Government to assist Shah Shujah with troops.[90] He, however, gave a vague verbal assurance of pecuniary assistance to Mulla Jaffar,[91] but did not corroborate it in another draft of a treaty which he presented to Shah Shujah at a later date under changed circumstances, when the danger of Napoleon Bonaparte's advance towards India had become remote and the critical internal situation in Afghanistan enhanced the importance of British financial help to the Afghan monarch.

The subsequent events made Shah Shujah revise his attitude. His troops, sent to Kashmir, met with severe reverses. Not more than two thousands of them could return safely, dismounted, disarmed and wholly disorganized.[92] Taking advantage of this weak military position of the Kabul Government, Shah Mahmud immediately resumed the offensive, occupied Kandhar and threatened the gates of Peshawar. The King's army was not in a position to checkmate such an advance. His exchequer was almost deplected and his means of mustering any considerable force were utterly defiant.[93]

In this emergency, Shah Shujah urgently solicited pecuniary assistance from the British Government as it was thought to be the only way to ensure the stability of his throne. He asked for a grant of rupees fifteen lacs.[94] Considering this demand to be too heavy for the Company's resources, Elphinstone recommended only rupees three lacs.[95] By promising this financial aid, he hoped to gain certain advantages for his Government; such as, command of the Northern route from Persia to India; control over the navigation of the Indus; the British influence over the chiefs of Seestaun and Mekraun and over the hilly tract between their states and the Indus.[96] The chiefs of all these places were, in different degree, subject to the King of Kabul.[97]

Acutely pressed by the need for more money, Mir Abdul Hasan and Mulla Jaffar made an overture to Elphinstone offering Sind to the British Government in mortgage for a sum of rupees two lacs per annum.[98] But this proposal was rejected by the British envoy as its acceptance would have spoilt the British Government's relations with the Ameers of Sind.[99]

But unhappily for Shah Shujah, events in Europe took such a turn that the policy of the British Government underwent a change.[100] Nepoleon Bonaparte had to suspend the execution of his designs upon India on account of his involvement in Spain and the Peninsular War.[101] The danger of a French invasion having thus become remote, the British Government changed its mind and did not think it necessary to purchase the goodwill and cooperation of Shah Shujah at a heavy price[102] as no advantages were any longer hoped for from Kabul.[103] This decision of the British Government was applauded by the Court of Directors[104] as the disabusement of the financial aid to the Afghan King might have unnecessarily involved the British in the internal complications in Afghanistan and jeopardized the changes of establishing relations with the future Government of Kabul in the event of the subversion of Shah Shujah's authority.

Notwithstanding disappointment at the marked change in the British attitude and having even lost all hopes of extracting advantageous terms from them, Shah Shujah considered a friendly alliance with a big power as of some gain to him. He, therefore, because inclined to accept the terms which Elphinstone offered soon after. In these terms, it was stipulated that Shah Shujah would oppose the Franco-Persian march towards India through Afghanistan; that the British Government would defray the expenses of such opposition and both the parties would act on these articles till the Franco-Persian confederacy continued; that the contracting parties would not interfere in each other's internal affairs; that the Shah would not allow any French to enter his territories and that friendship and union would ever subsist between the two countries.[105]

This Treaty was intended to establish friendship between the British India and Afghanistan with an assurance of complete non-interference in the internal affairs of each other. By it, British Government was assured of the cooperation of the Court of Kabul in checkmating the probable French advance towards India without incurring any reciprocal obligations of rendering any assistance to Shah Shujah against his deadly internal enemies. The promise of the Afghan monarch to prevent any future French establishment in Afghanistan relieved the British Government of its constant headache on the North-Western Frontier of India for some time. Besides, the British Government got in Afghanistan a buffer state between India and Persia, although its potentiality and stability were of an uncertain quantity. These were the solid advantages to the British from this Treaty.

But to Shah Shujah, this Treaty hardly proved to be of any great advantage, besides his friendship with the rising foreign power in India. It simply assured him of British financial assistance against the apprehended. Franco-Persian incursion into his country with the ultimate object of invading India. This gave Shah Shujah a partial sense of security against an external danger from the Western side.

The Treaty was undoubtedly a diplomatic victory for Elphinstone's mission which was of great historical importance. It marked the beginning of British relations with Afghanistan. It opened the channel of communication between the British Government and the State of Kabul, and removed the prejudices of the latter against the former, thus paving the way for the establishment of good understanding and cordial relations between the two States. Besides, it inculcated in the minds of the Afghan monarch and his ministers a just sense of the equal danger of the friendship or the enmity of France, and thus laid the foundation of future defensive arrangements in that quarters. Above all, this mission procured for the British an extension of their knowledge about the geography, topography, politics, ethnology and resources of Afghanistan, which was embodied in a valuable treatise compiled by the leader of the mission.

The successful mission and the advantageous Treaty were very much applauded in the British press. In India, the Governor-General put his signature on the Treaty on June 17, 1809.[106] Before its ratified copy could reach Peshawar to be handed over to Shah Shujah, neither the King nor the British envoy was found these to exchange its authentication.[107] All of a sudden, the affairs in Afghanistan took a very serious turn. The king was obliged to take the field with his small disorderly army against the rebels under Shah Mahmud. In this critical situation, Elphinstone considered the continuance of his mission at Peshawar extremely risky and, on June 14, 1809, he commenced his return towards the Indus, accompanied by his retinue. Soon after, he received the unhappy news of the reversal of the fortunes of Shah Shujah.[108]

On the defeat and deposition of Shah Shujah, Shah Mahmud established his ascendancy in Kabul.[109] But peace and order could not return to Afghanistan, because the prevalence of clannish rivalries could not be brought to an end. Among the wild people it was difficult to establish a strong and stable authority for any one. Other equally ambitious tribal chiefs did not acknowledge Shah Mahmud's overlordship. They soon revolted against him and made confusion worse confounded. While some of them waged war upon Shah Mahmud at his headquarters at Kabul, the others made the position of his representative untenable at the other political centres of his authority. Thus the Afghan monarchy, which had once been so powerful under the dynasty of Ahmad Shah Abdali, was completely broken up. Nearly every mountain-chief and every powerful Khan became a sort of pseudo-king in his tribal locality. Under these circumstances it was indeed idle for the British to think of forming another treaty of a binding character with a State subject to such vicissitudes. Hence the Treaty with Kabul was rendered nugatory by the collapse of one of the contracting parties and the work of the mission, which was eulogized as very useful and advantageous, was completely effaced by a sudden political outburst of a devastating nature in Afghanistan. This was the unexpected and melancholy end of the fabric of Anglo-Afghan friendship so cleverly woven by Elphinstone. During the subsequent years of Lord Minto's Governor-Generalship in India, there was neither an occasion not an opportunity for renewing friendly intercourse with Afghanistan.

(d) Mission to Persia

Lord Minto sent his fourth mission to Persia on April 17, 1808. He appointed Brigadier-General John Malcolm, a rising young soldier of the Coast army on this diplomatic mission.

The Government of England was no less alarmed by the sudden developments in Persia. Swayed by the apprehension that the British interests in the East might be jeopardized by French infiltration into Persia, its Foreign Office decided to take immediate and effective measures to counteract the sinister designs of the reckless Corsican adventure. Without waiting for the reactions of the Calcutta Government and quite unaware of what was transpiring in Lord Minto's mind and what attempts he was making for checkmating the Napoleonic peril to India, Lord Canning, the Foreign Minister of England despatched Sir Harford Jones and His Majesty's Envoy Extraordinary and Plenipotentiary to Persia.

Instead of equipping Harford Jones with instructions to proceed straightway on a mission to Persia, Lord Minto thought of the unwisdom and uselessness of sending a duplicate mission. Without any misgivings in his mind and disrespect to the decision of the cabinet, he advised Harford Jones to stay on at Bombay until he was in a position to get the appraisal of the manner in which John Malcolm's mission was received and entertained in Persia.[110] He felt that Harford Jones' presence in Persia simultaneously with that of John Malcolm might exhibit to the Government of that country an appearance of conflicting British interests and impede the attainment of Malcolm's mission itself.[111]

Meanwhile, John Malcolm executed the plan of his mission with interest and vigour. On his arrival at Bushire on May 10, 1808, he addressed a memorial to the ministers of the King of Persia explaining the sentiments of his Government with regard to the King's reception to General Gardanne's mission and exposing the dangers of his new policy in relation to France.[112] From there, he deputed his secretary, Captain Pasley, to proceed to Teheran, the capital of Persia, in the capacity of a special messenger with a copy of this memorial and a separate letter to the King.[113] After eight day's journey Captain Pasley reached Shiraz,[114] where, on various pretexts, he was prevented from prosecuting his journey to Teheran.[115]

Subsequent to the departure of Captain Pasley from Bushire, John Malcolm received intelligence that his secretary would be detained at Shiraz by the Persian Officials till they received orders from the King for his advance.[116] He, did not therefore give up the attempt to find out ways and means of obtaining permission for the successful prosecution of his mission to Teheran without being held up at Shiraz for a long time. He approached Jaffer Ali Khan, the Governor of Bushire and sought his help in this matter.[117] John Malcolm also intervened and informed Nasrulla Khan, the Prime Minister, that Captain Pasley's impediments in that way might have serious consequences.[118] To this Nasrulla Khan replied that it was the custom of his country that if an accredited agent of a foreign Government reached his country with the intention of negotiating with the Court of Teheran, he was required first to communicate the objects of his mission to the Governor of the Province he visited, to get his advice in respect of the procedure which he was to adopt and the etiquette and the details of ceremonies of reception which he was to observe.[119]

Meanwhile, the King's order was announced, fixing Shiraz as the seat of negotiations and deputing the Royal Prince of Shiraz to conduct negotiations with the British mission.[120] In taking this decision, the Shah was largely influenced by his hope of recovering the Northern Province of Georgia from Russia with the military assistance of France and also by the fear that the presence of the British mission at his Court in Teheran might annoy the French and lead to the loss of their friendship and support on which he was banking considerably for the attainment of his political object and restoration of lost honour.[121] Naturally, therefore, he did not want to foil his negotiations with the French envoy which had reached an advanced stage. Jammed between the two giants—France and England—the King of Persia, at that time preferred the friendship of the former with which he had already formed a friendly alliance.[122]

This indifferent treatment on the part of the King of Persia was taken as insulting and derogatory to the interests of the British Government. John Malcolm who was not inclined by temperament to submit, at once represented to the Court of Persia that he would not negotiate with a subordinate authority as desired by the King, while the French ambassador was allowed to conduct the affairs of his mission in direct communication with the King.[123] But having got no satisfactory reply and being disgusted with the cold and discriminatory behaviour of the Government of Persia, he found it useless to stay at Bhushire and withdrew from the Persian soil and returned to India in order to seek the advice of Lord Minto, lacing his representative, Captain Pasley, behind with orders to hold on as best as he could.[124]

The discriminatory attitude shown by the King of Persia to John Malcolm's mission was not due to any malice in his mind. It was, in fact, prompted by his self-interest which is the most important determining factor in the formation of foreign policy of a national state. His country was exposed to an invasion from his powerful European neighbour, Russia, which had already committed aggression in the past. The mind of the King of Persia was, therefore, absorbed by the terror of the Russian arms and he was disposed to make any sacrifice for any one who promised security against their 'further progress' and the restoration of the provinces which Russia had wrested from his dominion.[125]

Before leaving Persia, John Malcolm had already written to Lord Minto about the difficulties in the successful prosecution of his mission and his desire to quit Persia, if he was not allowed to proceed to the Persian capital to transact the diplomatic work assigned to him.[126] Later on, when Lord Minto received another communication from John Malcolm indicating the failure of his mission and his departure from Persia, he ordered Sir Harford Jones on August 12,1808 to proceed to Persia and prosecute the mission which the Crown had entrusted to him.[127]

A week after the despatch of this order, John Malcolm landed at Calcutta on August 20,1808, breathing vengeance against the Persian Court for the fancied indignity inflicted on him. He apprized Lord Minto of the state of affairs in Persia and persuaded him and his Council to reinforce the diplomatic mission by a military demonstration in the Persian Gulf, as it was the only 'effectual mode of defeating the intrigue of the French' at Teheran.[128] Convinced of the gravity of the situation in Persia, Lord Minto accepted this advice after full deliberation. He decided to from without delay a military establishment in the Island of Karrack, in the territories of Turkish Arabia, and selected John Malcolm for this new assignment.[129] For this purpose, a force was collected at Bombay to accompany John Malcolm to the Island of Karrack for enabling him to conduct his military and political duties at that end. Soon after this decision, John Malcolm embarked from Madras to Bombey on his way to the Persian Gulf.[130]

Having decided upon this plan of exerting pressure upon Persia with a view to counteracting the French influence at Teheran, Lord Minto deemed it proper, as a precautionary measure, to instruct Sir Harford Jones to suspend the execution of his mission to Persia.[131] But by the time, the Governor-General's letter of August 22, 1808 reached Bombay on September 14, 1808.[132] On receipt of information of Harford Jones' departure to Persia and without waiting for his reply, Lord Minto addressed another letter to him apprizing him on his new approach to the Persian problem and ordering him to withdraw from Persia immediately as military demonstration might endanger his mission.[133]

Lord Minto's letter put Sir Harford Jones to a quandary.[134] His mission had already reached Bushire on October 14,1808 and was accorded due reception.[135] The withdrawal of the mission without adequate cause would have been the height of discourtesy to the accredited country.[136] He wrote, therefore to Lord Minto that having officially announced to the Persian Minister the arrival of His Britannic Majesty's Mission, it would be highly improper to withdraw, until either the object of it was completed or the conduct of the Persian Court towards it became sufficiently offensive to justify such a step.[137] Thus he decided to remain in Persian in defiance of the Governor-General's command probably with the consciousness that he was the Crown's nominee.

Sir Harford Jones's reply was most unpalatable to Lord Minto. It made him furious, and critical of his official demeanour. He took a very serious view of his defiant conduct and criticized his behaviour as undignified and unworthy of a Briton. He felt that the situation created by him would tarnish British reputation and might endanger their interests in persia as he would be working without any authority and instructions from him.[138] He sent, therefore, a strong note to him in which he condemned his ways; expressed his loss of confidence in him; disavowed his mission and ordered him not to transact any diplomatic business in persia.[139]

Besides this drastic action against him, the Calcutta Government addressed a communication to the King of Persia informing him of its order for the withdrawal of Sir Harford Jones[140] and intimating to him that any commitment or engagement which Harford Jones might make with him, would not be valid and binding on the British Government. It also requested him to advise Harford Jones to retire from his country.[141]

To this communication of the Calcutta Government the Shah of Persia did not reply. But he simply communicated the views of the British Government to Harford Jones. At this the British envoy tried to clarify his position by stating that he was the direct representative of His Majesty, the King of England, not of the Governor-General of India, whose order to him was ultra vires and was based on John Malcolm's representations to him about the treatment meted out to him in Persia.[142]

On knowing this attitude of Sir Harford Jones, Lord Minto suspended the plan of military demonstration, lest it might precipitate a diplomatic crisis and result in open conflict between him and the Home Government.

Unmindful of what Lord Minto had written and what was communicated to him by the King of Persia, Sir Harford Jones engaged himself in diplomatic negotiations at Teheran under changed circumstances in Persia, finding its King better disposed to entertain British overtures. The change in the attitude of the Government of persia was the outcome of new developments in the international situation. After the bloody battles of Eylan and Friedland, the two armies of France and Russia had fraternized and the two Emperors had formed a project of conjoint campaign for 'centre les possessions de la campagne de Indes', dividing the territories of the East India Company among themselves. It was believed that attack would be made by land rather than by sea and that Persia would become a base of operations against India.

Sir Harford Jones did not miss this favourable opportunity to bring persia into the British alliance. For this purpose he started preliminary negotiations for a Treaty with that country which was to become the basis of Definite Treaty to be signed at a later date.[143]

The preliminary Treaty was concluded on March 12,1809.[144] It was agreed that the articles of this Treaty would form the basis for establishing a sincere and everlasting Definite Treaty of friendship and amity, which would be binding on the two Kings, their heirs, successors, subjects and dominions. The King of Persia declared his previous agreements or treaties with any other European power as null and void; and promised not to grant passage to any European force through his country towards India. If Persia was attacked by any European power, the British undertook the obligation to provide military assistance or a subsidy and a loan of officers. Such fores on the Persian soil in the Persian Gulf would work under the directions of the King of Persia, who would look after their welfare and provide necessary facilities to them. If, however, India was attacked by the Afghans or any European Power, the King of Persia promised to render military assistance to the British. In case of an outbreak of war between Persia and Afghanistan, the British Government would observe neutrality unless they were asked for mediation by both the parties. The King of Persia, on his part, promised not to enter into any engagement with any power inimical to the British; and to defray the expenses of the British troops if they had already landed on the Islands of Karrack with the consent of the King of Persia. The British Government was not to occupy any island or port in the Persian gulf. This Treaty was of a purely defensive nature and was signed by two ministers of Persia on behalf of their King.

Sir Harford Jones' activities in Persia were an eye-sore to Lord Minto who had withdrawn sanction to his mission. When he came to know about the negotiations for a Treaty by him, he felt terribly annoyed and his pride was greatly hurt. Sir Harford Jones on the other hand, had altogether removed Lord Minto from his mind and considered himself as a representative of the King of England who alone was competent to ratify or refuse the Preliminary Treay which he had negotiated. Lord Minto was therefore, impelled to write a strongly-worded letter to Harford Jones telling him about Johan Malcolm's appointment as envoy to Persia and asking him to retire from that country on his arrival there.[145] The Governor-General made it clear that no public act of his would be recognized by his government nor would any bills drawn by him be accepted.[146] The Shah of Persia was also informed of this new appointment and was requested to relieve Harford Jones as his continuance at his court would be " Productive of no advantage whatever to the combined interests of Persia and the British Government".[147] Mortified by Lord Minto's comments and assessment of his work in Persia, Harford Jones sought the permission of Foreign Secretary Canning[148] and Court of Directors to allow him to return to England as he did not conceive his services in that country could be any 'longer useful to the King'.

On getting the appraisal of the whole matter, the Foreign Office and the Court of Directors recognized the status of Sir Harford Jones as a representative of His Britannic Majesty to the Court of Persia and approved of the proceedings of his mission.[149] They communicated their views to Lord Minto that Harford Jones was an authorized agent of the

Government of England and he was perfectly justified in carrying out their order to a satisfactory conclusion.[150] They also directed him to honour the bills drawn by Sir Harford Jones under his original powers and to transfer to the Company's account his other bills, which his Government had placed to his private debt.[151]

Lord Minto agreed to these directions of his superiors, although they appeared quite unpleasant to him. He paid off the bills of Sir Harford Jones and did not interfered with his work in Persia. Soon after, he again despatched John Malcolm on January, 10,1810 to Persia to resume his old inconclusive misson.[152] The British envoy was required to put an end to the state of degradation into which the Government of India had fallen in the estimation of the Court of Persia.[153] This act of Lord Minto was in contradiction to his past views that the presence of two simultaneous British missions might create an impression upon the Court of Teheran that their sponsors did not hold identical views and were probably at loggerheads.

This time John Malcolm was warmly received at Bhushire, Shiraz as well as Teheran.[154] At Shiraz the Royal prince presented to him a sword two horses, a *khilat;* and a dress to each gentleman of his suite. He talked to him in a very friendly and flattering tone and evinced keen interest in the success of his mission. At Teheran, the King extended honours and courtesies to him expressing his friendly feelings towards the British Government in India.[155] John Malcolm was fully satisfied with his reception and communicated to Lord Minto the conviction that he would be able to accomplish the object of his mission as the conduct of the King of persia was marked by great respect and cordialities towards the Government to India.[156]

The presence of two missions at the Court of Teheran put the British Government in an awkward position. It appears that something transpired between the Cabinet and the authorities of the East India Company in England, and it was decided that the sponsoring authorities might withdraw their missions and the Court of Directors might appoint another mission to replace them. Accordingly, the Court of Directors announced the appointment of Sir Gore Ousley as the Ambassador Extraordinary and Plenipotentiary at the Court of Persia in place of Harford Jones who had earlier asked to be relieved of his post.[157] On this announcement, John Malcolm and Harford Jones withdrew from Persia. The former engaged himself in the compilation of his famous 'History of Persia' on the basis of the material he had collected during his stay there. The latter went back to England where his Government lavished high praises in him for the valuable services his mission had rendered under the most untoward circumstances of the Governor-General's disavowal of his work and the threat of his dismissal from Persia.[158] The new envoy was empowered to convert the Preliminary Treaty into a Definite Alliance and to obtain detailed information about the military and financial resources of Persia during peace and war times.[159] He reached Teheran on November 9, 1811 and was well received by the Royal Court.[160] As a result of Sir Gore Ousley's prolonged negotiations with the Court of Persia, a Definite Treaty consisting of 12 articles was concluded on March 14,1812.[161]

The main purpose of the Treaty was to afford mutual assistance and thereby to 'strengthen, consolidate and extend their power and dominions for the purpose of defeating the aggressions of their enemies'. The British interest was to provide effective safeguards for their interests in India against much apprehended Napoleonic peril by creating a strong and formidable buffer state between Europe and India. The containing parties entertained very high hopes from this Treaty and concluded with a conviction that it would 'produce the fairest and most beneficial results.[162]

After this Treaty, British relations with the Persian Court remained cordial and friendly during the remaining period of the Governor-Generalship of Lord Minto in India.

REFERENCES

1. Metcalfe to Edmonstone, Sept. 23, 1808, For. Deptt. Secret and Separate, Oct. 17, 1808, Cons. 19.
2. Metcalfe to Edmonstone, Sept. 23, 1808. For. Deptt. Secret and Seprate, Oct. 17, 1808, Cons. 19.
3. *Ibid.*
4. Metcalfe to Edmonstone, Sept. 24, 1808, For. Deptt. Secret and Seperate, Oct. 17, 1808, Cons. 20.
5. Metcalfe to Edmonstone, Sept. 25, 1808, For. Deptt. Secret and Separate, Oct. 24, 1808. Cons. 68.
6. Metcalfe to Edmonstone, Sept. 25,1808, For. Deptt. Secret and Seperate, Oct. 24. 1808, Cons. 68.
7. Metcalfe to Edmonstone, Oct. 5, 1809. For, Deptt. Secret and Seperate, Oct., 31, 1808, Cons. 2.
8. Plan of a Treaty transmitted by Metacalfe on Oct. 4,1808, For. Deptt. Secret and Seperate, Nov. 14, 1808, Cons. 15.
9. Metcalfe to Edmonstone, Oct. 5, 1808, For. Deptt. Secret and Seperate, Oct. 31, 1808, Cons. 2.
10. Metcalfe to Edmonstone, Oct. 5, 1808, For. Deptt. Secret and Seperate, Oct. 31, 1808, Cons. 2.
11. Proposal delivered by Ranjit Singh to Metcalfe on Oct. 8, 1808, For. Deptt. Secret and Separate, Nov. 14, 1808, Cons. 2.
12. *Ibid.*
13. *Ibid.*
14. *Ibid.*
15. *Ibid.*
16. Metcalfe to Edmonstone, Nov. 20, 1808, For. Deptt. Secret and Separate, Dec. 12, 1808, Cons. 27.
17. Metcalfe to Edmonstone, Oct. 26, 1808, For. Deptt. Secret and Separate, Nov. 14, 1808, Cons. 20.
18. *Ibid.*
19. *Ibid.*
20. Metcalfe to Edmonstone, Nov. 20, 1808, For. Deptt. Secret and Seperate, Dec. 5, 1808, Cons. 8.
21. Note transmitted by Envoy to the Maharaja, Dec. 12, 1808, For. Deptt. Secret Cons. Jan. 2, 1809, Cons. 94.

22. *Ibid.*
23. *Ibid.*
24. Note transmitted by Envoy to the Maharaja, Dec. 12, 1808, For. Deptt. Secret, Cons. Jan. 2, 1809, 94.
25. Note transmitted by Envoy to the Maharaja, Dec. 12, 1808, For,. Deptt. Secret, Cons. Jan. 2, 1809, 94.
26. Metcalfe to Edmonstone, Dec. 1, 1808. For. Deptt. Secret Cons. Jan. 30, 1809, Cons. 102.
27. Metcalfe to Edmonstone, Dec. 22, 1808, For. Deptt. Secret Cons. Jan. 30, 1809, Cons. 105.
28. *Ibid.*
29. Edmonstone to Lieut. Colonel Ochterlony, Dec. 29, 1808, For. Deptt. Secret, Cons. Jan. 2, 1809, Cons. 96.
30. Metcalfe to Edmonstone, Jan. 12, 1809, For. Deptt. Secret. Cons. March 13, 1809, Cons. 45.
31. *Ibid.*
32. *Ibid.*
33. Metcalfe to Edmonstone, March 7, 1809, For. Deptt. Secret Cons. April 3, 1809, Cons. 49.
34. A religious festival of the Muhammedans.
35. Metcalfe to Edmonstone, March 7, 1809, For. Deptt. Secret Cons. April 3, 1809, Cons. 49.
36. Metcalfe to Edmonstone, March 22, 1809, For. Deptt. Secret Cons. April 29, 1809, Cons. 30.
37. *Ibid.*
38. Metcalfe to Edmonstone, March 27, 1809, For. Deptt. Secret Cons. April 29, 1809, Cons. 29, 1809, Cons. 31.
39. *Ibid.*
40. Metcalfe to Edmonstone, March 27, 1809, For. Deptt. Secret Cons. April 29, 1809, Cons. 29, 1809, Cons. 31.
41. Metcalfe to Edmonstone, April 3, 1809, For. Deptt. Secret Cons. April 29, 1809, Cons. 39.
42. Metcalfe to Edmonstone, April 5, 1809, For. Deptt. Secret Cons. April 29, 1809, Cons. 40.
43. Aitchison, C. U., *op. cit.*, Vol. I, p. 34.
44. Secret letter to Court of Directors, May 3, 1808.

45. Aitchison, C. U., *op. cit.*
46. Secret letter to Court of Directors, Dec. 15, 1808.
47. Secret letter to Court of Directors, Dec. 15, 1808.
48. *Ibid.*
49. Edmonstone to N.H. Smith, Nov. 28, 1808, For. Deptt. Secret and Separate, Nov. 28, 1808, Cons. 10.
50. Smith to Edmonstone, Aug. 23, 1809, For. Deptt. Secret. Cons. Oct. 17, 1809, Cons. 16.
51. Smith to Edmonstone, Aug. 24, 1809, For. Deptt. Secret Cons. Aug. 7, 1812, Cons. 3.
52. Smith to Edmonstone, Aug. 24, 1809, For. Deptt. Secret Cons. Aug. 7, 1812, Cons. 3.
53. Smith to Edmonstone, Oct. 1, 1809, For. Deptt. Secret Cons. Aug. 7, 1812, Cons. 5.
54. *Ibid.*
55. *Ibid.*
56. *Ibid.*
57. Smith to Edmonstone, Oct. 1, 1809, For. Deptt. Secret Cons. Aug. 7, 1812, Cons. 5.
58. *Ibid.*
59. *Ibid.*
60. Smith to Edmonstone, Oct. 1, 1809, For. Deptt. Secret Cons. Aug. 7, 1812, Cons. 5.
61. Smith to Edmonstone, Aug. 23, 1809, For. Deptt. Secret Cons. Oct. 17, 1809, Cons. 16.
62. *Ibid.*
63. *Ibid.*
64. Smith to Edmonstone, Aug. 23, 1809, For. Deptt. Secret Cons. Oct. 17, 1809, Cons. 16.
65. *Ibid.*
66. Smith to Edmonstone, Oct. 1, 1809, For. Deptt. Secret Cons. Aug. 7, 1812, Cons. 5.
67. *Ibid.*
68. *Ibid.*

69. Smith to Edmonstone, Oct. 1, 1809. For. Deptt. Secret Cons. Aug. 7, 1812, Cons. 5.
70. Aitchison, C.U., *op. cit.*
71. Persian Secy. to Shah Shujah, Aug. 19, 1808, For. Deptt. Sect. and Seperate, Aug. 23, 1808, Cons. 3.
72. Edmonstone to Elphinstone, Aug. 19, 1808, For. Deptt. Sect. and Seperate, Aug. 23, 1808, Cons. 1.
73. Treaty of Finkenstein dated May 4, 1807.
74. Elphinstone to Lord Minto, March 8, 1809, For. Deptt. Secret and Seperate, April 29, 1809, Cons. 2.
75. Elphinstone to Lord Minto, March 8, 1809. For. Drptt. Secret and Separate, April 29, 1809, Cons. 2.
76. Elphinstone to Lord Minto, March 15, 1809, For. Deptt. Secret and Seperate, April 29, 1809, Cons. 5.
77. *Ibid.*
78. *Ibid.*
79. Translation of a Newspaper from Kabul received on March 10, 1809, Foreign Deptt. Secret and Seperate, April 29, 1809, Cons. 4.
80. Elphinstone to Lord Minto, March 15, 1809, For. Deptt. Secret and Separate, April 29, 1809, Cons. 5.
81. *Ibid.*
82. *Ibid.*
83. Elphinstone to Lord Minto, March 19, 1809, For. Deptt. Secret and Separate, April 29, 1809, Cons. 6.
84. *Ibid.*
85. *Ibid.*
86. Elphinstone to Lord Minto, March 22, 1809, For. Deptt. Secret and Separate, April 29, 1809, Cons. 9.
87. *Ibid.*
88. *Ibid.*
89. Elphinstone to Lord Minto, March 19, 1809, For. Deptt. Secret and Separate, April 29, 1809, Cons. 6.
90. *Ibid.*
91. *Ibid.*
92. Secret letter to Court of Directors, April 20, 1809.

93. *Ibid.*
94. Secret letter to Court of Directors, April 20, 1809.
95. *Ibid.*
96. Elphinstone to Lord Minto, March 28, 1809, For. Deptt. Secret and Separate, May 13, 1809. Cons. 4.
97. *Ibid.*
98. Elphinstone to Edmonstone, June 7, 1809, For. Deptt. Secret and Separate, July 24, 1809, Cons. 1.
99. *Ibid.*
100. Edmonstone to Elphinstone, April 15, 1809, For. Deptt. Secret and Separate, April 29, 1809, Cons. 10.
101. *Ibid.*
102. Secret letter to Court of Director, April 20, 1809.
103. Edmonstone to Elphinstone; April 15, 1809, For. Deptt. Secret and Separate, April 29, 1809, Cons. 10.
104. Secret letter from Court of Directors, March, 6, 1812.
105. Aithchison, C.U., *op. cit.,* vol. XIII, pp. 233-34.
106. Secret letter to Court of Directors, Jan. 21, 1810.
107. *Ibid.*
108. Elphinstone to Lord Minto, July 27, 1809, For. Deptt. Secret and Separate, Sept. 5, 1809, Cons. 26.
109. *Ibid.*
110. Secret letter to Court of Directors, May 3, 1808.
111. *Ibid.*
112. Malcolm to Ministers of the King of Persia, dated nil, For. Deptt. Secret and Separate, Aug. 15, 1808, Cons. 20.
113. Malcolm to King of Persia, dated nil, For. Deptt. Secret and Separate, Aug. 15, 1808, Cons. 6.
114. Pasley to Malcolm, May 30, 1808, For. Deptt. Secret and Separate, Aug. 15, 1808, Cons. 29.
115. Secret letter to Court of Directors, Sept. 17, 1808.
116. Malcolm to Edmonstone, June 8, 1808, For. Deptt. Secret and Separate, Aug. 15, 1808, Cons. 17.
117. Pasley to Jaffar Ali Khan, May 24, 1808, For. Deptt. Secret and Separate, Aug. 15, 1808, Cons. 21.

118. Malcolm to Nasrulla Khan, June 4, 1808, For. Deptt. Secret and Separate, Aug. 15, 1808, Cons. 29.
119. Nasrulla Khan to Malcolm, June 4, 1808, For. Deptt. Secret and Separate, Aug., 15, 1808, Cons. 27.
120. Malcolm to Minto, June 10, 1808, For. Deptt. Secret and Separate, Aug. 15, 1808, Cons. 38, Secret letter to Court of Directors, Sept. 17, 1808.
121. *Ibid.*
122. Treaty of Finkenstein.
123. Pasley to Minto, July 12, 1808, For. Deptt. Secret and Separate, Sept. 19, 1808, Cons. 2.
124. Secret letter to Court of Directors, September 17, 1808.
125. *Ibid.*
126. Secret letter to Court of Directors, Sept. 17, 1808.
127. Secret letter to Court of Directors, Sept. 17, 1808.
128. *Ibid.*
129. *Ibid.*
130. Minto to Barlow, Aug. 7, 1808, For. Deptt. Secret and Separate, Aug. 7, 1808, Cons. 8.
131. Minto to Jones, Aug. 22, 1808, For. Deptt. Secret and Separate, Dec. 26, 1808, Cons. 19.
132. *Ibid.*
133. Secret letter to Court of Directors, Dec. 21, 1808.
134. Jones to Minto, Nov. 1, 1808, For. Deptt. Secret and Separate, Dec. 26, 1808, Cons. 2.
135. *Ibid.*
136. *Ibid.*
137. *Ibid.*
138. Minto to Jones Jan., 30, 1809, For. Deptt. Secret Cons. Jan. 30, 1809, Cons. 27 and Secret letter to Court of Directors, April 3, 1809.
139. *Ibid.*
140. Persian Secy, to King of Persia, Jan. 30, 1809, For. Deptt. Secret, Cons. Jan. 30, 1809, Cons. 28.
141. Persian Secy. to King of Persia, Jan. 30, 1809, For. Deptt. Secret, Cons. Jan. 30, 1809, Cons. 28.

142. Jones to King of Persia, Feb. 5, 1809, For. Deptt. Secret. Cons. March 20, 1809, Cons. 57.

143. A Definite Treaty in conformity to the stipulations of the Preliminary Treaty was concluded on March 14, 1812.

144. Aitchison, C.U., *op. cit.*, Vol. XIII, pp. 53-55.

145. Minto to Jones, Oct, 26, 1809, For. Deptt. Secret and Separate, Nov. 28, 1809, Cons. 24.

146. *Ibid.*

147. Edmonstone to King of Persia, Oct. 26, 1809, For. Deptt. Secret and Separate, Nov. 28, 1809, Cons. 25.

148. Jones to Canning, Jan. 12, 1810, For. Deptt. Secret, Cons. Aug. 16, 1810, Cons. 53.

149. Jones to Court of Directors, Jan. 2, 1810, For. Deptt., Secret, Cons. Aug. 16, 1810, Cons. 55.

150. Secret Committee of Court of Directors to Minto, Jan. 26, 1810. For. Deptt. Secret, Cons. Aug. 16, 1810, Cons. 184.

151. *Ibid.*

152. Secret letter to Court to Directors, Jan. 10, 1810.

153. *Ibid.*

154. Translation of a Royal Firman to Malcolm, July 22, 1810, For. Deptt. Secret, Cons. Sept. 25, 1810, Cons. 65.

155. *Ibid.*

156. Countess of Minto, *Lord Minto in India,* p. 139.

157. Secret Committee of Court of Directors to Jones, April 9, 1810, For. Deptt. Secret, Cons. Sept. 25, 1810, Cons. 63.

158. Principal Secretary of State in Foreign Office to Jones April 7, 1810, For Deptt. Secret, Cons. Sept. 25, 1810, Cons. 61; and East India House London to Jones, Apr. 9, 1810, For. Deptt. Secret, Cons. Nov. 30, 1810, Cons. 4.

159. Instructions to Sir. Gore Ousley, Ambassador-designate to Persia, July 13, 1810. For Deptt. Secret, Cons. Feb. 4, 1811, Cons. 2.

160. Ousley to Marquess Wellesley, Nov. 9, 1811, For. Deptt. Secret, Cons. Oct. 1, 1813, Cons. 10.

161. Aitchison, C.U., *op. cit.,* Vol. XIII, pp. 56-60.

162. *Ibid.*

6

The Travancore Rebellion

The first political treaty of a subsidiary character with Travancore was concluded in 1795 by which its Raja, Vanji Bala Ram Varma, engaged to pay an annual subsidy adequate to maintain three battalions of sepoys, together with a company of European artillery and two companies of lascars, to be stationed in his capital or on its frontiers or in British districts contiguous to it.[1] In return, the integrity of his state was guaranteed. By a subsequent Treaty, concluded in 1805, his successor, Raja Rama Varma Perumal, agreed to pay annually an additional subsidy, for the maintenance of one more infantry regiment, in six equal instalments commencing from January 1, 1805.[2] In case of need for greater military assistance for its defence against aggression, a reasonable proportion of his net revenues was to be contributed.[3] In lieu of it, the Raja surrendered his foreign relations to the East India Company agreed to pay the utmost attention to British advice and promised not to recruit any European national in his service or to provide shelter to him within his territories without previous British sanction.[4] Eventually, the total subsidy payable by him was fixed at eight lacs of rupees per annum.[5]

When Lord Minto took over office as Governor-General, the subsidy to the tune of Rs. 626,669 was found to be in arrears.[6] On the demand being pressed, the Raja apprized the Governor-General of his distressed financial condition and the inadequacy of the resources of his state to defray the expenses of the additional subsidiary force posted in his capital by the last treaty, in the hope of getting the financially burdensome stipulations of the existing engagements abrogated. Some time later, he addressed a similar appeal to the Governor of Madras.[7] But these requests evoked no favourable response from them. The latter, however, conveyed to the Raja through his Resident that any relaxation in the existing engagement was beyond his jurisdiction and that he should fulfil the engagement as it was.[8]

Consequently, Colonel Macaulay, the British Resident in Travancore pressed the Raja for payment of the arrears of subsidy with relentless severity. It is alleged by Vailu Thampi, the Dewan of the state, that Dr. Macaulay, the nephew of the Resident, met him several times in this connection and remarked discourteously that 'something must happen' in the event of non-compliance; and asserted the British right to advise the Raja of Travancore on every point connected with the administration of his state.[9]

The Chief Secretary of the Madras Government ascribed the delay in the payment of subsidy not to the want of Raja's means, but to his disinclination to comply with the British demands.[10] But the Resident was of the view that the Raja's difficulty was mainly due to the diversion of his resources to the formation and maintenance of the Carnatic Brigade[11], which the British Government viewed with suspicion. The real question in dispute, thus, was whether the subsidiary force of the Carnatic Brigade should be reduced, the Raja advocating the former and the Resident the latter.[12] He threw the blame for this contingency on the Dewan to whom the British interference in the affairs of Travancore was inconvenient.[13] He was convinced that so long as the Dewan was at the helm of affairs, British position in Travancore would not be safe.[14] He considered the Dewan to be guilty of inattention to and disregard of British advice, and addressed repeated reminders to him to pay the arrears of subsidy without further delay. The Dewan did make frequent and solemn promises, but they were never fulfilled. In this procrastination of the Dewan, the Resident suspected some serious design on his part to disturb the existing relations between the two states. He was, therefore, asked to advise the Raja to disband the expensive Carnatic Brigade.[15]

The Dewan, however, dwelt upon the heaviness of the British financial demand and the inadequacy of the resources of the Raja to pay it. Moreover, the Raja was reluctant to reduce or discharge the Carnatic Brigade as he looked upon it as an essential part of his honour and dignity. He treated the British proposal to disband it as a preliminary step to the 'seizure of his person and the annihilation of his authority.[16] Enumerating the services, which the personnel of the Carnatic Brigade had faithfully rendered to the British in the past in the region between Madura and Cavery and the valuable assistance he had received from them in the collection of revenues, he did not feel morally justified in throwing them out of employment and making them a prey to poverty and hunger.[17]

The Governor of Fort. St. George did not give credence to these views of the Dewan and finding no substantial reason for the non-payment of subsidy, threw the entire blame on him for the delaying tactics, as it was evident to him that the management of the affairs of Travancore was exclusively in his hands; and the Raja's views were unnecessarily dragged into the controversies. Thus Vailu Thampi was held responsible for the strained relations between the British Government and the State of Travancore; and was considered the chief obstacle in the restoration of cordial relations with the Raja.[18] He was alleged to be strong-willed, courageous, arrogant and headstrong. Finding himself in this predicament, Vailu Thampi became exasperated and decided not to yield to the pressure of the Resident which he thought would not be in the best interests of the State.[19] Instead, he prepared to meet the critical situation with the full conviction, that in so doing, he was simply discharging his duty with courage and firmness. He revived the key post of Generalissimo of the military forces of the state and appointed his younger-brother to that exalted office.[20] Under him the state forces were reorganized and made more efficient by regular and proper training.[21] The Resident alleged that Vailu Thampi had issued instructions to the several district officials to train a portion of the population under their charge in the use of offensive weapons.[22] A large number of people were employed day and night in the manufacture of powder, the cleaning of arms and the fabrication of bows and arrows and lances in every district. Several officers in charge of Divisions were furnished with orders to keep certain classes of people ready for assemblage, and their names were registered, and security was taken from them. On a given signal, they were required to repair to some fixed rendezvous.[23] It was also whispered that the Dewan had sought French help by sending emissaried to the Island of Mauritius to solicit a reinforcement of 500 men of artillery to meet any eventuality of British attack on Travancore for the recovery of arrears of subsidy.[24] It was suspected that the Dewan of Cochin, who enjoyed as much authority in his state as Vailu Thampi in Travancore, was in agreement with the views of his counterpart and was in league with him.[25] For want of an impartial verdict on the conduct of Vailu Thampi by a committee of enquiry, it is difficult to judge the veracity of the allegations made by the British Resident against him.

The alarming reports received from the Resident of Travancore soon engaged the serious attention of the Madras Government. The conduct of Vailu Thampi was looked upon with suspicion and distrust; and the sincerity of his intentions and the motives of his actions were suspected. His activities were considered dangerous and subversive to British interests in Travancore.[26] Effective measures were, therefore, adopted to nip in the bud the suspected plan of defiance by the Dewan; and his early removal from his vantage position was considered indispensable. Consequently, the Resident was authorized to take action for placing him under restraint in order to save the situation from deteriorating. Under the assumption that the conduct of the Dewan was at variance with the wishes of the Raja of Travancore, the Resident was advised to explain to the Raja that, under the administration of his Dewan, the essential provisions of the existing Treaty had not been scrupulously observed, while the British Government had fulfilled its part of the engagement.[27] Consequently, a large arrear of subsidy had accumulated and was daily increasing. The repeated remonstrances addressed to the Dewan had brought forth only fresh excuses and promises, but no fruitful results.[28]

Under these circumstances, the Government of Madras felt that it would not be in the British interest to let the state of affairs continue in Travancore with its dangerous effects on the neighbouring British districts. Realising the seriousness of the situation, it gave orders to the officers, commanding the Southern Division, and the Coast of Malabar for immediate movement of a considerable body of troops towards Travancore with ammunition, camp equipage and stores.[29] Similar orders were issued to the officers, commanding the British detachments at Trichinopoly and Seringapatam.[30] To strengthen the British position in Travancore, the subsidiary force was reinforced with a strong contingent of artillery and was furnished with adequate supplies of ammunition and provisions in order to meet any eventuality.[31] The movements of the Malabar and Southern Divisions were directed with a view to launching a two-pronged attack on Travancore; and with this end in view, all possible devices were employed to ensure quick success in their projected military campaign.[32] Lord Minto fully approved of the policy.[33]

These British military preparations inside and outside Travancore convinced Vailu Thampi that the British Government would not, at any cost, allow the state administration to have its own way. Sensing the impending danger of British military action against his ascendancy in the state administration, and knowing the futility of a conflict ruinous to him, he felt disgusted and informed the Resident through Colonel Dally, the Commandant of the Carnatic Brigade, expressing his willingness to resign and quit the state, if his personal safety was guaranteed.[34] The Resident lost no time in acceding to his desire. Thinking that his exit from Travancore would well serve the British purpose, he assured him protection and residence in the Company's territories; and also promised him a handsome allowance for his maintenance.[35] To ensure his undisturbed and secret exit from Alleppey to Calicut, he despatched palanquins, conveyances and a strong military escort under a European officer on the night of December 28, 1808.[36] Palpanah Pillai, his confidential friend and Tombi, his brother, were the only persons of distinction who were to accompany him, and Colonel Dally was to attend the quitting party.[37]

This plan, however, could not materialize as the Dewan changed his mind and decided to resist the unjustice done to him. He was bent upon destroying the British influence in Travancore root and branch. A little after mid-night of the same day, a party of Nairs numbering about one thousand, headed by Palpanah Pillai and the Dewan of Cochin, surrounded the house of the British Resident and opened musketry fire at every attempt by the inmates to escape. Thereafter, they disarmed the guards, broke into the house, pillaged it and ultimately withdrew at the break of day without getting hold of the Resident.[38]

The attack on the Resident's house was the expression of an open defiance of the British authority. It was reinforced by creating excitement among the people of Malabar against the British. This incident made the Madras Government alive to the imminent danger of an immediate rebellion. Prompt and effective measures were, therefore, taken to meet the serious situation. Besides ordering the march of troops to Travancore, the Government of Fort St. George issued a proclamation on January 5, 1809 to the people of Malabar, asking them not to be excited by the Dewan's anti-British propaganda and cautioned them against taking law in their hands and bringing calumny to them.[39] The Raja of

Travancore was also apprized of the situation created by his Dewan's rebellion and was assured of the security of his position and authority, as British manoeuvres were directed entirely against the rebellious elements in the state; and not against him and his royal house.[40]

In the meantime, Sir George Barlow, the Governor of Madras received intelligence of a desperate plan of Vailu Thampi and his rebel associates to attack the British military station at Quilon and excite rebellion all over Malabar. Therefore, Colonel Gibbs of His Majesty's 59 Regiment was ordered to march to Malabar with a sufficient force to foil the intrigues of the rebels.[41] A European Regiment was called in with the greatest promptitude from Ceylon to cope with the grave situation and to maintain law and order in Travancore. The British force under Colonel Picton and Colonel Chalmers met the Carnatic Brigade at Quilon and ascending the heights to the west of Cantonment, opened fire on it and forced its soldiers to surrender their guns. This victory was won on January 15, 1809 with 41 casualties on the British side and a larger number on the rebel side.[42]

After this reverse at Quilon, Vailu Thampi concentrated his attention on Cochin which was then held by a strong British force under Major Hewitt. Here the Cochin troops joined hands with him and attacked the British force under Major Hewitt on January 19, 1809.[43] The battle lasted for an hour and ended in the rout of the insurgents with considerable slaughter and the loss of a field piece.[44]

After these two military encounters in which the rebels were beaten and dispersed with considerable losses, a concentrated two-pronged drive was made against Travancore to capture its territories and denude it of the rebels. Colonel Cuppage, along with his forces, marched through the Northern frontier and advanced to the South without meeting any oppisition. Colonel St. Leger pushed on towards Aramboly with a force composed of one regiment of European soldiers, another of the Indian cavalry and three battalions of Indian infantry. A detachment of artillery and a regiment from Ceylon joined him. Two divisions, commanded by Colonel Wallace and Colonel Gibbs were stationed in the Tinnevelly district, in the vicinity of Wynad, to keep the Travancoreans in check, and eventually to cooperate with Colonel St. Leger who arrived from Trichinopoly with his forces and encamped near the Aramboly pass on February 6, 1809. The pass was protected by a strong wall, supported by well built bastions mounted with guns. The ascent was reached with enormous difficulty and it took six hours to reach the foot of the walls.[45] Ultimately, the Aramboly Lines were captured the next morning and the fortifications on both sides of the gate were dismantled.[46] This success of the British demoralized the rebels who ran helter-skelter for safety. Their leader, Vailu Thampi, found his cause lost, and quitted Travancore which he was not destined to see again.[47]

Thus Travancore was now completely under British possession. Its ruler accepted humiliating terms on March 1, 1809[48] and the state was allowed to continue as a separate subordinate political entity under him. He agreed to pay all the expenses of war and also the arrears of the subsidy. The Carnatic Brigade and some Nair battalions in the Raja's service were disbanded and dismissed. The defence of the state became the exclusive responsibility of the subsidiary troops. Womanah Thampi, who enjoyed the confidence of the British Resident, was appointed Dewan in place of Vailu Thampi who was dismissed. On the conclusion of this engagement, the British occupation troops were withdrawn immediately, and a part of the subsidiary force was permanently quartered in the proximity of Trivandrum. This arrangement received the approval of the Governor-General who sent cordial congratulations to the Government of Madras on the successful termination of hostilities in Travancore.[49] He also praised the wisdom shown in planning the military operations and the skill, energy and valour which distinguished the execution of them.[50]

The ruler of Travancore was not completely absolved of the responsibility of the rebellious proceedings of his Dewan. The course of events convinced the British that the Raja acquiesced in the doings of his minister. They did not find any evidence of an attempt on the part of the Raja to prevent his minister from the open exhibition of his resentment. Hence the interests of the Raja were not treated as distinct from those of his Dewan. To the Calcutta Government, the spirit of hostility in Travancore appeared to have been deeply rooted and originated not so much in the pecuniary burden of the subsidy, nor in personal enmity towards the Resident, as in a systematic design to shake off its connection with the British Government and the subversion of British power and authority in that region.[51] The Dewan was condemned as unscrupulous, barbarous and cruel and his rebellious conduct was considered to be a project conceived long back, systematically pursued and precipitated by the demand for arrears of subsidy.[52]

The Dewan fled into the thickets towards the Northern frontier of the state.[53] He was closely pursued by the parties detached by the Raja to apprehend him.[54] He was obliged to move from place to place to avoid the disgrace of surrendering and falling a victim to the vindictiveness of the British. At last, he was found out from the pagoda of Bhagwadi, where he had put an end to his life rather than to be captured alive by the British. On entering that edifice, his pursuers found the corpse of Vailu Thampi.[55] His brother, found in the same premises, was taken captive to Quilon and was hanged as an accessory in the murder of the British, in the presence of the 12th Regiment, drawn out to witness his execution. The Dewan's body was taken to Trivandrum where it was exposed on a common gibbet.[56] This act of the Resident was not appreciated by the Governor-General[57], as it was likely to excite more dissatisfaction in the section sympathetic to him and his cause; and might lead to acts of exasperation. Thus the unpleasant episode in Travancore, created by the systematic British interference into it, ended favourably for the British.

The successful military operations against Travancore served the British ends in view in that quarter of India, but the state could not be freed from difficulties altogether for a long time. The military resources of the state were crippled. There remained no body of troops in the absolute control of its Raja or Dewan which could be used as an instrument by either of them to execute their wishes unhampered by the British. The elimination of the Carnatic Brigade, which was an eye-sore to the British and a source of strained relations with the Dewan, was an undoubted achievement of the Madras Government. The entire Peninsula, south of the Tungbhadra, no longer sheltered any organized bands of armed men under any political leader to challenge the British supremacy in that region. Now the British will, expressed by their Residents and plans executed by their subsidiary troops, could prevail to shape the destiny of the subjugated tract. The other notable British achievement was the removal from the helm of affairs of the strong-willed and inconvenient Dewan who had kept the ruler under his control and was disinclined to subordinate state policies to the Resident's interests. In his place, a person amenable to British advice who could be used to infiltrate British influence deeper into the internal polity of the state, was appointed as the highest executive authority under the Raja. Under this regime, the uncertainty about the regular payment of subsidy and its arrears was removed. The resistance offered to the British revealed to them the sources of anti-British sentiment in the state that needed greater suppression and also the knowledge of the pro-British element which needed greater patronage. A part of the subsidiary force, permanently stationed at Trivandrum, accorded greater safety to the British Residency against any future attacks of which there was hardly any further danger. Greater vigilance was shown by keeping a closer watch over the activities of the Raja and the Dewan as a guarantee against future trouble. Thus, by all possible means, the future security of British interests in Travancore was ensured permanently. To avoid any danger to British interests from its neighbouring state of Cochin, whose Dewan had made cause with Vailu Thampi, the state was brought rigorously into the web of a subsidiary alliance, and opposition to the British was rooted out by adequate punishment to the hostile elements.

REFERENCES

1. Aitchison, C. U., *op. cit.*, Vol. X, Arts III & IV, p. 130.
2. Treaty of 1805, Aitchison, C. U., *op. cit.*, Vol. XI, Art. 3, p. 136.
3. Arts. IV and V of the Treaty.
4. Articles VII, VIII.
5. Barlow to Lord Minto, Aug. 5, 1808, For. Deptt. Secret, Cons. Jan. 2, 1809, Cons. 24.
6. *Ibid.*,
7. Raja to Lord Minto, received on Feb. 13, 1808, For. Deptt. Secret, Cons. Dec. 26, 1808, Cons. 30.
8. Chief Secretary, Madras to Colonel Macaulay, Resident in Travancore, June 25, 1803, For Deptt. Secret, Cons. Jan. 2, 1809, Cons. 27.
9. Dewan to Chief Secretary, Madras, July 8, 1808, For. Deptt. Secret, Cons. Jan. 2, 1809, Cons. 28.
10. Chief Secretary, Madras to Dewan, May 30, 1808, For. Deptt. Secret, Cons. Jan. 2, 1809, Cons. 31.
11. *Ibid.*
12. *Ibid.*
13. Macaulay to Chief Secretary, Madras, No. 3, 1808, For. Deptt. Secret, Cons. Jan. 2, 1809, Cons. 40.
14. Macaulay to Chief Secretary, July 13, 1808, For. Deptt. Secret, Cons. Jan. 2, 1809, Cons. 30.
15. *Ibid.*
16. Dewan to Chief Secretary, Nov. 23, 1808 For. Deptt. Secret, Cons. Jan. 2, 1809, Cons. 45.
17. Dewan to Chief Secretary, Nov. 23, 1808, For. Deptt. Secret, Cons. Jan. 2, 1809, Cons. 45.
18. *Ibid.*
19. Macaulay to Chief Secretary, Dec. 5, 1808, For. Deptt. Secret, Cons. Jan. 2, 1809, Cons. 59.

20. *Ibid.*

21. Macaulay to Chief Secretary, Dec. 2, 1808, For. Deptt, Secret, Cons. Jan. 2, 1809, Cons. 56.

22. Macaulay to Chief Secretary, Dec. 22, 1808, For. Deptt. Secret, Cons. Jan. 2, 1809, Cons. 49.

23. Macaulay to Chief Secretary, Dec. 22, 1808, For. Deptt. Secret, Cons. Jan. 2, 1809, Cons. 49.

24. Macaulary to Chief Secretary, dated nill, For. Deptt. Secret, Cons. Jan. 23, 1809, Cons. 33.

25. *Ibid.*

26. Chief Secretary to Macaulay, Dec. 7, 1808, For. Deptt. Secret, Cons. Jan. 9, 1809, Cons. 14.

27. *Ibid.*

28. Chief Secretary to Macaulay, Dec. 7, 1808, For. Deptt. Secret, Cons. Jan. 9, 1809, Cons. 14.

29. Chief Secretary to Officer Commanding, Southern Division, Dec. 18, 1808, For Deptt. Secret, Cons. Jan. 9, 1809, Cons. 11, and Chief Secretary to Officer Commanding, Malabar, Dec. 18, 1808, For. Deptt. Secret, Cons, Jan. 9, 1809, Cons. 12.

30. Chief Secretary to Officer Commanding, Seringapatam, *op. cit.*, Cons. 13.

31. Barlow to Minto, Dec. 27, 1808, For. Deptt. Secret, Cons. Jan. 23. 1809, Cons. 28.

32. Chief Secretary, Madras to Edminstone, Dec. 16, 1808, For. Deptt. Secret, Cons. Jan. 2, 1809, Cons. 53.

33. Lord Minto to Barlow, Dec. 19, 1808, For. Deptt. Secret, Cons. Jan. 2, 1809, Cons. 40.

34. Macaulay to Chief Secretary, Dec. 27, 1808, For. Deptt. Secret, Cons. Jan. 23, 1809, Cons. 40.

35. Macaulay to Dewan, Dec. 26, 1808, For. Deptt. Secret, Cons. Jan. 23, 1809, Cons. 41.

36. Macaulay to Chief Secretary, Dec. 28, 1808, For. Deptt. Secret, Cons. Jan. 23, 1809, Cons. 42.

37. *Ibid.*

38. Macaulay to Chief Secretary Dec. 29, 1808, For Deptt. Secret, Cons. Jan. 23, 1809, Cons. 30.

39. Proclamation of Chief Secretary, Madras, Jan. 5, 1809, For. Deptt. Secret, Cons. Feb. 8, 1809, Cons. 5.

40. Barlow to Raja, Jan. 5, 1809, For. Deptt. Secret, Cons. Feb. 6, 1809, Cons. 10.

41. Chief Secretary to Colonel Cuppage, Jan. II, 1809, For. Deptt. Secret, Cons. Feb. 13, 1809, Cons. 30.

42. Chief Secretary to Edmonstone, Feb., 10, 1809, For. Deptt. Secret, Cons. March 6, 1809, Cons. 9.

43. Chief Secretary to Edmonstone, Feb. 20, 1809, For. Deptt. Secret Cons. March 6, 1809, Cons. 10.

44. Chief Secretary to Edmonstone, Feb. 20, 1809, For. Deptt. Secret, Cons. March, 6, 1809, Cons. 10.

45. Chief Secretary to Edmonstone, Feb. 23, 1809. For. Deptt. Secret, Cons. March 13, 1809, Cons. 27.

46. *Ibid.*

47. Macaulay to Chief Secretary, Feb. 26, 1809, For. Deptt. Secret, Cons. March 27, 1809, Cons. 22.

48. Aitchison, C. U., *op. cit.*

49. Edmonstone to Chief Secretary, Madras, April 10, 1809, For. Deptt. Secret, Cons. April 10, 1809, Cons. 14.

50. *Ibid.*

51. *Ibid.*

52. Macaulay to Edmonstone, June 9, 1809, For. Deptt. Secret, Cons. July 15, 1809, Cons. 6.

53. Chief Secretary to Edmonstone, March 4, 1809, For. Deptt. Secret, Cons. March 20, 1809, Cons. 5.

54. Chief Secretary to Edmonstone, March 4, 1809, For. Deptt. Secret, Cons. March 20, 1809, Cons. 16.

55. Macaulay to Barlow, March 29, 1809, For. Deptt. Secret, Cons. April 29, 1809, Cons. 16.

56. Macaulay to Chief Secretary, April 2, 1809, For. Deptt. Secret, Cons. April 9, 1809, Cons. 18.

57. Edmonstone to Chief Secretary, April 29, 1809, For. Deptt. Secret, Cons. April 29, 1809, Cons. 19.

7

Socio-Economic Consequences of British Rule

I. INDUSTRIAL AND COMMERCIAL SUPREMACY OF INDIA IN THE SEVENTEENTH CENTURY

The supremacy of India in the industrial field reached its high-water mark towards the end of the seventeenth century when there was a sudden spurt in the demand for Indian cotton goods in England, induced by a remarkable change in English fashions and modes of dress. The English people developed a preference for light cotton garments in place of the coarse woollens that they had worn for centuries. Among the ladies there was a craze for Indian chintzes and calicoes. "On a sudden," reports a publication of the early eighteenth century, "we saw all our women, rich and poor, clothed in calico, printed and painted, the gayer and the more tawdry the better". Coarse varieties of Indian cloth had been imported into England in the past, but they were little used for purposes of dressmaking. The change in the fashion of dress led to the chintzes being "advanced from lying upon their floors to their backs, from the foot-cloth to the petty-coats".[1]

Defoe bewailed the fact that "it (Indian cotton cloth) crept into our houses, our closets and bed chambers; curtains, cushions, chairs, and at last beds themselves were nothing but calicoes or Indian stuffs". The effect was that "almost everything that used to be made of wool or silk, relating either to dress of the women or the furniture of our houses, was supplied by the Indian Trade".[2]

The East India Company seized the opportunity offered by this new demand and began to import large quantities of cotton cloth from India. Originally, as is well known, the Company had been established in 1600 for competing with the Dutch in the pepper trade, and for a long time pepper and other spices constituted the principal items of import into England. About 1670, there was a sudden increase in the demand for textiles and this was immediately reflected in the orders placed by the Directors for purchases in India. In view of their popularity, import duties on them were abolished in England in 1684 and this gave further impetus to the demand. Finally, with the prohibition of imports from France in 1688, the Indian calicoes emerged as the biggest item of the Company's imports from India. Hitherto the Company's lists were primarily made up of saltpetre, indigo, pepper and other commodities, but after 1688 textile goods of various kinds almost monopolised the space on the list; indigo and spices were relegated to a corner.[3]

The change in the composition of India's trade led to the revival of opposition in Britain to the East India Company. The attack came from two quarters—from the mercantilists and from the woollen and silk manufacturers. The former attacked the Indian trade on the ground that it led to the export of treasure from England. What the country obtained in exchange for gold and silver was Indian Muslims, "a shadow of a commodity". "If European countries agreed not to deal in Indian goods," writes Davenants, "this side of the world would save a great and continual expense of treasure". Another writer cries, in perfect Biblical style, "O Jerusalem, Jerusalem, thy destruction is of thyself. . . O England, strangers devour thee, strangers eat there up. Thou art fond of novelties which will be thy ruin".[4]

The other line of attack on the Company's trade with India was that the import of cotton goods destroyed the ancient woollen and the nascent silk industries and thus caused unemployment and suffering among the weavers. While there can be no doubt that the displacement of British textile manufactures by Indian cotton piece-goods, both in England and in the European markets, must have caused unemployment in the textile industries, the pamphleteers of the time painted a grim and probably exaggerated picture of the suffering of the artisans. They succeeded in making the imposition of restrictions on imports from India a national issue. It was stated that, by the end of the seventeenth century, half the working men of the weaving trade "were running up and down the nation seeking bread from Canterbury to London, from London to Norwich".[5]

The suffering was not confined to weavers alone. The public finances were affected because of the decline in revenue and the increase in expenditure on poor relief.[6] The profits of the landlords were diminished by the decline in the rents of land and houses. Under the circumstances, it was natural for the agitation to assume nation-wide dimensions. One of the first effects of the agitation was that the Company withdrew from India the weavers, pattern makers and artists who had been sent from England to advise Indian weavers about European tastes and fashions and to persuade them to produce the patterns of cloth in great demand in Europe. But popular opinion was not satisfied by this minor concession. The national temper was so aroused that legislation to prohibit or restrict the East India Company's import trade in Indian cotton goods could not be long evaded.[7]

British Protectionism before the Conquest of Bengal

Accordingly an Act was passed in 1700 which laid down that from Michaelmas (September 29, 1701) "all manufactured silks, Bengals, and stuffs mixed with silk or herba, of the manufacture of Persea, China or East Indies and all Calicoes painted, dyed, printed or stained there which are or shall be imported into this kingdom of England, dominion of Wales and town of Berwick-on-Tweed, shall not be worn or other wise used within this kingdom".[8] The Act excluded from its operation calicoes painted or printed in England thereby saving "the various subsidiary industries that subsisted on working up Indian calicoes". The Act also provided for the establishment of bonded warehouses which separated imports for the purchase of the carrying trade from imports for home consumption. In this way not only profits from the carrying trade were retained, but positive encouragement was given to the British navigation and shipping industry.[9]

But the Act of 1700 failed to stop completely the imports of Indian calicoes into England. In 1702, therefore, an import duty of fifteen per cent was imposed on plain cottons. This shifted the demand from coarse and cheap calicoes to superior Muslims.

The imports of Indian white calicoes rose to the phenomenal figure of 2,088,451 pieces in 1719 as against 247,214 pieces in 1698, 951,109 pieces in 1701 and 1,220,324 pieces in 1718. The imported cloth was worked up, that is "stained, dyed and printed" in England for sale. Consequently, a flourishing dyeing and printing industry developed. If protection had benefited anybody, it was this new British industry. The weavers failed to benefit except where they gave up the traditional woollen trade and took to weaving cotton, an industry which was just establishing itself in England at the time.

The agitation against Indian goods was revived in 1719 and a new Act was passed in 1720 which prohibited the wear and use of Indian silks and calicoes painted, stained, or dyed in England under the penalty of £5 for each offence on the wearer, and of £20 on the seller.

The new Act did not prove more successful than its predecessor. The imports of white calicoes fell to 718,678 pieces in 1722, but rose to 1,115,011 pieces in 1723, and

1,291,614 pieces in 1724.[10] Similarly, the imports of Bengal silks which stood at 55,491 pieces in 1721 fell to 18,439 pieces in 1722, but rose to 58,729 pieces in 1723 and 79,602 pieces in 1727. The pamphleteers once again started denouncing the use Indian fabrics. Lamenting the failure of legislation in putting a stop to the imports of Indian goods, the ingenious author of *A Plan of the English Committee* wrote in 1728, "two things amongst us are ungovernable : our passions and our fashions".[11]

England was not alone in adopting the protectionist policy against Indian manufactures. The mercantilist spirit was rampant at the time, and all European countries, with the sole exception of Holland, either prohibited totally or imposed heavy duties on the import of Indian cotton goods. Louis XV's edict of 1726 is typical of the spirit of the time. By this law, the penalties for the use and sale of Indian cotton goods in France were made stringent. Smuggling was to be met, under the law, by the imposition of capital punishment on the third offence!

Meanwhile, the cotton industry in England was developing rapidly. By the middle of the eighteenth century it was well established. In 1744 the Directors of the East India Company wrote to India, "printing here hath come to so great perfection that unless you can keep to these instructions, you must lessen the quantity".[12] About the excellence of British printers it was said at the time, "it was reserved for the English to attempt the imitation of the best Indian work in prints and to arrive at a degree of perfection which no one would have thought possible".[13] In 1754, a printed piece which a dealer presented to the Princess of Wales is said to have greatly excelled Indian chintz in workmanship.[14]

Under the combined influence of the restrictions on imports into Europe and the growth of the English industry, the Indian cotton trade with Europe began to suffer a decline from the middle of the eighteenth century. Nevertheless, it speaks highly of the resilience of the Indian industry and of the high quality of its products that substantial quantities of both cotton piece-goods and silk continued to be imported into Europe even after 1750. In 1760, which may be taken as a normal year, after the battle of Plassey, the exports to England alone amounted to 988,709 pieces of white calicoes, 51,108 pieces of wrought silk from Bengal, 212,910 pieces of stained calicoes and 665 pieces of sooseys. In the same year, other goods exported to England from India were: pepper 3,133,884 lbs., coffee 186 lbs. (the previous year's figure for coffee was 971,464 lbs.), wool 75,543 lbs. and saltpetre 37,780 cwts.[15]

But it was not till foreign rule was firmly established in India and political power was abused by the new rulers to strangulate the arts and crafts of the subject people that Indian industries suffered final extinction. They held their own till about the first decade of the nineteenth century. It was after 1820 that they suffered a heavy blow in the form of the fall in the foreign demand for their products. The following table[16] shows the fall in the export of cotton piece-goods from India during the period of thirty-five years between 1795-96 and 1829-30:

Export of Cotton Piece-Goods from the Port of Calcutta

(Pieces)

Year	*United Kingdom*	*America*	*Hamburgh*	*Copen-hagen*	*Portugal*	*Total for all countries*
1795-96	198,750	434,412½	344,286	186,549	527,068	2,122,089½
1796-97	162,195	522,692	104,574	307,073	185,077	1,712,247
1797-98	161,276	457,945	28,532	64,374	401,391	1,466,142
1798-99	177,197	239,928	86,277	8,415	183,125	1,454,463
1799-1800	305,119	776,919	3,744	169,473	1,122,853	3,026,253
1823-24	106,516	38,440	—	—	—	2,189,926
1824-25	167,524	123,748	—	9,178	112,165	1,543,095
1825-26	111,295	146,184	—	1,646	123,514	1,256,573
1826-27	47,572	21,648	—		83,867	970,223
1827-28	50,654	10,521	—		54,002	978,858
1828-29	32,626	23,780	—		20,045	819,170
1829-30	13,043	3,771	—		—	695.725

II. INDIA'S INDUSTRIAL DECLINE

During the early decades of the nineteenth century neither the existing import duties nor the fall in the cost of production of cotton piece-goods resulting from the use of steam power and machinery enabled England to compete with goods from India in the markets of Europe. India prices continued to be from fifty to sixty per cent lower than English prices. In order, therefore, to create favourable conditions for its own goods, Britain used her political power to smother the manufactures of her defeated rival. The duties on Indian imports were made prohibitory and Indian producers were saddled with crippling burdens. The rates of duties on some of the Indian imports into England were as follows in 1812:[17]

Calicoes, plain, white Dimities, plain, white	£68 6s. 8d. per cent ad valorem, plus an additional warehousing duty of £3 6s. 8d.
Articles of manufactures of cotton, wholly or in part made up, not otherwise charged with duty	£27 6s. od. per cent ad valorem plus £10 0s. od.
Mats and matting	£68 6s. 8d. per cent ad volorem, plus £2 13s. 4d.
Silk manufactures	Prohibited for home use
Taffaties and other plain or figured silks not otherwise described	"
Warehousing duty on above when imported for purposes of re-export	£3 6s. 8d. per cent ad valorem
Hard soap	£68 6s. 8d. plus £2 13s. 4d. per cent ad valorem
Sugar	£1 13s. od. per cwt
Indigo	£o 14s. 4d. per 100 lbs. of weight plus £2 13s. 4d. per cent ad valorem

"It consequently became necessary," writes Wilson, "to protect the latter (the British manufactures) by duties of seventy and eighty per cent on their value or by positive prohibition"[18] "Had this not been the case," he continues, "the mills of Paisley and of Manchester would have been stopped in their outset and could scarcely have been again set in motion, even by the powers of steam. They were created by the sacrifice of the Indian manufacture. Had India been independent, she would have retaliated, would have imposed preventive duties on British goods, and would thus have preserved her own productive industry from annihilation. This act of self-defence was not permitted her; she was at the mercy of the stranger. British goods were forced upon her without paying any duty; and the foreign manufacturer employed the arm of political injustice to keep down and ultimately strangle a competitor with whom he could not have contended on equal terms".[19]

The enormous increase in the exports of British manufacturers to India after 1813, when the trading monopoly of the East India Company was withdrawn and the Indian trade was thrown open to all, was therefore not merely due to the fall in the prices of British manufactures, as was made out by some of the witnesses before the Select Committee[20], but largely because of the commercial policy of Britain and her political domination over India.

Use of Political power to Destroy Industry

As a sovereign power, the interest of the East India Company lay in promoting the wealth of the subjects by encouraging their productive activity; but as a body of merchants it was interested in increasing its profits. "It is the interest of East India Company considered as sovereigns," wrote Adam Smith, "that European goods which are carried to their Indian dominions should be sold there as cheap as possible; and the Indian goods which are brought from thence should bring here as good a price, or should be sold here as dear as possible. But the reverse of this is their interest as merchants. As sovereigns, their interest is exactly the same with that of the country which they govern. As merchants their interest is exactly opposite to that interest".[21] The

Company manipulated prices to the detriment of the artisans; it oppressed the weavers and followed other restrictive policies which ruined Indian industries, particularly the cotton industry of Bengal. As William Bolts, a contemporary critic of the East India Company observed in 1767, "the whole inland trade of the country, as at present conducted, and that of the country's investment for Europe in a more peculiar degree, has been one continued scene of oppression: the baneful effects of which are severely felt by every weaver and manufacturer in the country, every article produced being made a monopoly: in which the English with the *banyans* and black *gmashtas*, arbitrarily decide what quantities of goods each manufacturer shall deliver and the *prices* he shall receive for them."[22]

The mechanism of making purchases of Indian goods and providing the Company's investments in India was so contrived as to result in oppression and in the "defrauding of the poor weaver". Agents called *gomashtas* were engaged by the Company mostly on monthly wages. Each *gomashta* accompanied by a clerk and a cashier paid visits to the interior as regular intervals for the purpose of making purchase. When Mir Jafar was installed on the gaddi in 1757, the *gomashtas* of the English had already become so powerful and had acquired such jurisdiction that "even the authority of the Rajas and Zamindars in the country durst not withstand". After 1765, when the veil of the Nawab's sovereignty in Bengal was finally cast aside, they came to derive their authority directly from the sovereign of the country and exercised powers on his behalf. They were not only commercial agents, but also law-givers and magistrates from whose decisions there was no appeal. "The assent of the poor weavers," adds William Bolts, "is in general not deemed necessary; for the *gomashtas* when employed on the Company's investment frequently make them sign what they please; and upon the weavers refusing to take the money offered, it has been known they have had it tied to their girdles and they have been sent away with a flogging".[23]

A number of weavers were also registered in the books of the Company, and they were not permitted to work for any one else. They were transferred from one *gomashta* of the Company to another, "as so many slaves, subject to the tyranny and rougers of every succeeding *gomashta*".[24] Peons and watchmen were employed to supervise them, so that they did not sell goods to any one other than the Company's *gomashta*, and on the slightest suspicion of the weaver's intention of doing so, pieces of cloth were cut out of the loom even before they had reached the finished stage.[25] If in spite of this watchfulness, any weaver dared to sell his goods to any one else with the connivance or support of *dallals*, both the broker and the weaver were "seized and imprisoned, confined in irons, fined considerable sums of money, flogged and deprived, in the most ignominious manner of what they esteem most valuable, their caste".[26] With the Company's investments, the *gomashtas* combined personal and private business and made use of their arbitrary powers for buying goods on their account on the same favourable terms on which they purchased goods for the Company. "The rougery practised in this department," concludes William Bolts, "is beyond imagination but all terminates in the defrauding of the poor weaver; for the price which the Company's *gomashtas*, and in confederacy with them, the *Fachendars* fix upon the goods, are in all places at least fifteen per cent and in some forty per cent less than the goods manufactured would sell for in the public bazar or market upon a free sale".[27]

Another sharp practice was the manipulation of prices of raw materials to the detriment of Indian producers. One such instance may be quoted: Bengal obtained its supplies of finer varieties of cotton from Bombay and Surat. The servants of the Company formed a private company consisting of the members of the Council at Calcutta in order to corner the supplies and to raise the prices in Bengal. They purchased cotton worth Rs. 25 lakhs from Surat, causing the shooting up of prices immediately from the prevailing range of Rs. 16 to 18 per maund to that of Rs. 28 to 30 per maund. This was ruinous to the weaver. He could not charge higher prices for his products because they were arbitrarily fixed down for him by the Company's purchase agents, while he was forced to pay exorbitant prices for his raw materials.

The effect of the practices followed by the Company and its servants was bound to prove destructive. The craftsmen were ruined. The few adventurers in the service of the Company, no doubt amassed great fortunes and retired to England to lead lives of cause and plenty. But they did so by killing the proverbial goose that laid the golden eggs. The prices of Indian manufactures were inflated without any corresponding increase in the wages of labour. The quality of Indian products was debased. The history of the early period of British rule in India is thus, a sordid tale of vandalism, plunder, oppression and destruction of Indian handicraft and manufactures. The once flourishing industrial towns were depopulated and the artisans diverted from their traditional occupations into agriculture in order to find employment as wage labourers.

In 1769, Mr. Becher, the Company's Resident at Murshidabad, reported: "this fine country which flourished under the most despotic and arbitrary Government, is verging towards its ruin while the English have really so great a share in the Administration...With concern I now see its present ruinous conditions, which I am convinced, is greatly owing to the monopoly that has been made of late years in the Company's name of almost all the manufactures in the country".[28] A responsible member of the British Parliament, William Fullarton, was even more forthright in his denunciation of the Company's rule in Bengal. In 1787 he described the transformation of Bengal after twenty years of the Company's rule in these words: "In former times the Bengal countries were the granary of nations, and the repository of commerce, wealth and manufacture in the East...But such has been the restless energy of our misgovernment that within the short space of twenty years many parts of these countries have been reduced to the appearance of a sert. The fields are no longer cultivated; extensive tracts are already overgrown with thickets; the husband man is plundered; the manufacturer oppressed; famine has been repeatedly endured; and depopulation has ensued".[29] By 1789, the prosperous industrial province of Bengal had been so ruined that "one-third of the Company's territory in Hindustan" had been converted, according to Lord Cornwallis, into "a jungle inhabited only by wild beasts".[30]

Internal causes of Economic Decline

Howsoever strong the industrial structure of the country might have been, it could hardly withstand the hostility of its foreign rulers. But in fact there were weaknesses in the industrial structure itself which must share part of the blame for the decline of industries. In the first place, Indians did not evince any interest in the extension of markets for their goods, a factor which, as Adam Smith points out, limited the division of labour and, therefore, industrial progress. What is worse, most of India's foreign trade even before the British conquest, had passed into the hands of foreigners. The result was that Indian artisans and producers were at the mercy of foreign merchants so far as sales in foreign markets were concerned.

Secondly, against the aggressive Mercantilism of the West, India had no national commercial policy of its own. Even in the heyday of their power, the Mughal emperors remained merely silent spectators to the establishment of "factories" and to the scramble for the capture of Indian trade and markets by European powers. When heavy import duties were being imposed on Indian goods in England in the seventeenth and eighteenth centuries, India, though it was a sovereign power, did not retaliate against England. The fact is that in India economic questions had not yet begun to be viewed from a national standpoint, and it is doubtful whether the country would have considered the question of external trade differently from what it did even if political circumstances had not changed for the worse.

Thirdly, the Indian weakness at sea was as much responsible for the industrial decline of the country as for its political subjugation. In the seventeenth and eighteenth centuries, European powers combined maritime trade with piracy. It was hazardous for any merchants to sail with cargo to another country without adequate armed protection against the pirates. On account of the lack of sea power, India failed to maintain the overseas markets, which were forcibly acquired by the European nations. The result was that while Europe speedily went through the industrial revolution, India suffered industrial decline and was converted into a backward agricultural country.

Fourthly, the gild organisation which characterised medieval industry and commerce in Europe, was very weak in India. The caste system which did duty for the gild, failed to protect industry from external attacks. When the foreign trader appeared on the scene for making purchases of industrial goods, the individual artisan was pitted against the organised monopolies of foreign buyers. He depended very often on advances of money from the purchaser for executing the latter's orders for the products. In the absence of an independent gild and financial organisation, the Indian producer was unable to hold his own in settling prices and in producing commodities independently of advance orders from the foreigner.

Finally, India did not possess a class of industrial entrepreneurs such as England had. If there were no inventions or technological advances in India, it was not because of the inferiority of Indian talent or skill, but because that progressive class which, in the West, first captured the markets and then organised production to supply those markets with manufactures of their own country, did not exist.

Decline of Agriculture

The ruin of Indian industry proceeded simultaneously with the decline in agriculture and commerce. The factors responsible for this were mainly political.

Agriculture suffered because the State levied an oppressive land tax and because the servants of the Company forced the villages to raise crops which benefited them rather than the cultivator. It was said about the Dutch that in the Spice Islands they "burn all the spiceries which a fertile season produces beyond what they expect to dispose of in Europe with such a profit as they think sufficient".[31] The English Company followed the same destructive policy in Bengal. "It has not been uncommon," wrote Adam Smith, "for the chief, that is the first clerk of a factory, to order a peasant to plough up a rich field of poppies, and sow it with rice or some other grain. The pretence was, to prevent a scarcity of provisions; but the real reason, to give the chief an opportunity of selling at a better price a large quantity of opium which he then happened to have upon hand. Upon other occasion the order has been reversed; and a rich field of rice and other grain has been ploughed up, in order to make room for a plantation of poppies, when the chief foresaw that extraordinary profit was likely to be made by opium".[32]

Disruption of Trade

India's trade suffered equally with agriculture and industry. Its destruction was wrought by the institution of monopolies—sometimes legal, but very often illegal—by the servants of the Company, and its diversion from its natural channels.

(a) *Internal Trade*: The East India Company had obtained exemption from the payment of transit and customs duties since the times of Farrukh Siyar. But they absurd this concession. They defrauded the treasury of its legitimate dues on the private goods belonging to the Company's servants who frequently issued *parwanas* over their signatures to allow them to pass from one part of the country to the other without paying the transit duties. The *dastaks* (signed passes) of the servants of the Company became a vendible commodity and even the Indian traders frequently purchased them from the Company's servants in order to secure exemption from duties.

On the assumption of political power in Bengal, the Company came to control the country's commercial activity. Indian and foreign merchants were then systematically ousted from their business by discriminatory taxation and the institution of trade monopoly in the more important commodities. Under Clive almost the whole of the inland trade was monopolised by the Company and its servants. "The whole inland trade, in almost everything else that country produces, and even the trade in some of the principal of foreign import," writes William Bolts, "has been carried on as monopolies, by a few of the superior servants of the Company with their Banyans and favourites: and not only has every public measure of late years adopted by the Government at Calcutta been calculated to favour the establishment of such monopolies, but even the contradictory, and the injudicious orders of the Court of Directors, on some occasions from want of local knowledge, and on others from a connivance at the proceedings of their servants abroad, or from the state of parties in the Leaden Hall, have promoted such shameful measures".[33] The system of transit duties was used as a prop to maintain these monopolies and save the monopolists from losses on their transactions. For instance, the crop of cotton in Upper India (Uttar Pradesh) turned out to be extraordinarily good in the year the superior servants of the Company in Bengal formed a monopoly in the import of Bombay cotton. The native merchants in Bengal began to import cotton in large quantities from northern and southern India. The Company's monopoly was threatened in consequence, with the prospect of heavy loss. Immediately, a thirty per cent duty on the inland import of cotton passing through Bihar into Bengal was levied and prices were forced up to save the monopolist from loss.[34]

The internal trade was in the hands of the servants of the Company and the profits from it went to enrich its corrupt employees rather than the Company itself. Great fortunes were made by the higher servants of the Company. Even the Governor General took part in this traffic. Such activities not only pushed out the Indians from the internal trade, but also defrauded the producer and the consumer by forcing the former to sell cheap and the latter to buy dear.[35] The Bengal famine of 1770 was the direct outcome of these monopolistic practices in trade. "The English manufactured a famine by buying up all the rice, and refusing to sell it again, except at fabulous prices".[36]

In other ways, too, the Company used its political power for driving out its rival merchants from trade. There were frequent instances "of the goods of private merchants, even Europeans, but particularly of those belonging to Armenians, Mughals, and Gentoos (Hindus), being in consequence of this monopoly, stopped on the public road, and by force carried to the freight warehouse".[37] The proprietors of these goods were often "obliged, contrary to their will, to see their goods shipped on vessels they had not a good opinion of and going on voyages whose destination and management were often contrary to their private schemes of trade.[38] The goods were often damaged by being left at out of the way and unfrequented ports and were sometimes lost. The Armenians who were the principal traders in Bengal for exports to Persia and Arabia were completely ruined, their place being taken by the Company and its servants.[39]

Transit and customs duties, had been levied on the inland trade even under Mughal rule. The British on their acquisition of power in Bengal substantially increased the rates, imposed customs duties on commodities that had hitherto been exempt and raised new tariff and toll barriers.

An elaborate machinery of transit and customs duties was thus built up in the country. These imposts were instrumental in achieving two important objectives. First, they ousted the rivals of the East India Company—the Dutch and the French, as also the Indian merchants—from the country's inland trade; and secondly they made a useful addition to the revenues of the Company, which were used partly for meeting the military and civil expenses of the Company and partly in making purchases of Indian goods for export to England. As always happens with high protective duties, the two objectives proved somewhat contradictory, for the duties which are high enough to have protective effect cannot bring much revenue.

Ultimately transit duties on the inland trade began to be lowered towards the end of the eighteenth century and were finally abolished after the Parliamentary enquiry into East India affairs in 1838.

(b) *Foreign Trade*: The English at home had a clear understanding of how the resources of India were to be used for promoting the prosperity of Britain. As early as 1769, the Directors of the East India Company had issued instructions desiring that the manufacture of raw silk should be encouraged in Bengal and that of manufactured silk fabrics should be discouraged.[40] In the same letter, it was recommended that the silk-winders should be forced to work in the Company's factories and prohibited from working in their own homes. This letter contained the essence of the policy of moulding the Indian economy into the colonial pattern, the main function of which was to buy cheaply raw materials for the home industries and to sell dearly its manufactured goods. "This letter," the Select Committee of 1783 rightly observed, "contains a perfect plan of policy both of compulsion and encouragement which must in a very considerable degree operate destructively to the manufactures of Bengal. Its effects must be to change the whole face of the industrial country in order to render it a field of produce of crude materials subservient to the manufacture of Great

Britain".[41] The plan was in accord with the well-established commercial policy of Britain in the eighteenth century. As early as 1721, it was pointed out in the Kings' speech that "if by encouragement the colonies could be induced to produce the naval stores which were imported from foreign countries, it would not only increase the riches and powers of the nation but by employing the colonies in this useful service *would divert them from carrying on manufactures* which interfered with those of England".[42] The policy was put through in North America in the first instance, but after the loss of those colonies, Britain turned to India so that it might play the role that American colonies had played in her economy before 1776. The aim of turning Indian economy into the classical colonial mould was vigorously pursued in the early period of British rule.

The Company had obtained the monopoly of English trade with India and China. So long as the Company was without political power in India, the monopoly only operated against the English merchants not connected with the Company. With the conquest of India, the East India Company acquired the power to exclude rival European companies from the Indian trade. The Dutch and the French were prevented form making purchases of Indian goods from the Company's territories; the producers and artisans were prohibited from selling their products to the agents of the non-British companies, and the *gomashtas* of the Dutch and the French companies were often beaten up and molested by the agents of the English Company. It was only in the China trade in opium and tea that the other European companies were encouraged to participate, but this was dictated by the necessity of securing the maximum quantities of Chinese silver to purchase "investments" in India.[43]

With the appointment of Cornwallis, a sharp change began. Furber describes it as "a shift from unregulated to regulated imperialism". "In the last years of Hastings we watch Europeans scramble to get their wealth home in any way they can. In the last years of Cornwallis there is a similar scramble for wealth but it is more orderly".[44] Pitt's India Act and the administrative reforms of Cornwallis helped considerably to further the cause of imperialism.

Changes were taking place which were destined to make the East India Company wholly subservient to the State.[45] Under the circumstances, the emphasis in the British commercial policy in India naturally shifted from securing a favourable balance of trade together with annual remittances of the surplus from India, to an increase in the volume of trade by the exploitation of the Indian market for the benefit of the British industry. The Parliamentary probes made into the affairs of the East India Company, at intervals of twenty years beginning from 1773, provided opportunities to the industrialists to influence Parliament in formulating England's commercial policy. From 1813, systematic attempts were made to extend the market for British goods in India.

The value of trade between England and India over the period of twenty years from 1793 to 1813 stood at the average annual figure of £2 million. Considering the vastness of the country and judged by the accounts of its riches that had reached England in the eighteenth century, this was a poor record. At the time of the revision of the Charter in 1813, therefore, the Company's monopoly came in for a severe attack and the demand for the withdrawal of its trade privileges became insistent. As a result of the revision, the Company lost its monopoly and Indian trade was thrown open to all Britons. Shortly afterwards, the restrictions on the settlement of British nationals in the interior of India were withdrawn and permission was given to the British capitalists to settle and invest their capital in the cultivation of land and in the plantation industries.

III. THE ERA OF LAISSEZ FAIRE

A new era in the relations between England and India with the ending of the monopoly of the Company and the throwing open of trade to private enterprise. The withdrawal of the monopoly produced a spectacular increase in British exports to India. From £I.8 million in 1814, the value of British merchandise imported into India rose to £4.5 million in 1829. Even these figures do not adequately express the extent of the increase which Mr. Crawford described as "unparalleled in the history of Commerce,"[46] for the currency in 1814 showed a depreciation in value of 25 or 26 per cent below its standard value. If that fact is taken into consideration, the figure for 1814 would be reduced to £1.4 million.[47] Besides, prices in 1814 were high on account of the French wars; in 1828-29, the prices had fallen to their normal peacetime level. In quantitative terms, therefore, the British exports to India during the period of fifteen years must have increased fourfold. This is borne out by the following table of increase in the quantity of some of the more important items of British exports to India[48]:

Article	*1814*	*1828*	*Absolute increase*	*Increase per cent*
Copper (wrought and unwrought) cwt.	37,619	41,742	4,123	11
Iron, bar, bolts and cast (cwt.)	186,454	438,629	252,175	135
Broad-cloth, stuffs and camlets (pieces)	17,790	49,502	31,712	178
Calicoes, plain and printed (yards)	680,234	34,843,110	34,162,876	5,022
Cotton wrist (lbs.)	8	4,558,185	4,558,177	56,977,213

It had been confidently asserted on behalf of the East India Company in 1813 that "there was little probability either of increasing the quantity or of multiplying the number of commodities suited to the consumption of the people of India, and as little of augmenting the amount, or increasing the variety of articles which India could furnish in exchange".[49] The assertion, so far as India's capacity to absorb British manufactures was concerned, proved wrong in the face of the vigrous export drive that the British launched during the period.

Change in the structure of India's trade

One of the most important steps taken by Britain to extend its market in India was the imposition of the free trade policy on the country at a time when her industries were on the decline. India was forced to admit British imports either free or at nominal rates of duties, while Indian manufactures continued to be subjected to high import duties in England.[50] The policy immediately bore fruit. There was a rapid increase in India's foreign trade. The average annual value of India's foreign sea-borne trade rose from Rs. 18.64 crores (£18.64 millions) to Rs. 35.87 crores in the quinquennium 1846-51. The increase over the next five years was still more impressive. The average annual value of trade rose to Rs. 52.70 crores of which exports accounted for Rs. 26.85 crores and imports for Rs. 25.85 crores.

Ordinarily expansion in trade is an advantage to a country. But because of the radical changes in the structure of her trade, the expansion of trade proved ruinous to Indian industry, and resulted in the impoverishment of the people. From the world's principal producer and exporter of cotton fabrics in the eighteenth century, India was reduced in the short period of seventy years to the position of one of the largest consumers of foreign manufactures. Cotton textiles came to form the major item of imports, instead of the largest item of exports that they were in the eighteenth century. The following table shows the remarkable change wrought in the industrial position of India in the period of twenty years from 1814 to 1835:[51]

Year	*British cotton manufactures exported to India*	*Indian cotton piece-goods imported into Great Britain*
	(yards)	*(yards)*
1814	818,208	1,266,608
1821	19,138,726	534,495
1828	42,822,077	422,504
1835	51,777,277	306,068

Between 1814 and 1835, the exports of Indian cottons to Britain fell from nearly 1.3 million yards to a little over 0.3 million yards. Meanwhile there was a decline in India's exports to other countries as well; for instance, the exports to America fell from 13,633 bales of cotton piece-goods to 258 bales in 1829 and Denmark which took 1,457 bales in 1800 never took more than 150 bales after 1820.

Not only did India lose foreign markets for its manufactures but its domestic market was inundated with foreign imports. The following table shows the increase in the value of British cotton exports to India:[52]

	In million pounds
1813	0.11
1831	1.65 (Exports to China are included in this figure.)
1835	1.79
1840	3.86
1845	4.21
1850	5.22
1855	5.84
1856	6.30

Silk and woollen fabrics, machinery and metal manufactures were the other commodities of imports into India. Competition with imported goods destroyed the Indian industry, deprived the artisan of his income and narrowed down the avenues of employment for labour. On the other hand, the exports which came to consist of raw cotton, raw silk, food-grains, opium, indigo, and jute denuded the country of her agricultural surplus, raised the prices of raw materials and laid the foundation of future agricultural shortages and famines which held the country in their grip over the next one hundred years. Foreign trade in India was thus an instrument of exploitation of the resources of the country and of her economic enslavement.

Henry St. George Tucker,[53] George Thompson[54] and other Englishmen of their way of thinking rued the commercial policy that Britain was following in India. "What is the commercial policy," wrote Henry St. George Tucker in 1833, "which we have adopted in this country in relation to India? The silk manufactures and its piece-goods made of silk and cotton intermixed, have long since been excluded altogether from our markets; and of late, partly in consequence of the operation of a duty of 67 per cent but chiefly from the effect of superior machinery, the cotton fabrics which heretofore constituted the staple of India, have not only been displaced in this country but we actually export our cotton manufactures to supply a part of the consumption of our Asiatic possessions. India is thus reduced from the state of a manufacturing country to that of an agricultural country".[55] The East India Company represented to the Parliament in 1840 against the import duties in England on Indian goods which discouraged Indian industries. But such belated protests were of little avail, for the process of reducing India from an industrial to an agricultural country which was a part of the imperial design had, by then, been nearly completed.

IV BALANCE OF PAYMENTS

One obstacle in the way of increasing British exports to India still remained. If India was to absorb the ever-increasing quantities of British manufactures, it must be enabled to produce and give something in return for the imports. The balance of payments problem was not easy to manage.[56] The increase in production in India did not keep pace with the increase in imports. India's lack of purchasing power was proving an obstacle in the way of pushing forward the sale of British manufactures. Its principal foreign exchange earning industry, cotton-weaving, had been destroyed and instead of exporting cotton piece-goods, India itself was being flooded with cheap machine-made cotton cloth. Raw cotton was another commodity which it could sell to England, but the price of India cotton was higher and its quality poorer than that of the American cotton.[57] The demand for pepper, sugar and cinnamon had also fallen off considerably.

Besides there was a heavy recession in the prices of Indian products in the world market so that the terms of trade had turned heavily against the country. The following table gives some idea of the extent of the fall in the prices of the principal commodities of export from India.[58]

Article	*1793*	*1815*	*Increase or decrease per cent*	*1831*	*Decrease per cent over 1815*
	s.d.	s.d.		s.d.	
Cottonwool per lb.	1-3/4	0-11½	—9	0.5	56
Indigo per lb.	7-4½	8-10	+9	4-0	54
Rice per cwt.	None	23-9	—	14-10	39
Saltpetre per cwt.	59-9	87-0	+45	36-0	58
Raw silk per lb.	21-0	18-1	—13	13-7½	24
Cinnamon (Ceylon) per lb.	12-0	13-8	+13	8-9	35
Pepper black, per lb.	1-2½	0-10½	—27	0-3¼	64
Sugar per cwt.	66-6	49-1	—26	26-2	46

The fall was attributed to the withdrawal of monopoly and the establishment of free trade with India.[59] But the major cause appears to have been the weakening of the demand for Indian products in the British market. The structure of India's export trade had undergone a radical change. Cotton and silk manufactures, which had in the past formed the bulk of Indian exports, were now the principal commodities of import. The demand for raw silk had declined, while raw cotton of India, as already pointed out, was considered to be of inferior quality. Demand for pepper and sugar had also fallen on account of the opening of new sources of supply. Besides, there was the problem of making payments of annual charges that arose out of India's political connections with England and which, in the absence of gold and silver, had to be remitted in the form of commodities. Under the circumstances, it was not surprising that the terms of trade moved against India.

Commenting on the balance of payments situation at the time of the revision of the Company's Charter in 1832, Mr. Mackillop stated before the Parliamentary sub-committee, "......very great difficulties exist in effecting remittances from India. To illustrate how this difficulty operates, I may observe that a great portion of the indigo, and also other articles imported during the last two years, have not realised here more than is. 3d. Per rupee, while the mint value of that coin may be stated at IS. 11¾d.; and hence it is that individuals as well as the Company, latterly have effected remittances by bringing home silver instead of goods".[60] For centuries India had exported its staples and other countries had to give gold and silver in exchange. Now the tables had been turned: India could give nothing but gold and silver in exchange for its imports. But India does not produce gold and silver, and as Mr. Mackillop stated, "this mode of remittance form India and China if continued, must check the import of goods from this country (England)".[61]

Remedies for adverse balance of payments

(a) Development of agriculture

One way to solve India's balance of payments problem and provide her with the necessary purchasing power to buy British goods was to develop her agricultural resources. Various trade associations of England urged before the Parliamentary Select Committee (in 1832) that every effort should be made to develop the agricultural resources of the country. The Manchester Chamber of Commerce, for instance, stated: "The improvement and increase of the exportable productions of India would doubtless be a great good to India and, not to India merely, but to this country. The improvement in the quality of Indian cotton is an object of paramount importance to the prosperity of cotton manufactures of Great Britain so much so that every facility should be afforded to the speedy development of whatever India is capable of accomplishing this way".[62] The Glasgow Chamber of Commerce similarly thought that "every improvement or increase of the exportable productions of India would, no doubt, have that effect (of extending market for British goods in India)".[63]

In 1840 it had come to be widely recognised that Britain could not indefinitely continue to inundate India with her manufactures unless she enabled the latter to produce some commodities for exchange. Public agitation was set afoot in England for bringing pressure on the East India Company to develop the agricultural resources of India. It was suggested that land-tax should be reduced, means of irrigation be developed, improved varieties of commercial crops, particularly cotton, be introduced, and the raw cotton produced in India be given preference in the import trade of England over raw cotton produced in America which had ceased to be an English colony and where cotton was produced with the help of slave labour. This agitation, of which the six lectures delivered by George Thompson in 1839 to the East India Association[64] are a typical example, did not achieve much in the matter of the development of Indian agriculture or of the diversion of the British demand from the American to the Indian produce. But it helped in exposing the injustices perpetrated by England on India and the injury that its policy had caused to Indian agriculture.

Commenting on the bad quality of Indian cotton and its unsuitability for fabricating fine cloth in the British mills, Thompson said: "The soil of India lies under a curse. It is viewed by the cultivator not as a source of wealth to himself, but the scene of his thankless toil; from which he must reap a crop not to enrich himself but a stranger in the land who claims a proprietary right by virtue of conquest and deprives him of the entire surplus produce of his industry. It is hardly surprising that industry languishes and the march of improvement is stayed. The people are in the condition of serfs; they are virtually tenants-at will. They are at the mercy of men whose sole aim is the collection of revenue. The maximum tax is too heavy to be borne: it never has been reached, it never can be reached; the ryots, the cultivators, fall into arrears; they are from that moment liable to be crushed by the collector of the district who thinks he deals most mercifully with them, when he takes the last pound of cotton or grain of rice and leaves them to supplicate 'with bated breath and whispering humbleness' the assistance of the village banker to enable them to purchase a little seed to scatter upon the earth and to enable them to keep together the bodies and the souls of their beggared families until the next harvest appears".[65] What improvement, asked Thompson, could be expected in Indian agriculture under such conditions?

(b) Colonisation of India

As the Government would not extend protection to agriculture or aid to the development of other productive occupations in India, the remedy that suggested itself to the British manufacturers was the colonisation of India and the stimulation of production by the settlement of British nationals in the interior of the country, and the investment of British capital. The Liverpool East India Committee stated before the Parliamentary Select Committee: "We would, in particular, suggest that encouragement be give to men of talents, particularly acquainted with best modes of raising and improving the different products of India, to settle in the interior of the country; that encouragement and protection be given to men of capital to invest their property in land by grants in perpetuity on easy terms; and that facilities be afforded for the establishment of a free intercourse between different parts of the country, by the construction of bridges and roads".[66] The Glasgow Chamber of Commerce, similarly, desired that "every encouragement and facility consistent with the safety and tranquillity of India will be granted to British subjects going there, from whose skill, capital, enterprise, most beneficial results may reasonably be expected".[67] According to the Manchester Chamber of Commerce the "obvious" measure to increase the products and trade of India was "permitting British subjects to hold land".[68] "If injurious restrictions be removed," the Chamber continued, "and latitude given for the natural operation of British capital, skill, and enterprise in aid of the fertility of the soil of India and the industrious habits and peaceable disposition of its inhabitants, everything will be one that is requisite".[69] Holt Mackenzie, when asked to state specifically the advantages to be derived in revenues by the Indian Government from the settlement of Europeans in that country, remarked: "I consider that every European who settles in any part of India must add something to the revenue; for he will be a profitable consumer, that is, he will consume articles capable of taxation. He will, I should hope, greatly improve the means of production, thereby adding largely to the general wealth of the country. His example will introduce among many of the natives some European habits, which are habits of greater comfort and expense than native habits, which are habits of greater comfort and expense than native habits and without any change in the habits of the people, the miscellaneous taxes must increase with the increase of wealth, and the more abundant production of the objects of internal and external commerce. In the unsettled districts, every improvement in agriculture must add to the land rent of Government. To introduce irrigation where it is not now practised is to render highly productive land that is now comparatively unproductive; and since the rent of all waste land not specially assigned belongs to the Government, there would be immediately, or at no distant time, an accession of revenue in all cases in which such land might be brought under tillage. I believe intercourse with Europeans leads to indulgence in the use of wine and spirits, which, though it may be lamented on the score of morals, must be beneficial to the revenue; their servants are generally better clothed, and the articles of clothing being subject to taxation, that would increase the revenue".[70] There was, besides, the great political advantage to be gained from stationing the nationals of the ruling country in the interior, for this would prevent the combination of people against the foreign rulers and scotch any intention on their part to revolt.

The restrictions regarding residence and settlement of Europeans in the interior of the country had been removed in 1824. During the following years vigorous attempts were made to encourage the penetration of India by British nationals and their capital. Land was offered to them either as freehold or on long leases of sixty years for purposes of cultivation and the establishment of plantation industries. Transit duties on the inland trade were withdrawn and the whole trade and industry of India was thrown open to foreign enterprise.

Failure of the policy of colonisation

But India could not be colonised in the sense that America, Canada, Australia and New Zealand were, for it was a well-populated and highly developed country, whereas the latter were, at the time of settlement, just vast tracts of waste land awaiting development.

Moreover, Englishmen could not undetake the cultivation of small strips of land in competition with Indian farmers. The only crops that they found suitable for their enterprise were coffee and tea. The rest of the farming business was closed to them because of the peculiar agricultural situation in the country.

Secondly, the climate of India was very different from what an Englishman was used to at home. In the early days of British occupation of India, the death rate among those to this me to this country was very high. Dysentery, smallpox, malaria and stomach complaints took a heavy toll of life. Those who escaped death suffered deterioration in health as a result of disease and the rigours of the Indian summer.

Finally, the Europeans could not succeed in competition with the Indians in business enterprises located in the interior of the country. The people of India are frugal, industrious and intelligents. Once an industry was established by a foreigner in the country, Indians would not lag behind; and their cost of living being lower, they would undersell the goods produced by Europeans. This difficulty had been foreseen by Munro who, in his evidence before the Parliamentary Committee of 1813 on East India Affairs, stated: "The people of India are as much as nation of shopkeepers as we are ourselves; they never lose sight of the shop, they carry it into all their concerns, religious and civil; all their holy places and resorts for pilgrims, are so many fairs for sale of goods of every kind; religion and trade are in India sister arts, the one is seldom found in any large assembly without the society of the other. It is this trading disposition of the natives, which induces me to think it impossible that any European traders can long remain in the interior of India, and that they must sooner or later all be driven to the coast; what the European trader eats and drinks in one month, would make a very decent mercantile profit for the Hindoo for twelve, they do not, therefore, meet on equal terms; it is like two persons purchasing in the same market, the one paying a high duty, the other paying none... it is impossible, therefore, that he (the European) can long carry on the competition upon such an unequal footing; he may for a time with a large capital carry on some new manufacture, or improve some old one, such as indigo or sugar; the Hindoo will wait till he sees the success which follows the undertaking; if it is likely to be successful and to be permanent, he will engage in it and the European must quit the field. There can be no doubt, I thin, that this cause will in time operate so as to force all Europeans to the sea-coast, and I can have little doubt but hereafter, when the Hindoos come to correspond directly with the merchants in England, that many of the agents now settled upon the coast, will, from the same cause, the superior economy and diligence of the Hindoos, be obliged to leave India".[71]

That subsequent events worked out exactly in accordance with these anticipations, speaks highly of the foresight of Munro. The British failed to convert India into an English settlement. Their capital flowed only into those industries and commercial activities from which Indians were excluded on account of the special privileges accorded to the British Tea and coffee plantations, indigo manufacture, shipping, foreign exchange banks and insurance were the main objects of attention of foreign capital. Instead of solving this aggravated the balance of payments problem, for it added to the list of invisible imports which had to be paid for by the export of raw produce and food-stuffs from India.

(c) Development of transport

The improvement of the internal means of communication and transport and Dalhousie's plan for the construction of a network of railways in India fitted well into the British plans of subordinating Indian economy to the purposes of Britain. If the products of India were to be collected from the interior and if the consumption of British manufactures was to permeate the interior, it was necessary to provide cheap and easy means of transport in the country. The construction of railways would have another advantage also: it would provide a profitable channel of investment for British capital. It is true that the work of construction of railways was taken up in right earnest only after the administration had passed from the Company to the British crown, but the policy of the East India Company was already pointing in that direction. The policy remained the same, only the pace was quickened after the upheaval of 1857.

V. The Drain of Wealth

The feature of India's foreign trade which had consequences of a far-reaching character for the economy of both India and England was the unrequited surplus of exports from India. The East India Company adopted the policy of purchasing Indian goods out of the revenue collected from Bengal and exporting them to England. The purchases were known as "investments". They constituted the "drain" of wealth from India. According to a statement[72] of the revenues and of Bengal during the first six years of the Company's administration, the net revenue of the country was £13,066,761 and the total expenses £9,027,609, leaving a net balance of £4,039,152, which was remitted in the form of goods to England. But this annual unrequited outflow of one-third of the country's net revenue did not represent the total drain on the economic resources of Bengal. Vast private fortunes were made in India and remitted home by the servants of the Company. No account of these remittances can be drawn up, but some idea of its extent may be obtained from the figures of exports and imports for the three years between 1766 and 1768 compiled by Harry Verelst, the then Governor of Bengal[73] According to these figures, the total imports in the three years amounted to £624,375, while the total exports were valued at £5,311,250, leaving a balance of £4,686,875, or an annual average of £1.5 millions. The volume of this drain grew steadily over the years. In course of time it became a prominent point of attack on British rule by the Indian nationalists.

Opinions with regard to the extent of this drain in the later years differ. William Digby, after taking into account the transfer of treasure on private accounts, together with export surplus appearing in official trade statistics, estimates, that "probably between Plassey and Waterloo a sum of £1,000 million was transferred from Indian hoards to English banks".[74] This gives an average of £17.2 millions per annum. Professor Furber, on the basis of figures of trade for ten "trading seasons". Reaches the conclusion that "although there can be no doubt that a drain of Indian wealth in the sense above defined existed, it certainly did not reach vast proportions. The drain towards the West should not be reckoned as exceeding £1.9 million annually during the period 1783-93".[75] John Strachey thinks that "Professor Furber is nearer the mark," because "he is a recent and American investigator with no motive for minimising the figure".[76]

In the absence of the necessary data for making exact quantitative measurements, it is presumptuous for any one to take sides in the controversy over the precise amount of the annual transfer of funds from India to England. If Digby's estimate appears exaggerated, Furber's is surely an underestimate. For as he himself acknowledges, his conclusion lacks the basis of "full and accurate statistics of exports and imports for the entire continent".[77] Be that as it may, there is hardly any question about the fact that as a result of the conquest of India by Britain, the foreign trade of Indian was rendered an instrument of exploitation of the people of India.

India's loss and England's gain

The drain of wealth from India was a contributory factor in the industrial development of England. The available evidence leaves little doubt that the magnificent industrial structure of England which began to rise after Plassey was largely built up on the ruins of Indian manufactures. There was, according to the British historians themselves, a close relation between the Industrial Revolution in England and the establishment of British rule in India.

It was the Indian loot by the East India Company and its servants in the early days of British rule in Bengal that provided the funds which administered the necessary stimulus to industrial production in the initial stages of the Industrial Revolution[78] Books Adams affirms: "the influx of the Indian treasure, by adding considerably to the nations' cash capital, not only increased its stock of energy, but added much to its flexibility and the rapidity of its movements.

"Very soon after Plassey, the Bengal plunder began to arrive in London and the effect appears to have been instantaneous... . Plassey was fought in 1757, and probably nothing has ever equalled the rapidity of the change that followed. In 1760 the flying shuttle appeared, and coal began to replace wood in smelting. In 1764 Hargreaves invented the spinning-jenny, in 1779 Crompton contrived the mule, in 1785 Cartwright patented the power-loom and, chief of all, in 1768 Watts matured the steam engine... . But, though these machines served as outlets for the accelerating movement of time, they did not cause that acceleration. In themselves inventions are passive, many of the most important having lain dormant for centuries, waiting for a sufficient store of force to have accumulated to set them working. That store must always take the shape of money and money not hoarded, but in motion... . Before the influx of the Indian treasure and the expansion of credit which followed no force sufficient for this purpose existed; and had Watts lived fifty years earlier, he and his inventions must have perished together.

"Possibly since the world began, no investment has ever yielded the profit reaped from the Indian plunder, because for nearly fifty-years Great Britain stood without a competitor".[79]

From 1694 to 1757 the growth had been relatively slow; between 1760 and 1815 it was rapid in speed and prodigious in volume.

Cunningham is not explicit on the sources of finance for the Industrial Revolution in England, but as regards the reasons why the Revolution occurred after 1760 and not before, he supports Brooks Adams. He writes, "Inventions and discoveries often seem to be merely fortuitous; men are apt to regard the new machinery as the outcome of the special and unaccountable burst of inventive genius in the eighteenth century. But... to point out that Arkwright and Watts were fortunate in the fact that times were ripe for them, is not to detract from their merits. There had been many ingenious men from the time of William Lee and Dodo Dudley, but the conditions of their day were unfavourable to their success. The introduction of expensive implements, or processes, involves a large outlay; it is not worthwhile for any man, however energetic, to make the attempt, unless he has a considerable command of capital, and has access to large markets. In the eighteenth century these conditions were being more and more realised".[80]

On the other hand, it has been held in some quarters that it is wrong to call this export surplus a drain of wealth, for the payments from India represented the cost of "good" government, and peace and order that the British gave to India. As for the earlier period the testimony of John Strachey, whose ancestors held high posts in India, is conclusive. He writes, "But it may be asked did not Bengal at least receive some recompense by way of good government and law and order for the tribute thus paid to its conquerors? No doubt it did and in the fulness of time regular government and law and order were to be of value. But for some fifteen years after the conquest the fact that Bengal was now protected from being ravaged by its neighbours was of no advantage to the unhappy province. For it was now ravaged far more systematically by its new rulers. No Maratha raid ever devastated a countryside with the thoroughness with which both the Company. And above all, the Company's servants in their individual capacities, sucked dry the plains of Bengal. In fact in their blind rage for enrichments, they took more from Bengali peasants than those peasants could furnish and live. And the presents duly dird".[81]

Even the view that the good government and law and order established by the British were ultimately of value to the country needs qualification. For the British military and civil administration was used more for the benefit of England than for the development of the resources of India and the enrichments of its people. There can be little doubt about the injustice to India involved in these payments or about the fact that the flow of wealth from India did help Britain in the process of her economic development in the initial stages of the Industrial Revolution.[82]

VI. CONCLUSION

Sir Stampford Raffles, the English Governor of Java, said of the old Dutch Company: "The Dutch Company, actuated solely by the spirit of gain, and viewing their subjects with less regard or consideration than a West India planter formerly viewed a gang upon his estate, because the latter had paid the purchase money of human property, which the other had not employed all the existing machinery of despotism to squeeze from the people their utmost mite of contribution, the last dregs of their labour, and thus aggravated the evils of a capricious and semi-barbarous Government, by working it with all the practised ingenuity of politicians, and all the monopolising selfishness of traders".[83] The English Company in India followed the ways of her Dutch sister in the East Indies.[84] It destroyed the trade and industry of the country. It started by excluding the Indian products from the European markets. It then "broke up the Indian handloom, and destroyed the spinning wheel" and, finally, "inundated the very mother country of cotton with cottons".[85] It oppressed the weavers and other artisans and perpetrated inhuman crimes to crush the rival producers; instances of thumb of workmen being cut off to prevent them from winding raw silk or weaving fine cloth were not unknown. Over and above this, the British exacted a cruel and unjust annual tribute from India, which prevented any accumulation of capital or improvements in agriculture or industry. The productive organisation of India was destroyed and the country which was once known for its riches all the world over was reduced to a state of poverty, disease, misery and starvation.

The economic decline of the country was accompanied by a social revolution. The village community which fostered cooperative living was destroyed. New economic relations based on the Western ideas of individual property and enterprise, competition, and marked economy began to prevail. Marx saw in this social revolution a means for the fulfilment of man's destiny. "England it is true, in causing a social revolution in Hindustan," he wrote, "was actuated only by the vilest interests and was stupid in her manner of enforcing them. But that in not the question. The question is, can mankind fulfil its destiny without a fundamental revolution in the social state of Asia? If not, whatever may have been the crimes of England she was the unconscious tool of history in bringing about that revolution".[86]

REFERENCES

1. A Brief Deduction of the Oriental Progress and Immense increase in Woollen Manufactures (London 1727), p. 50, quoted by Thomas, P. J., *Mercantilism and East India Trade*, p. 26.
2. *Weekly Review*, January 31, 1708, quoted by Thomas, P. J., *op. cit.*, p. 30.
3. Thomas, P. J., *op. cit.*, p. 38.
4. *Ibid.*, p. 47.
5. *Ibid.*, p. 55.
6. Poor relief at the time fell among the duties of parishes. In some of the parishes, like Gloucester, for instance, one-fifth of the whole annual value of land was distributed to the starving poor. See *Ibid.*, p. 56.
7. For an interesting and detailed account of the struggle between free traders and protectionists and the role of the East India Company in delaying legislation against Indian goods, see *Ibid.*, pp. 67-117.
8. *Ibid.*, p. 115.
9. *Ibid.*,
10. See Balkrishna, *op. cit.*, Appendix C (Table) to Chapter VII, pp. 308-09.
11. Quoted by Thompson, *Six Lectures on the Resources of India* (London, 1842), p. 48; also Balkrishna, *op. cit.*, pp. 263-64.
12. Vide Thomas, P. J., *op. cit.*, p. 163.
13. Baines, *History of Cotton Manufactures*, p. 261.
14. Thomas, P. J., *op. cit.*, pp. 163-64.
15. Vide Balkrishna, *op. cit.*, pp. 308-310.
16. *Select Committee Report*, 1833, Vol. II, Part II, pp. 883-87.
17. *Ibid.*, Vol. II, Appendix 5, pp. 592-607.
18. Mill, James, *History of British India* (continued by Wilson), Vol. VII (London 1858), p. 385, note I.
19. *Ibid.*,
20. *Select Committee Report*, 1833, Vol. II, Mr. Mackillop's evidence, p. 516.
21. Adam Smith, *The Wealth of Nations* (Modern Library edition), pp. 602-3.

22. Belts William, *Considerations of Indian Affairs*, p. 191.
23. *Ibid.*, p. 193.
24. *Ibid.*,
25. *Ibid.*,
26. *Ibid.*, p. 194.
27. *Ibid.*, p. 193.
28. See Dutt, R. P., *India Today* (Bombay, 1947), p. 92.
29. *Ibid.*, p. 93.
30. Lord Cornwallis Minute dated 18th September, 1789, vide Firminger, *Fifth Report*, Vol. II, p. 512.
31. Adam Smith, *op. cit.*, p. 600.
32. *Ibid.*, p. 601.
33. Bolts, William, *op. cit.*, p. 195.
34. *Ibid.*, p. 196.
35. Macaulay, T. B., *Critical and History Essays*, Dent's double volume edition (1933), p. 528.
36. Marx, *Capital* (Moscow edition), Vol. I, p. 753.
37. Bolts, William, *op. cit.*, p. 197.
38. *Ibid.*, p. 197.
39. *Ibid.*,
40. General Letter to Bental, dated March 17, 1769, vide Dutt, R. G., *Economic History of India under Early British Rule*, p. 256.
41. *Ninth Report of the Select Committee*, 1783, p. 64.
42. Rees, R. F., 'The Commercial Policy of England in the Eighteenth Century,' *Economic*, London, 1925.
43. Sir John Macpherson, head of the British Government in India at the time, privately offered to the Dutch in 1785 every facility for shipping opium to Batavia. "He clearly saw that the English Company would benefit by selling opium to the Dutch Company to be paid for in China and not in Bengal. Herklot's (Dutch Representative) inability to bind the Dutcch Governor General at Batavia to pay the English Company large sums in silver prevented this private offer from being accepted. Macpherson did his best to give the Dutch as large allowances as possible of opium and saltpetre".—Furber Holden, *John Company At Work*. (Cambridge, Harvard University, 1948), p. 87.

44. Furber, Holden, *op. cit.*, p. 227.
45. *Ibid.*, p. 302.
46. *Evidence before the Select Committee on East India Affairs*, 1833, *Report*, Vol. II, Part II., p. 511.
47. *Ibid.*, p. 511.
48. *Ibid.*
49. *Ibid.*, p. 512.
50. Beauchamp, Joan, *British Imperialism in India*, p. 29.

    After the decline of Indian industry and the rise of the cotton industry in Manchester, the danger to British manufactures from competition of Indian textiles disappeared. The duties on Indian goods were consequently gradually lowered. In 1840, British cotton goods exported to India paid a duty of 3½ per cent while Indian cotton goods imported into England paid a duty of 10 per cent.
51. *Ibid.*, p. 29.
52. *Ibid.*, p. 30.
53. Tucker, G. *Memorials of Indian Government*, London, 1852.
54. Thompson, *Six Lectures, op. cit.*
55. Letter to Huskisson, 1823, reprinted in *Memorials of Indian Government, op. cit.*, p. 494.
56. Some idea of the balance of payment difficulties on India may be had from the following figures: In 1806, through the port of Calcutta, piece-goods of the value of £1,460,000 were exported, in 1836, the quantity of cotton piece-goods exported was worth £108,000. In 1805, the raw cotton exported was valued at £400,000; in 1835 at £487,000.
57. *Select Committee Report*, 1883. Vol. II. Part II. p. 716.
58. *Ibid.*, p. 514.
59. *Ibid.*, p. 515.
60. *Ibid.*, p. 577.
61. *Ibid.*, p. 577.
62. *Ibid.*,
63. *Ibid.*, p. 578.
64. Thomson George, *Six Lectures on the Resource of India London.*
65. *Ibid.*, p. 70.

66. *Select Committee Report* Vol. II, Part II, p. 578.
67. *Ibid.*,
68. *Ibid.*,
69. *Ibid.*
70. *Select Committee Report* (1833), Vol. II, Part I, question No. 89, p. II.
71. *British Parliamentary Papers: House of Commons Returns etc.*, 1812-13, Vol. VII, Pt. Pages 150-51; Minutes of Evidence...on the Affairs of the East India Company (Evidence by Colonel Thomas Munro).
72. *Fourth Report of the Houe of Commons*, 1773; see also Beauchamp, loan *op. cit.*, p. 25.
73. Harry Verelst, *Vies of the Rise, etc. of the British Government in India*, quoted in Beauchamp, *op. cit.*, p. 26.
74. Digby, William, *Prosperous British India*, p. 33.
75. Furber, *John Company At Work* (Cambridge, 1948), p. 305.
76. Strachey, John, *The End of Empire*, p. 63.
77. Furber, *op. cit.*, p. 305.
78. Strachey, John, *op. cit.*, p. 67.
79. Brooks Adams, *The Laws of Civilization and Decay*, op. 259-60.
80. Cunningham, W., *Growth of English Industry and Commerce: Modern Times*, Part II, p. 610.
81. Strachey, John, *The End of Empire, op. cit.*, p. 41.
82. *Ibid.*, p. 60.
83. Quoted by Marx, *The British Rule in India*, vide Marx-Engels, *Selected Works* (Foreign Language Publishing House, Moscow), Vol. I, p. 313.
84. *Ibid.*,
85. *Ibid.*, p. 315.
86. *Ibid.*, p. 317.

8

Expeditions to Persian Gulf and French Islands

Besides the despatch of missions to the Courts four Asian States, West of British India, to counteract the threat of a French invasion, another important phase of Lord Minto's Foreign policy was to have effective control over the Persian Gulf and the French Islands on the African coast. The main consideration in the adoption of this policy towards the former was to convert it into a British lake by destroying the hostile elements n that quarter and making it a safe and secure passage for British shipping and commerce and thus preventing the possibility of its coming under French influence at any future date. The policy towards the latter was motivated by dominant British anxiety to prevent the French from establishing military and naval bases there and using them as a springboard for hostile activities against British India.

Persian Gulf was, however, rendered an insecure and risky passage for the development of British commerce in the East. The man reason for this state of affairs was the alarming increase in piracy in the Persian Gulf, which had seriously affected the East India Company's trade through this region.[1] This Coast of America was known from the ancient times as the' Pirate Cost', which was haunted by the Jawasmee pirates.[2] Having embraced the tenets of

Muhammad Wahab, a Mohammedan reformer, they had added ferocity and fanaticism to the courage of their national character.[3]

When Lord Minto took over as Governor-General of India, the Jawasmees had started their aggressive activities. They captured no less than twenty British vessels during 1808.[4] Their atrocities near Qais on a British merchant-ship, the 'Minerva' proceeding from Bombay to Bushire, were most dreadful.[5] The captives were bound and brought singly to the gangway, where one of the pirates cut their throats 'in the name of God'. Another British cruiser, the 'Sylph' met the same fate. The greedy chief of Ras al Khaima, whose harbour had been the principal Government, if it desired its merchantships to traverse the waters of the Gulf unmolested.[6] These repeated aggressions and the insolent demand of Sultan bin Saqar, at length, opened the eye of the British Government in India and the Court of Directors to the fatal impolicy and absurdity of reliance on the crafty and faithless Jawasmee Chief. They realized that the safety of their shipping and commerce from the clutches of the pirates would not be ensured without complete extirpation of the nest of banditti.[7]

The British Government, therefore, became very keen to destroy these vagabonds.[8] With this end in view, the Bombay Government sanctioned a naval and military expedition to the Persian Gulf.[9] The expeditionary force consisting of 1000 men under the command of Lieutenant Colonel Smith and the naval force under Captain Weinwright sailed of the destination from Bombay on September 10, 1809.[10] Instructions were issued to them to get the captured British property and British subjects released from their bondage. They were also required to help the friendly chief Sayyid Said of Muscat whose territory was exposed to invasions by the Wahabees.[11] This Chief made common cause with the British by joining them on their arrival at Muscat.[12]

The two combined forces carried out their work successfully in four campaigns. Their first operation was directed against Ras al Khaima which was heavily bombarded.[13] The Jawasmees resistance was short and ineffectual. After bloody conflict their Chief was left with no other alternative but to surrender on November 13, 1809.[14] He was placed under the custody of the Imam of Muscat.[15] The effect of this expedition was highly disastrous to the Jawasmee pirates. About eighty of them were killed and their town, along with about fifty vessels, was burnt.[16] On the British side, only one officer was killed and three soldiers were wounded.[17]

After the subjugation of Ras al Khaima, the British forces launched a second operation against Lingeh, another flourishing port of the Jawasmees, where they destroyed twenty dows and boats without sustaining any loss.[18] From there they sailed to the Port of Luft, situated on the North of the Isle if Qishm, where they arrived on November 26, 1809. Mullah Husain, the Chief of that place, realized his helplessness, sent on board the British ship, the 'Chiffonne' and his messenger with an offer to surrender. But later on, he changed his mind and refused to comply with his promise. Annoyed at this duplicity, the British landed a force of 300 men on the Port of Luft on November 27, 1809 and launched their third operation against the Jawasmees.[19] their naval force on board the 'Fury' and the gun boats kept up an intermittent fire on the enemy's fort. The garrison in the fort made a stiff resistance, but was at last prevaild upon by Sheikh Dervish, head of the Benimen Arab tribe, attached to the forces of Imam of Muscat, to surrender all the property. All the Jawasmee dows and boats on the port were destroyed; but Mullah Husain was allowed to depart to a place of safety unmolested.[20]

Thereafter, the British expedition advanced ahead and launched its fourth operation on the pirate port of Shinas. Its castle was most formidable. The British troops, under Lieutenant Colonel Smith, maintained an unceasing fire which resulted in a breach in the wall of the castle, through which it was assaulted. The enemy, at length, given after sustaining huge loss of life. The loss of the Jawasmees was about 400 killed. On the British side, no casualty occurred except for one soldier who was slightly wounded. The town was delivered to the Imam of Muscat.[21] Lord Minto praised the 'brilliant capture' of the Port of Shinas.[22] Thus the pirate cost was occupied by the British forces. The subjugated coast was, however, given to the Imam of Muscat as a reward for his services. He assured the British Government to safeguard its commercial interests in the Persian Gulf.[23]

Having attained the object of the expedition to the Persian Gulf, the British forces returned to India on January 12, 1810. With the settlement of this problem, the Persian Gulf became the emporium of British trade and commerce. Although there were sporadic pirate-activities during the remaining period of Lord Minto's administration in India, he did not send any expedition on account of his involvement in matters of internal administration and in crushing the French influence in western and eastern islands. The evil of piracy continued even during the time of Lord Hastings.

(A) EXPEDITIONS TO FRENCH ISLANDS

The second oversea expedition launched by the Government of India during the Governor-Generalship of Lord Minto was directed against the French islands of Bourbon and Mauritius. These islands had been the centres of French political and naval activities against the British since the war of Austrian Succession in Europe. From these islands were directed anti-British movements and activities in India under Haider Ali and Tipu Sultan. Moreover, they were also the haunts of French pirates who received direct encouragement from their Government, whenever France was at war against England anywhere in the globe. So long as the French ships and privateers possessed the means of ingress into and egress from the ports of French islands unobserved by the ships of the British squadron, the Company's interests were constantly exposed to great risks. This history of the French islands, their commercial and strategic importance and the frequent use their owners made of them to inflict injuries on the British shipping, commerce and political interests in India, was quite vivid in Lord Minto's mind, when he took over office as Governor-General of India. He very well realized the gravity of the danger which the British interests in India were exposed by the political manoeuvrings and designs of the son of the French Revolution. Safety of the oversea route was considered no less necessary than of overland route. Entertaining apprehensions of a possible French naval drive against India from their sea-nests in the Indian ocean, he decided to destroy them altogether and to afford permanent security to the British in the Indian waters.

With these ends in view, a firm decision was taken to deprive the French of these islands as the only means of effective defence to India.[24] This was to be accomplished by military expeditions to these islands.[25] As a measure of safety, it was considered necessary to have a port of call near the French islands to enable the British ships to maintain effective blockade of these islands and to establish a convenient base for supplies to the expeditionary force nearer them. To implement this policy, elaborate naval preparations were made with the help of the Government of St. George[26] and a plan was prepared with the approval of the Admiralty[27] to occupy the small island of Rodriguez 750 miles from Bourbon and about three hundred miles from Mauritius; and to establish upon it British magazines and stores with a view to using it as base for refitting and revictualling of British expeditionary force for the reduction of Bourbon and Mauritius.[28]

To put this plan into execution, an expeditionary force consisting of two hundred Europeans and two hundred sepoys under Lieutenant Colonel Keating and a naval force under Commodore Rowley has dispatched on May 16, 1809, with instructions to occupy the french island of Rodriguez. This small island, inhabited by three French men and about eighty slaves, was captured on August 4, 1809 without any opposition, and was converted into a base for further naval expeditions to other French islands. But effective blockade of the French islands was still remote. Hence with full preparations and adequate knowledge of French military positions in the adjacent islands, another expedition was despatched to the Isle of bourbon.[29]

(i) Expedition to Bourbon

The plan of the naval expedition ot the Island of Bourbon was made by commodore Rowley with the approval of Vice-Admiral Bertie, the British naval commander at the Cape. On September 16, 1809, 368 soldiers started from Rodriguez on board the 'Nereide', the 'Otter' and the 'Wasp', and were joined by two other British vessels, the 'Raisonable' and the 'Sirius' off Port Louis on September 18, 1809. This force of about 600 strong disembarked at St. Paul, the chief French town on the western coast of the island of Bourbon, on September 21, 1809. The French were taken completely by surprise. Their batteries defending the town were poorly manned, and there was little hope of prompt reinforcement from their capital, St. Denis, where General Des Bruslys, its Governor, had a very small force.[30] St. Mihiel, the French Commandant, however, put up a very stubborn resistance till he was forced to capitulate on the same day. The Governor felt disheartened and committed suicide on the next day. After about ten days' stay at St. Paul, the British troops went back to Rodriguez on October 2, 1809, with vast booty, including the French frigate, the 'Caroline', the 'Streathan', the 'Europe' and a few small trading vessels.[31]

This victory was highly significant for the British.[32] It enabled them to gauge fully the French military resources on the island of Bourbon and the external help they might receive during an emergency.[33] On the other hand, the British military and naval activities in that quarter made the French Commander Decaen realize that they were determined to capture all the French islands. Ever since the capture of Rodriguez by the British, Decaen had been sending frantic appeals to Decres, the French Minister of Marine, of reinforcements to checkmate British assault on the isles. But the response to this request was only nominal due to the serious diversion of Napoleon's attention to gave European affairs.[34]

Encouraged by the success at St. Paul, Lord Minto decided to send an expedition to Isle of Bourbon under the military and naval commands of Colonel Keating and Commodore Rowley.[35] The British blockading squadron was immediately reinforced by three ships from the Cape of Good Hope, the 'Iphigenia' under Captain Lambert, the 'Magicienne' under Captain Curtis and the 'Nercide' under Captain Willoughby.[36] With elaborate arrangements and large reinforcements from India, the expedition consisting of 1800 Europeans and 1850 native troops started for St. Denis, the capital of the Isle of Bourbon, on July 3, 1810 and effected landing in its vicinity on July 7, 1810.[37] Colonel Saint Suzanne, the Governor of the Isle, with his small force of 480 men capitulated after a stubborn resistance on July 8, 1810.[38] By the terms of capitulation, the Island of Bourbon was ceded to the British with all the State property, and ts Governor was permitted to proceed to the Isle of France on parole. The France troops taken as prisoners of war were to be sent to the Cape or to England.[39]

Robert Townsend Farquhar of the Bengal Civil Service was appointed Governor of Bourbon,[40] and Colonel Keating was stationed as the Commandant of the British forces.[41] Soon after the occupation of Bourbon, the British Governor issued a Proclamation to its dependents on July 28, 1810, severely criticizing the French system of Governments and assuring them of protection, friendship, religious liberty, peace, tranquillity and better administration.[42] This rich, extensive and valuable colony with a population of about one hundred thousand was added to the British Dominions with trifling losses.

(ii) Expedition to Mauritius

The ease with which the British captured the Island of Bourbon greatly strengthened their expectations of succeeding in launching an expedition against the Island of Mauritius also. Naval reconnaissance in its vicinity was made by the British naval force under Captain Pym who explored a convenient Ianding place on its coast. As a preliminary measure, a small British contingent was landed on the Isle de la Passe, about three miles from the main island on August 13, 1810. It was easily captured and a military out-post was established on it with a small garrison of 130 men to facilitate advance on Mauritius.[43]

After a week, on August 20, 1810 three French vessels under Duperre arrived at Grand Port, a harbour on the South-East coast of the Isle of Mauritius. As soon as they passed close to the Isle de la passe, they were fired upon by the British frigate on the Port. Duperre, however, succeeded in reaching the Grand Port, with the loss of one ship, the 'Windhan' and anchored on an advantageous position, protected by the coast battery.[44]

Under these circumstances, a clash between the two navies became imminent. Four British frigates, viz, the 'Sirius' under Captain Pym, the 'Nereide' under Captain Willoughby the 'Iphigenia' under Captain Lambert and the 'Magicienne' under Captain Curtis were despatched to attack the French vessels. Scenting immediate danger, Decaen ordered the naval division under Captain Hamelin at Port Louis, consisting of three frigates, the 'Astree', the 'Manchee' and the 'Venus' to reach him at the Grand Port at once. But before these French ships could reach the rendezvous, the naval combat had already started, resulting in the victory of the French.[45] Three of the British frigates were captured and sunk. Among others, the 'Iphigenia' and the garrison on the Isle de la Passe also surrendered on the arrival of Captain Hamelin. The combat lasted from August 23, 1810 to August 28, 1810, causing great damage to the British navy. Sixteen hundred soldiers a and sailors, including Captains Pym, Lambert, Willoughby and

Curtis were taken prisoners, and the Isle de la Passe was surrendered to the French.[46]

The naval combat off Grand Port seemed to be a turning point for the French fortunes. Greatly encouraged by this success, Decaen thought of taking an offensive. He had two plans before him; either to attack the Island of Rodriguez, the base of British naval operations, and intercept their naval reinforcement proceeding to it, or to blockade the Isle of Bourbon and starve the British garrison into submission. Ultimately, the second plan was adopted. But this time, the french plan failed as a larger British reinforcement from India and a naval force under Vice-Admiral Bertie from the Cape of Good Hope reached Rodriguez for launching an immediate attack on Mauritius.[47]

This large concentration of British forces on the Island of Rodriguez greatly alarmed Decaen. He became apprehensive of the British naval superiority in the French waters, and feared a massive British naval attack on his forces. With his few frigates and less than 2000 troops, he could hardly think of effective resistance. He therefore, sent an urgent note to Decres, the Minister of French Marine, for immediate reinforcements.[48] But it did not evoke a satisfactory response from him due to the union of France and Holland, and the despatch of the French naval reinforcements to the Dutch Island of Java to counteract British manoeuvres at that end.[49]

Decaen was thus left to meet the approaching crisis with the meagre resources at his command. Of the six French frigates, only one, the 'Astree', was fit for active service, and the others required repairs. In all, he had about 900 officers and men in the army, besides 300 marines and artillery men and 800 men of the National Guard. Among them, there were a large number of Irishmen on whose loyalty Decaen could not obviously count as they were recruited forcibly from amongst the war prisoners. Moreover, there were as many as five suitable landing points on the coast of Mauritius, whose defence with the limited resources at the command of Decaen was practically impossible. Nevertheless, without losing heart, he fortified every post as far as possible.[50]

With full knowledge of French obligations to defend the dutch settlement in South-East Asia and of their limited resources in Mauritius, Lord Minto decided to send a large expeditionary force to Mauritius without loss of time in order to destroy the French navy before reinforcements could reach there for its help.[51] He thought that it would be of great consequence for the British, if they instead of Monsieur Decaen, could be at Port Louis in time to receive supplies from France. To implement this plan, five British frigates reached Rodriguez from India; the first under Colonel Picton, the second under Colonel Gibbs, the third under Colonel Kelso, the fourth under Colonel Macleod, and the fifth under Colonel Keating. The entire force consisted of 21 frigates under Vice-Admiral Bertie and 11,300 fighting men under general Abercromby. The expedition for Mauritius started from Rodriguez on November 22, 1810.[52]

After a week, on November 29, 1801, the British ships landed at Grande Baye, fifteen miles North of Port Louis and anchored in the narrow passage between a small island known as Coin de Mir and the mainland. From this vantage point, they marched towards Port Louis on November, 30, 1810 and met with heroic resistance.[53] It was, however, difficult for Decaen with his limited military force to resist the massive attack successfully for long. On the advance of British troops to the outskirts of Port Louis on December 1, 1810, the French forces retired with the town. At this stage, the British ships took up position to cannonade the capital from the seaside. At this critical juncture, realizing the futility of an unsuccessful resistance leading to incalculable losses and enormous sufferings to its distressed population, Decaen capitalated on December 2, 1810.[54]

By the terms of capitulation, the Isle of Mauritius was surrendered to the British with all the naval vessels and public property. The French troops and crews were not to be taken as prisoners of war, but were to be transported to

France with their arms and equipments.[55] With the fall of this French island disappeared the last vestiges of French power in the East, and the might of British military and naval prowess in Asia was amply demonstrated. The British interests in the Indian ocean and the Arabian Sea became fully secure. The fear of these islands being used as bases for operations against India no longer lurked in the British mind. The chances of the success of anti-British French intrigues in Persia and the Persian Gulf also became remote. The British India could now breathe a sigh of relief. These British victories and French losses continued the climax of Lord Minto's successful foreign policy. They added a new feather to his cap and earned plaudits for him in the British press.

(B) EXPEDITIONS TO EASTERN IS ISLANDS

Simultaneously with the British attempts to safeguard their Indian Empire and shipping and commerce in the Arabian Sea from possible French incursion, their attention was also diverted towards the Eastern islands in the Indian Ocean in order to prevent any damage being caused to their interests from those quarters. The South-East Asian islands originally belonged to Holland. But they had lately come under French hegemony with the subjugation of Holland by the French revolutionary forces in 1794 and the consequent transfer to their colonial Empires to France. By virtue of the geographical location of these islands on the way from Europe and India to the Far East, their strategic importance was immense for a growing world power like England which had overseas commercial, colonial and imperial interests, spreads all over the eastern hemisphere.

The hold over the Eastern islands by friendly Holland had not posed any danger to British interests in the East. But the establishment of French hold over them created the fear in their minds that the French might hamper British cimmerce with the Far East, and use Java as a convenient and safe military and naval base against their Indian Empire. This danger became magnified, when Napoleon Bonaparte reached the height of his glory in Europe and concentrated his attention on the ruining of British sources of wealth and power outside Europe. Therefore, safety to British commerce with the Far East and their Empire in India naturally necessitated the elimination of those spheres by having control over the islands of Amboyna, Banda, Ternate and Java.

(C) EXPEDITIONS TO AMBOYNA, BANDA AND TERNATE

(a) Soon after the successful extirpation of piracy in the Persian Gulf, Lord Minto diverted his attention towards them directing his first naval and military attack against the island of Amboyna. It was an important island among the Moluccas and was well-known to the British due to the melancholy event of 1623.[56]

A naval squadron consisting of four hundred men under Captain Tucker and land force under Captain Court embarked from Madras in the 'Dover', the Cornwallis' and the 'Samarang' on October 16,1809 and reached there on February 16,1810[57] Soon after achoring they started a brisk connonade on the Dutch sea-force consisting of 1300 men, and forced it to surrender. This resulted in the military occupation of the island under Captain Tucker to whom an adequate garrison was, supplied for this purpose.[58] By this naval victory, the British felt that the massacre of 1623 was avenged.

(b) The next Spice Island which attracted British attention was Banda, situated on the South-East of Amboyna. It was a cluster of islands with Great Banda and Banda Neira as the principal ones. A naval force under Captain Cole and a land force under Captain Tucker embarked in the 'Carolina', the 'Piedmontaise' and the 'Barracouta' from the coast of Madras on May 6, 1810,[59] and reached the coast of Banda on July 14, 1810 after encountering adverse monsoons and traversing the intricate waters of the pitts Strait.[60] They landed under the bluff points of Great Banda on August 9,1810 within a hundred yards of the Dutch battery with ten guns, facing the fury of monsoons and tempests.[61] However, Captain Keunah of the 'Barracouta' overpowered the Dutch, and captured their guns. Thereafter, Fort Belgica was attacked and taken after a well-directed fire and stiff resistance. With its fall, the entire island of Banda fell into the British hands.[62] Its administration was entrusted to William Bryan Martin of the Bengal Civil Service[63] and the military command to Major Samuel Kelly.[64]

(c) The third expedition with a naval force of 170 men under Captain Tucker sailed from the Island of Amboyna in the 'Dover' on August 20,1810 to attempt the reduction of the Island of Ternate.[65] On reaching within striking distance of it on August 27,1810, they had to face a barrage of Dutch musketry. With heavier shelling in reply, they manoeuvered their way amidst the booming of guns to the outskirts of the Fort of Kyomirah, the principal Dutch post on the island. Here the enemy opened a much heavier fire of grape and musketry. But notwithstanding this stiff resistance, the British scaled its walls with considerable daring, and the fort was taken with one officer and sixty eight soldiers as prisoners.[66] Thereafter the forts of Kota Bara and Fort Orange also met the same fate after feeble resistance.[67]

By August 31,1810, the entire island of Ternate surrendered to the British on certain conditions laid down in the capitulation-engagement signed by both the contending parties.[68] By it, the British Commander promised to respect private property, and permitted the Dutch officers and men to leave for Java on parole. After their departure, the British banner was hoisted on Fort Orange on August 31,1810 with a royal salute from the 'Dover'.[69] With the fall of this island, British control over all the Spice Island was established.

(d) Expedition To Java

This success greatly encouraged the British to launch a grand and massive expedition against Java, a larger and more important island in the Eastern Archipelago. On the successful termination of the expedition against the French island of Mauritius and Bourbon on December 3,1810, elaborate preparations were made for the execution of this object.[70] The over-all command of the expeditionary force was entrusted to Sir Samuel Auchmuty, the Commander-in-Chief of the Madras army.

The British expeditionary forces of the Bengal and Madras Presidencies were collected at Malacca by the Ist of June, 1811. Lord Minto took so great an interest in the expedition that he accompanied the British forces to Java in the frigate, the 'Modeste' as a 'volunteer'.[71] This action of the Governor-General was appreciated by the Court of Directors.[72]

The first embarkation of the British troops took place at a small place called Chillinching in Batavia Bay without any opposition on August 4,1811.[73] All the troops, a few field pieces and part of the stores were landed that evening and in the course of the night. The horses, ordnance and additional stores were put on shore next day. This village was principally Chinese, and they accorded the British a welcome.[74]

Thereafter, the British army moved forward to a place about three miles from Batavia, the capital of Java. From there the British General sent a summon to the citizens of the town asking them to surrender.[75] The approach of the British troops so close to the capital greatly surprised the French Governor who could not arrange for its timely defence.[76] He, therefore, ordered the army to set fire to the public stores and the citadel, and withdraw to Cornelis, a strong French post about six miles from Batavia on August 6,1811.[77] He also ordered the inhabitants under pain of death to evacuate the town and repair to the headquarters of the army, where arrangements could be made for their safety. Batavia thus fell into the hands of the British on August 8,1811 without any armed resistance.[78]

From Batavia, Lord Minto sent Captain Robinson, his aide-de-camp, to Cornelis with summons to the French Commander, General Janssens, to surrender. He proceeded up to the Cantonment of Weltevreeden unobstructed, but was not permitted to proceed further. He reported therefore the Lord Minto that the British troops would easily advance upto Weltevreeden, a magnificent unfortified Cantonment, without any fear of opposition as there were no French outposts upto that place.[79]

Upon this report, the British army moved forward on August 20,1811 and reached Weltevreeden without any opposition.[80] But immediately after it, they had to encounter a sharp French attack in which they suffered principally from their grape and musketry fire. But soon the superiority of the British forces became manifest, and the encounter proved decisive for them. They drove the French troops in utter confusion, and entrenched themselves almost under the guns of Cornelis.[81] This was the most significant British success. It gave them accommodation for their army, huge stores, magazines, some hundred pieces of artillery, horse, labourers and an easy conveyance for every article by water. In this encounter, the loss of enermy was great and of the British inconsiderable.[82]

The next British target was Cornelis, a place most formidable in strength. It had a fort in the centre of the city and was defended by a numerous and well organized artillery. The British plan to carry the fort by assault was entrusted to two daring officers, Colonel Gillespie and Colonel Gibbs.[83] They stormed the fort at day-break on August 26, 1811, causing dreadful slaughter of the enemy and forcing the rest of them to surrender.[84] In all about 5,000 were taken prisoners including three General Officers, 34 Field Officers, 70 Captains and 150 Subaltern Officers.[85] The French Commander General Jassens, however, escaped capture most narrowly by his precipitate flight to Buitenzorg, thirty miles from cornelis, with a few trusted men, the sole remnant of his army of 10,000 men.[86] Subsequently, pressed hard by the pursuing British army, he had to leave this place for Samarang. Here he was compelled to surrender before the British Commander-in-Chief, Sir General Auchmuty, and signed a Treaty.[87] By this Treaty, the surrender of Java and its dependencies to Great Britain was stipulated. All the captured forces were treated as prisoners of war. The future administration of the island devolved on the British without French interference. The guarantee of the public debt and the liquidation of the paper money was also undertaken by the British.[88]

The facility with which Java was captured by the British demonstrated the feebleness of the enemy's forces on that island and the su periority of the British arms in the East. Its reduction left the Eastern seas without an enemy, and the merchant-vessels of Great British and of British India were at liberty to purse their navigation and commerce peacefully without dread of molestation or fear of plunder. This colony, which for three centuries had contributed much to the power, prosperity and grandeur of Holland, was wrested from the short usurpation of the French and was added to the Dominion of the British Crown. From a seat of hostile mechinations and commercial competition, it was converted into a feature of British power and prosperity.[89] This achievement of Lord Minto received the highest approbation from the Court of Directors.[90]

Soon after the annexation of Java, Thomas Stamford Raffes, an able, active and judicious man, conversant with the interests and affairs of the Eastern States, took over as the Lieutenant Governor of Java.[91] His appointment was approved by the court of Directors.[92] Colonel Gillespie, the hero of this campaign, was vested with the command of the troops on the island.[93]

For the administration of Java, the Governor-General issued two proclamations on October, 1,1811.[94] and October 11, 1811.[95] By the first one, the island of Java and its dependencies were declared to be a part of the territorial possession of the East India company, and the form of the their Government was to be determined by the British Parliament. But meanwhile, they were to be adminstered by the Government of India. All the powers of the Government were to be exercised, and all acts and orders were to be issued in the name of the Governor-General of India. Lieutenant Governor Thoms Stamford Raffes was to act as the representative of the Governor- General-in-Council in Bengal.[96]

By the second proclamation, attempt was made to win over the inhabitants of the subjugated island by promises of promoting their prosperity and welfare. They were exhorted to consider their new connection with England as founded on principles of mutual advantage and to be conducted in a spirit of kindness and affection.[97] On the British side, a promise was given that they would be entitled to the same general privileges as were enjoyed by the naturnal born subject of Great Britain,[98] such as freedom of trade with the British Dominions, promotion of their commerce, righ to occupy offices of trust according to their merits.[99] and to be governed by an enlightened and liberal administration.[100] During the period of transition, the Dutch Code of laws was to remain in force till it was replaced by the British code.[101] Odious punishments such as torture and mutilation were abolished.[102] For a British-born subject, the law of England was to be applicable.[103]

After the completion of this work, Lord Minto sailed for Bengal on October 19, 1811, giving his parting instructions to Raffles to do all the good he could for Java. For the administration of Java, the British Lieutenant-Governor appointed British civil officials in the districts under him.[104] The legal system was based on the Indian pattern. Justice between natives was administered in accordance with the native laws. Criminal cases were entrusted to a circuit judge. For deciding the cases of Europeans, three courts were established at Batavia, Samarang and Sourabaya, the commercial centres of Java. Slavery was discouraged by measures like doubling of duty on import of slaves from outside, prohibiting trade in children under 14, and declaring slaveryas felony in law.[105] In this way, the sources of supply of slaves were virtually dried up.

By the aforesaid expeditions to the South-Eastern islands, the Spice Islands of Amboyna, Banda and Ternate and the important Dutch political settlement in Java, came under effective British control. British effectivess increased in South-East Asia and the danger of the Dutch islands becoming the centres of French military and naval activities, threatening British interests in the Indian oceans, was averted. This achievement of Lord Minto added a new feather to his cap.

REFERENCES

1. Marlow, John, *The Persian Gulf in the Twentieth Century*, p. 11.
2. *Ibid,* and Secret letter to Court of Directors, April 17, 1809.
3. Wilson, Arnold T., *The Persian Gulf*, pp. 196-197.
4. *Ibid.*, p. 202.
5. Resident at Muscat to Governor of Bombay, Feb. 8, 1809. For, Deptt. Pol., Cons April 3, 1809, Cons. 21.
6. Calcutta Monthly Journal, July-August, 1809, pp. 39 and 172.
7. Edmonstone to Rear Admiral Drury, April 3, 1809, For, Deptt. Pol., Cons. April 3, 1809, Cons. 110.
8. *Ibid.*, and Secret letter to Court of Directors, April 3, 1809.
9. Calcutta monthly Journal, Aug. 1809, p. 172.
10. Calcutta monthly Journal, Oct. 1809, p. 346.
11. Secret letter to Court of Directors, April 17, 1809.
12. *Ibid.*
13. Col. Smith to Governor of Bombay, Nov. 14, 1809, For Deptt. Pol., Cons. Feb. 20, 1810, Cons. 47.
14. *Ibid.*
15. Col. Smith to Governor of Bombay, Nov. 14, 1809. For Deptt. Pol., Cons. Jan. 9, 1810, Cons. 106.
16. *Ibid.*
17. *Ibid.*

18. Col. Smith to Governor of Bombay, Dec. 16, 1809. For Deptt. Pol., Cons. March, 6, 1810. Cons. 104.

19. Col. Smith to Governor of Bombay, Dec. 16, 1809, For. Deptt. Pol., Cons. March 6, 1810, Cons. 104.

20. *Ibid.*

21. Col. Smith to Governor of Bombay, Jan. 8, 1810. For. Deptt. Pol., Cons. Feb. 27, 1810, Cons. 37.

22. Edmonstone to Secy. Bombay Govt. Feb. 14, 1810, For, Deptt. Pol. Cons. March 6, 1810, Cons. 53.

23. *Ibid.*

24. Admiral Battie to Governor of Bombay, March 23, 1809. For, Deptt. Secret and Separate, June 26, 1809, Cons. 4.

25. *Ibid.*

26. Governor of Bombay to Minto, May 27, 1809, For. Deptt. Secret and Separate, June 26, 1809, Cons. 1.

27. Edward Parry and Charles Grant of the East India House to Governor of Bombay, Ec. 27, 1809. For Deptt. Secret and Separate, June 26, 1809, Cons. 2.

28. *Ibid.*

29. Political letter to Court of Directors, Feb. 10, 1809.

30. Edmonstone to G. Dowdeswell, Acting Chief Secretary, Fort William, Nov. 28, 1809. For. Deptt. Pol., Cons. Dec. 19, 1809, Cons. 12.

31. *Ibid.*

32. Minto to Commodore Rowley, March 26, 1810, For. Deptt. Secret and Separate, April 24, 1810. Cons. 22.

33. Edmonstone to Lt. Col. Keating, March 26, 1810. For Deptt. Secret and Separate, April 24, 1810, Cons. 24.

34. Lt. Col. Keating to Edmonstone, April 10, 1810, For. Deptt. Secret and Separate, April 10, 1810, Cons. 10.

35. Minto to Admiral Drury, March 12, 1810, For. Deptt. Secret and Separate August 25, 1810, Cons. 23.

36. Minto to Admiral Drury, March 12, 1810, For. Deptt. Secret and Separate, April 24, 1810, Cons. 13.

37. Col. Keating to Edmonstone, July 21, 1810, For. Deptt. Secret and Seprate, Aug. 25, 1810, Cons. 23.

38. R.T. Farquhar to Secret Committee of Court of Directors, July 24, 1810, For. Deptt. Secret and Separate, Sept. 25, 1810, Cons. 9.
39. R.T. Farquhar to Minto, July 21, 1810, For. Deptt. Secret and Separate, Aug. 25, 1810, Cons. 4.
40. Government order dated July 9, 1810. For. Deptt. Secret and Separate, Aug. 25, 1810, Cons. 11.
41. R.T. Farquhar to Col. Keating, July 16, 1810. For. Deptt. Secret and Separate, Aug. 25, 1810, Cons. 6.
42. Proclamation issued on July 28, 1810, For. Deptt. Secret, Cons. Oct. 5, 1810, Cons. 5.
43. R.T. Farquhar to Minto, Aug., 21, 1810. For. Deptt. Secret and Separate, Oct. 19, 1810, Cons. 11.
44. *Ibid.*
45. British Commander to Edmonstone, Aug. 30, 1810. For. Deptt. Secret and Separate, Aug. 30, 1810, Cons. 25.
46. British Commander to Edmonstone, Aug. 30, 1810, For. Deptt. Secret and Separate Aug. 30, 1810, Cons. 25.
47. *Ibid.*
48. *Ibid.*
49. *Ibid.*
50. British Commander to Edmonstone, Aug. 30, 1810. For. Deptt. Secret and Separate Aug. 30, 1810, Cons. 25.
51. Pol. letter to Court of Directors, Jan. 15, 1811.
52. *Ibid.*
53. British Commander to Edmonstone, Dec. 3, 1810, For. Deptt. Secret and Separate, Dec. 3, 1810, Cons. 4.
54. *Ibid.*
55. British Commander to Edmonstone, Dec. 3, 1810, For. Deptt. Secret and Separate, Dec. 3, 1810, Cons. 4.
56. The British were pushed out from the Island of Amboyna after their merciless slaughter by the Dutch in 1623.
57. Capt. Tucker to Chief Secretary, Madras, March 2, 1810, For. Deptt. Pol. Cons. May 15, 1810, Cons. 59.
58. *Ibid.*
59. Capt. Tucker to Chief Secretary, Madras, Sept 20, 1810, For. Deptt. Pol., Cons. Nov. 23, 1810, Cons. 29.

60. Calcutta Monthly Journal, November 1810, p. 338.
61. Capt. Tucker to Chief Secretary, Madras, Sept. 20, 1810, For. Deptt. Pol., Cons., Nov. 23, 1810, Cons. 29.
62. *Ibid.*
63. Edmonstone to W.B. Martin, Nov. 23, 1810. For. Deptt. Pol, Cons. Nov. 23, 1810, Cons. 105.
64. Edmonstone to Major Keely, *Ibid,* Cons. 110.
65. Calcutta Monthly Journal, Feb. 1811.
66. Capt. Tucker to Commander 'Dover' Sept. 1, 1810, For. Deptt. Pol., Cons. Feb. 16, 1811, Cons. 25.
67. *Ibid.*
68. Capt. Tucker to Commander at Amboyna, Sept. 9, 1810, For. Deptt. Pol., Cons. Feb. 16, 1811, Cons. 26.
69. Calcutta Monthly Journal, Feb. 1811, p. 665.
70. Lord Minto to LadyMinto, Oct. 3, 1810, quoted Countess of Minto, *Lord Minto in India,* p. 299.
71. Secret letter to Court of Directors, July 4, 1811.
72. Secret letter from Court of Directors, March 6, 1812.
73. Lord Minto to W.B. Martin, Oct. 27, 1811, For. Deptt. Pol, Cons. Dec. 26, 1811, Cons. 4.
74. Lord Minto to Lady Minto, Aug. 6, 1811, *op. cit.,* p. 284.
75. Lord Minto to Lady Minto, Aug. 9, 1811, *op. cit.,* p. 286.
76. Lord Minto to W.B. Martin, Oct. 27, 1811, For, Deptt. Pol., Cons. Dec. 26,m 1811, Cons. 4.
77. *Ibid.*
78. Lord Minto to W.B. Martin, Oct. 27, 1811, For. Deptt. Pol., Cons. Dec. 26, 1811, Cons. 4.
79. Lord Minto to Lady Minto, Aug. 12, 1811, *op. cit.,* p. 288.
80. *Ibid.*
81. *Ibid.*
82. Lord Minto to Lady Minto, Aug. 12, 1811, *op. cit.,* p. 289.
83. C-in-C to Lord Minto, Aug. 31, 1811, For Deptt. Pol., Cons. Oct. 25, 1811, Cons. 6.
84. Lord Minto to Lady Minto, Aug. 28, 1811, *op. cit.,* p. 290.

85. C-in-C to Lord Minto, Aug. 31, 1811, For. Deptt. Pol., Cons. Oct. 25, 1811, Cons. 6.

86. Lord Minto to W.B. Martin, Sept. 27, 1811, For. Deptt. Pol., Cons. Dec. 26, 1811, Cons. 4.

87. Treaty signed on Sept., 28, 1811, For. Deptt. Pol. Cons. Nov. 29, 1811, Cons. 61.

88. *Ibid.*

89. Lord Minto to Secretary of State, Sept. 2, 1811, For. Deptt. Pol., Cons. Oct. 25, 1811, Cons. 27.

90. Secret letter from Court of Directors, March 6, 1812.

91. Raffles to Lord Minto, Sept. 30, 1811, For Deptt. Pol., Cons. Jan. 25, 1812, Cons. 1.

92. *Ibid.*

93. *Ibid.*

94. Proclamation on Oct. 1, 1811, For, Deptt. Secret, Cons. Dec. 6, 1811, Con. 2

95. Proclamation on Oct. 11, 1811, For Deptt. Secret, Cons. Dec. 6.

96. *Ibid.*

97. Proclamation on Oct. 11, 1811, *op. cit.,* (Art. I.).

98. Art. II.

99. Art. III.

100. Art. IV.

101. Art. V.

102. Art. VI.

103. Art. VII.

104. Minute of Lord Minto, Dec. 6, 1811, For, Deptt. Secret, Cons. Dec. 6, 1811, Cons. 1.

105. *Ibid.*

9

The Madras Mutiny

On the arrival of Lord Minto, although danger from the native soldiery was over on account of the ruthless suppression of the Vellore Mutiny, the European element in the Madras army was far from satisfied. A state of excited feelings and bitter antagonism, caused by a series of regulations, unpalatable to them, prevailed among the officials. This created an ill-will and strife between the civil and military authorities. It was not altogether a new development. Even in the past, the East India Company's Government had received serious jolts by the sedition of European officers twice in the course of less than half a century. The white mutiny of 1765 was overcome by the zeal and firmness of Lord Clive. The flames of the Mutiny of 1796-97, fostered by the feebleness of Sir John Shore, were extinguished by Lord Wellesle's mandate.

During the period under review, discontent in the European section of the Madras army was not without some pertinently valid causes. After the second Maratha War, the directions from the Court of Directors for economy in military expenditure and the consequent pressure of the Government of Bengal upon the subordinate Presidencies for effecting retrenchments and the Commander-in-Chief of the Madras army Sir John Cradock's plans for reducing the military expenditure of the Madras army, deprived the European military officers of their several emoluments.

Besides, the differences in the military allowances between the Madras and Bengal services had long been a subject of discontent. The assignment of commands to officers of His Majesty's Regiments in place of East India Company's officers also caused frequent murmurs and grumblings among the latter. Moreover, the bitter personal feelings of Sir Hay Macdowall, the new Commander-in-Chief of the Madras army who was refused a seat in the Governor's Council and was replaced by a civilian officer added insult to injury and made him also a party to it.

Among the most unsavoury measures were the abolition of the Baggage Allowance, formerly granted to officers in command of Divisions and Stations; removal of full *batta* drawn by officers, commanding small ports and garrisons and the abolition of the Tent Contract system of June 7, 1807.[1] The last one heightened the discontent to its climax. This was an arrangement by which the British military officers, commanding native corps, received a permanent monthly allowance both in Cantonments and in the field in times of peace and war; and in lieu thereof, they provided men under them with suitable camp equipage, whenever required. This system was inherently vicious and was, therefore, open to serious objections. There was hardly any doubt about the reasonableness of its abolition, as it was a definite measure of economy. Colonel Munro, the Quarter-Master-General of the Madras army who had the overall charge of the department of camp equipage, was asked to investigate into the complaints against the Tent Contract and submit his report on it. He reported that the officers in command of the corps, concerned with the Tent Contract, consulted their own interest at the expense of the public service and drew the tent allowance without keeping up the requisite establishment.[2] This adverse report was approved by Sir John Cradock, the Presidency Commander-in-Chief and William Bentinck, the Governor of Madras. But on their sudden recall on account of the unsatisfactory handling of the Vellore Mutiny, their successors Sir Hay Macdowall and Sir George Barlow had to deal with the matter.[3]

The report of Colonel Munro was strongly resented by the British army officers of the Madras Presidency. They determined to wreak vengeance on him for his aspersions on their character as officers and gentlemen. In disgust, twenty-four officers, commanding the corps, addressed a letter to the Governor in which they charged Colonel Munro with conduct unbecoming of a British officer and a gentleman; and questioned the validity of his views on the matter.[4] The Governor referred these accusations against Colonel Munro to the Judge-Advocate-General for his expert legal opinion. To this, he replied that Commander-in-Chief of the army was within his rights to call for the advice and opinion of any officer under his command even on the subjects under him and that officer was bound to give his honest opinion on them. Discussing the circumstances of the case in all its bearings, he concluded that there was no reason for the army officers to question the propriety of Colonel Munro's advice to the Commander-in-Chief.[5] Thereupon, the Governor snubbed the army officers for their accusations against Colonel Munro, and decided to work out the suggestions given to him.

Dissatisfied with the reaction of the Governor, the British officers sent a Memorial to the Directors of the East India Company apprizing them of their case. Among their grievances, they mentioned the reductions made in their emoluments by the abolition of the Baggage Allowance and the removal of the full *batta* and the partiality shown in selecting officers for general commands. They also complained that, except a very few cases, a military officer serving in India had nothing else to look to, but his bare pay which was hardly adequate to his subsistence until after a period of twenty two years of actual service in India[6] The abolition of the Tent Contract was mentioned by them as the addition of an insult to the injury already caused to them by the reduction of their allowances. They denounced the proposal to abolish the Tent Contract as a 'spurious measure of economy'.[7] The Court of Directors rejected the Memorial stating that its transmission was objectionable and improper as it was not sent through proper channel. They suspected that the Commander-in-Chief of the Madras army excited a spirit of discontent and insubordination in the army by encouraging the officers to send a Memorial directly to the Court of Directors.[8]

General Macdowall, who was already dissatisfied owing to the loss of his seat in the Council, considered the remarks of the Court of Directors about him as derogatory to his dignity and authority. He took up the cause of the army officers, openly espoused their cause, and became the champion of their rights. On January 20, 1809, he placed Colonel Munro under arrest on a charge of casting imputations on the character of the army in the official report drawn by him.[9]

Finding himself thus disgraced. Colonel Munro, at first, appealed to the Commander-in-Chief on January 20, 1809 requesting him to communicate the news of his arrest to the Governor.[10] General Macdowall did not consider it and asked him to appeal to the succeeding Commander-in-Chief. General Gowdie.[11] He refused to forward his application to the Governor and stated that the latter could not interfere in such military matters.[12] On this refusal. Colonel Munro appealed to the Governor under whose authority he had acted and by whom the measures, he had recommended, had been approved and adopted. On this, the Governor of Madras asked the Commander-in-Chief to release Colonel Munro, but he did not comply with his request.[13] This attitude of General Macdowall was viewed seriously by the Governor and he was ordered to release Colonel Munro which he obeyed reluctantly.[14] He, however, did not appreciate the Governor's decision and argued that this kind of interference by the civil authority was 'unprecedented and it encouraged very dangerous example, proving destructive to every military discipline'. Beside this denunciation of the Governor's order, he charged Cononel Munro with violation of military discipline and disrespect to him in addressing the Governor directly. He felt that for this unbecoming conduct and insubordination, the Quarter-Master-General should be court-martialled.[15] Arrogating himself to be the custodian of military discipline and guardian of the rights of army under him, he deemed it his duty to set things right in the army by punishing an act of indiscipline.[16]

The dispute between the civil and military authorities was referred to the Judge-Advocate-General for his legal opinion. In his view, the Govenor right in his action as the whole civil and military Government of his Presidency was vested in him and his Council by the Act of Parliament and they were fully competent to protect their servants, in the discharge of their duties, from punishment by an inferior authority. In this respect, the Commander-in-Chief was himself subject to the orders of the Government as any other officer under his command and that officer could legally be released by a power superior to that of the person who ordered the arrest.[17] He conceded the Commander-in-Chief's contention that obedience to higher authority was undoubtedly an important part of military discipline and a great duty of a soldier; but in the event of a conflict in the orders of civil and military authorities, his first obedience was due to the civil laws of the country and second to the military. The proposed action of Commander-in-Chief against the Quarter-Master-General, therefore, appeared to be a transgression of his authority and disrespect to the government.[18]

The interference of the Civil Government in the military matters and the legal opinion of the Judge-Advocate-General in its favour, annoyed General Macdowall. He felt insulted and resolved to quit his office as a protest.[19] But a day prior to his departure, he issued a General Order on January 28, 1809 and directed Major Boles, the Deputy Adjutant General of the Madras army, to circulate it. In it was stated that his precipitate departure from Madras prevented him from bringing Colonel Munro to trial for disrespect and disobedience to him and for contempt of military authority he had shown by obeying an order of the Civil Government in defiance of that of the military authority. He therefore, expressed strong disapprobation of Colonel Munro's unexampled proceedings and reprimanded him in General Order.[20]

The Governor and his Council took a very serious view of this expression of dissatisfaction and disgust by General Macdowall in his General Order and its circulation among the British military officers under the signatures of Major Boles.[21] They interpreted the Commander-in-Chief's order as a piece of calculated mischief intended to encourage faction in the army against the superior civil authority of the Governor by misuse of his high official position and to subject the Government to dangerous criticism and ridicule. Similarly Major Boles was treated guilty of an act, offensive in nature and in direct violation of his duty to the Government by giving currency to the General Order of the Commander-in-Chief.[22] Therefore, by General Order issued by the Government on January 31, 1809, appointment of General Macdowall as the Commander-in-Chief of the Madras Presidency was annulled on the plea of his 'violent and inflammatory' proceedings on a number of occasions and Major Boles was suspended from service.[23] The latter defended his conduct in the Memorial to the Court of Directors,[24] but it evoked no response.

The action against Macdowall and Major Boles heightened the discontent already existing amongst British military officers in the Presidency. They took up the cause of Major Boles as their own, defended his conduct and condemned the Government's action as cruel and unjustified and the sentence as undeserved. They collected for him contributions equivalent to his pay and allowances and assured him of economic security and resolved to fight out his case. This afforded an encouragement to other officers to violate their duty towards the Government.[25] They addressed a Memorial to Lord Minto in which they enumerated their grievances and protested against the high-handedness of the

Governor of Madras in dealing with General Macdowall and Major Boles. They demanded the removal of the Governor to reduce the tension in the army; the grant of a seat to the Commander-in-Chief in the Governor's Council and the re-definition of the relations between the military and civil authorities.[26] The Governor-General did not reply to this Memorial, but made mention of it in his communication with the Government of Madras in which he defended the Governor's action, took a serious view of the whole agitation in the army and stated that the grant of a seat to the Commander-in-Chief of the Presidency armies lay within the purview of the Court of Directors.[27]

Re-enforced by the support from the Governor-General, the Governor of Madras advised Major General Francis Gowdie, the new Commander-in-Chief of the Madras army to suppress the refractory elements in his army.[28] Accordingly, he issued a circular on March 5, 1809 to the officer, commanding the Division of the army asking him to enforce the code of conduct rigidly on the officers under him; prevent them from circulating improper addresses and memorials and punish those guilty of such acts of indiscipline in the past.[29] But these efforts only added fuel to the fire. Discontent spread at a number of places and grievances became more vocal. Lieutenant Colonel Davis, Officer Commanding Mysore Division, noticed the circulation of papers highly improper in nature, against army officers in Mysore regarding the suspension of Major Boles.[30]

When Sir George Barlow came to know of the growing acts of indiscipline among the army officers, he issued another General Order on May 1, 1809, in which he praised the distinguished zeal, discipline and obedience shown by the military establishment of his Presidency in the past and censured the intemperate acts of the late Commander-in-Chief, General Macdowall as highly derogatory to military discipline. He took a strong exception to the Memorial they had addressed to the Governor-General in gross violation of the service conditions and code of conduct. He felt that this action was calculated to destroy discipline, obedience and fidelity in the army.[31] Strongly condemning the army officers responsible for sending addresses to Major Boles, encouraging him in his action and affording him percuniary inducement, he ordered the suspension of four officers of rank and removal of an equal number from their commands and staff appointments. The most notable among them were Colonel St. Leger, Colonel Chalmers and Colonel Cuppage who had performed distinguished services in Travancore. The drastic action of the Governor without giving an opportunity to the accused to defend their conduct ignited the accumulated discontent in the European section of the Madras army.

The first open expression of mutinous conduct was shown by the larger and most united division of the European army stationed in Hyderabad. Its officers condemned the General Order of the Government and made known their innate feelings on the suspension of eight officers to the rank and file of the army. A rumour gained currency that fifteen officers of their Division would also be suspended and multiplied their violence. They held daily secret meetings, pledged to remain united, organized themselves into committees for frequent communications with different Cantonments, encouraged open defiance of the civil authority and supported the cause of the suspended officers.[32]

On June 15, 1809, they transmitted a representation to the Government Fort St. George with 186 signatures in which they expressed their resolve of the whole army to uphold unitedly the cause of the victims of injustice and visualized the impending danger of conflict between the civil and military authorities, if the General Order of the 1st May was not rescinded and their genuine grievances were not redressed.[33] They also inserted in their representation a warming that in the event of their representation going unheard, the scenes of Vellore might be reacted with increased effect. But it was later on omitted. This was, however, known to the whole Presidency army.[34]

The officers of other European Regiments stationed at various Cantonments soon echoed their sympathy for the common cause. The European Regiment at Masulipatam mutinied on June 25, 1809 and Major-Storey, the leader of the revolt, put the Commandant, Colonel Innes, under arrest for not sharing views with the rebel officers and himself assumed its command. In accordance with the pattern set by the mutinous officers of the Hyderabad Division, he instituted, a small committee for developing contacts with other mutinous Divisions in the Presidency.[35]

The mutinous officers received applause and promises of cooperation and support from most of the Cantonments. This showed wide-spread dissatisfaction in the army and the shape its revolt was going to take. To counteract this design, the Government appointed Colonel Malcolm, an officer known for his popularity in the army, to take the command of Masulipatam Division, and hoped that he might be able to induce that garrison to return to a sense of duty. But he failed to restore the mutinous army to obedience. He found every European in the army overtaken by mutinous spirit and pledged to rise against Government until the common grievances were redressed.[36]

The British detachment at Jaulna seized the public treasure and interrupted the official correspondence. On July 5, 1809, it prepared an Address of a very intemperate nature meant to be forwarded to the Governor-General. But Colonel Montresor, its Commanding Officer, declined to forward it. On the same day, the officers of the Hyderabad Subsidiary Force refused to permit the march of a battalion which Government had ordered to proceed to Goa.[37]

Four days after, the orders issued to there Travancore battalions and a Seringapatam detachment to march to Bangalore were also disobeyed. At Quilon, the situation became much worse. The mutinous officers entered into a conspiracy to effect the murder of Colonel Macaulay, the British Resident, and the Pro-Government section of the European officers of that station. But the Resident and the

Commanding Officer, Colonel Hall, peremptorily suppressed the conspiracy without loss of life and punished the conspirators.[38] The British troops in Mysore were excited. They resisted the Government's orders, prepared an inflammatory Address and marched towards Madras in a state of open rebellion.[39] But here the timely action of the Commanding Officer, loyal to the Government, frustrated the plan.[40]

On July 21, 1809, the officers of the Hyderabad Regiment drew out their charter of demands in which they asked for the open repeal of the General Order; the restoration of officers removed or suspended; the trial of Colonel Innes for his general conduct at Masulipatam; the removal of officers of the General Staff and general amnesty for the coastal troops. Colonel Close who, on account of his great popularity with the army, had been sent to Hyderabad to take over the command of the ambitious Subsidiary Force, found the troops under arms and prepared for action. A rumour was afloat that 30,000 mutinous troops would march upon Madras from different directions.[41]

The open resistance of a considerable portion of the Madras army at different centres, their combination caused by the unity of sentiments and commonness of purpose, failure of Colonel John Malcolm and Colonel Close to prevent the Masulipatam and Hyderabad Battalions from becoming refractory and the alarming intelligence received from various Cantonments, reduced the Government to the alternative of either subduing the officers by force or granting to them the concessions, they demanded.

Fully conscious of the critical situation created by the white mutiny and gauging its aftermath, the distinguished officer like Colonel Malcolm who had kept temper and loyalty unshaken, counselled Sir George Barlow to tide over the storm by the revocation of the objectionable General Order and the restoration of the suspended military officers to their jobs. Such a concession might have moderated the violence of the tempest. But this advice produced no effect upon him. He relied upon the fidelity of the King's troops and planned to use the loyal section of the army against the mutinous elements. To test their loyalty, he asked for the signatures of the officers to a pledge of loyalty to the Government of Fort St. George on pain of transfer from the covetous military stations on the sea-coast to those in the interior. This, however, could not be established as not even one-tenth of the officers, consented to affix their signatures.[42]

In this alarming situation, an attempt was made to ensure the loyalty of the Indian officers and soldiers. For this purpose, the loyal European Commanding Officers of the Indian Corps were directed to assemble the Indian officers and explain to them and through them, to sepoys that the discontent of the European officers was mainly personal and the government had no intention to curtail the privileges. They enjoyed, but was rather anxious to improve them. This appeal to the Indian officers and men produced the desired result. Lord Minto considered this measure as wise decision. He decided to proceed to Madras to restore the mutinous white army to its sense of discipline by his personal influence. But encouraging news from Madras delayed his departure for some time.[43]

The firm decision of Sir George Barlow not to bend before the storm and to face the situation squarely with the aid of loyal European officers and the entire strong body of Indian officers and soldiers, made the leaders of the white mutiny at Hyderabad realize the gravity of the situation and introduce moderation in their attitude in full consciousness of their defiant conduct. On mature consideration, their temper and resolve underwent a change. They put their signatures on the required pledge or Declaration of Obedience and entreated their brethren through a circular elsewhere to do likewise under the changed circumstances stated therein. The Jaulna and Masulipatam Divisions also signed the pledge. In Travancore, Malabar, Canara and Bangalore, all the Divisions professed their attachment and loyalty. The change in the attitude of the army officers arrested the dangerous progress of the white mutiny.

In this favourable atmosphere, Lord Minto left for Madras on August 12, 1809.[44] On his arrival, he found that tranquillity had already been restored and that the officers engaged in fomenting the late commotions were prepared to receive the decision from him. On the 25th of the same month, a General Order announced to the army the Governor-General's reprobation of their past conduct, and his resolution to inflict such punishment as might be commensurate with the offences committed. This determination was expressed in language designed and calculated to assuage all irritated feelings. A few only of the offenders were selected; such as officers in command of stations; Commandants of Corps and individuals conspicuous for violent and forward behaviour. For the two first, Court-martial were ordered; to the others, the alternative was offered of investigation before the same tribunal or dismissal from the service.[45]

Shortly after the promulgation of this order, the trials of three Lieutenant Colonels, three Majors and fifteen Captains commenced. Lieutenant Colonel John Bell, the Commandant of the garrison of Seringapatam, was charged with joining in, and with heading, the mutiny of the troops. The defence set up was, that he had taken the command only to prevent excesses; that he had signed the test without hesitation, and that the garrison finally surrendered the fort peacefully. This did not satisfy the Court-martial. He was pronounced guilty and sentenced to be cashiered.[46] Lieutenant Colonel Doveton was charged with having moved his detachment from Jaulna with a mutinous and seditious design against the Government of Fort St. George.[47] The defence was the same. He was suspended from the service pending a reference to the pleasure of the Court of Directors. Major Storey was charged with holding the command at Masulipatam after the arrest of Colonel Innes. He was sentenced to be cashiered. Of the second category of officers, Lieutenant Colonel Munro and Major Kennyy, stood a trial and were cashiered; the rest accepted the alternative of dismissal. However, as a special case, all the officers of the Hyderabad Subsidiary Force were pardoned in consideration of the example, they had set by a 'welcome change' in their attitude. To the rest of the rank and file who had shown indiscipline under the influence of the discontented officers, a 'general and unqualified' amnesty was granted.[48]

Thus ended the serious conflict between the civil and military authorities which had taken an ugly turn, threatened a rupture between the two and endangered British position in the Madras Presidency. By its happy ending, the constitutional issue between the two authorities was resolved in favour of the former whose supremacy was tacitly accepted by the army.

REFERENCES

1. Parliamentary Papers, House of Commons, May 3, 1811, p. 95.
2. Countess of Minto, *Lord Minto in India*, p. 206.
3. Countess of Minto, *Lord Minto in India*, p. 206.
4. Judge-Advocate-General to Adjutant General of Army, Nov. 7, 1808, For Deptt. Secret, Cons. Feb. 20, 1809, Cons 66.
5. *Ibid.*
6. Memorial of army officers to Court of Directors Jan. 9, 1809, For. Deptt. Secret, Cons. Feb. 20, 1809, Cons. 70.
7. Memorial of Army Officers to Court of Directors, Jan. 9, 1809, For. Deptt. Secret, Cons. Feb. 20, 1809, Cons. 76.
8. Parliamentary Papers, House of Commons, Sept. 10, 1810, p. 20.
9. *Ibid.*, pp. 56-61.
10. Munro to C-in-C, Jan. 20, 1809, For. Deptt. Secret, Cons. Feb. 20, 1809, Cons. 62.
11. C-in-C to Munro, Jan. 21, 1809, For, Deptt. Secret, Cons. Feb. 20, 1809, Cons. 62.
12. C-in-C to Munro, Jan. 23, 1809, For. Deptt. Secret. Cons. Feb. 20, 1809, Cons. 63.
13. Chief Secretary, Fort St. George to C-in-C, Jan. 27, 1809, For. Deptt. Secret, Cons. Feb. 20, 1809, Cons. 75.
14. C-in-C to Chief Secretary, Jan. 27, 1809, For Deptt. Secret, Cons. Feb. 20, 1809, Cons. 74.

15. *Ibid.*
16. *Ibid.*
17. Judge-Advocate-General to Governor of Madras, For. Misc, Vol. 77, Feb. 20. 1809.
18. Judge-Advocate-General to Governor of Madras, For. Misc., Vol. 77, Feb. 20. 1809.
19. C-in-C to Barlow, Jan. 27, 1809, For. Deptt. Secret, Cons. Feb. 20, 1809, Cons. 51.
20. General Order of General Macdowall, Jan. 28, 1809, For. Deptt. Secret, Cons. Feb. 20, 1809, Cons. 80.
21. Barlow to Court of Directors, Feb. 28, 1809, For. Misc. Vol. 77.
22. *Ibid.*
23. General Order of Chief Secretary, Madras, Jan. 31, 1809, For. Deptt. Secret, Cons. Feb. 20, 1809, Cons. 81.
24. Memorial of Major Boles to Court of Directors, Feb. 23, 1809, For. Misc., Vol. 77.
25. Parliamentary Papers, House of Commons. Sept., 10, 1810. p. 76.
26. Memorial of the Madras Army Officers dated nil. For. Deptt. Secret Cons. May 27, 1809, Cons. 16.
27. Lord Minto to Barlow May 27, 1809. For. Deptt. Secret Cons. May 27, 1809 Cons. 29.
28. Gen. Gowdle to O. C., the Division of the Army, March 5, 1809, For. Deptt. Secret Cons, May 27, 1809. Cons. 13.
29. Gen. Gowdie to O. C., the Division of the Army, March 5, 1809. For. Deptt. Secret Cons. May 27, 1809, Cons. 13.
30. Commdg. in Mysore to Gen. Gowdie, April 24, 1809, For. Deptt. Secret Cons. May 27, 1809. Cons. 22.
31. General Order by Governor-in-Council, May 1, 1809. For. Deptt. Secret Cons. May 27, 1809, Cons. 24.
32. Commanding Subsidiary Force to Edmonstone: July 29, 1809, For. Deptt. Secret and Sept. September 5, 1809, Cons. 24.
33. Parl. Papers, House of Commons: Sept 10, 1810, p. 82.
34. *Ibid.*
35. *Ibid.*
36. Parl. Papers, House of Commons; Sept. 10, 1810, p. 82.
37. *Ibid.*

38. Governor of Madras to Court of Directors, June 20, 1809, For. Misc., Vol. 77.
39. Commdg. Subsid, Force Hyderabad to Edmonstone, July, 29, 1809, For. Deptt. Secret, Cons. Sept. 5, 1809, Cons. 24.
40. *Ibid.*
41. Parliamentary Papers, House of Commons, May 25, 1811, p. 33.
42. *Ibid.*
43. Parliamentary Papers, House of Commons, May 25, 1810, p. 83.
44. *Ibid.*
45. Parliamentary Papers, House of Commons, April 1, 1811, p. 353.
46. Parliamentary Papers, House of Commons, April 1, 1811, p. 353.
47. *Ibid.*
48. *Ibid.*

10

Relations with Nepal and Burma

Situated on the Southern parts of the Himalayas between British India and the Chinese dependency of Tibet, the landlocked state of Nepal occupied a unique strategic position. The strategic and commercial importance of Nepal was realized by the British soon after the establishment of their hold over Bengal. Maintenance of trade with this state and the countries across it through the traditional trade routes passing through it, so favourable to India, had never escaped British attention.[1] For its security, they had taken interest in its political affairs also. Several missions were despatched from time to time under Lord Cornwallis, Sir John Shore and Lord Wellesley in 1792, 1795 and 1801 respectively in the persons of Captain Kirkpatrick, Abdul Qadir Khan and Captain W. D. Knox[2] for having friendly political relations with the Nepal Government, and thereby affording security to their commerce. Commercial and political treaties were signed in 1792[3] and 1801,[4] but they hardly brought forth any result worth the name. The British residency established in 1801 could not function longer than two years, and was withdrawn in April 1802 due to the political troubles in that country.[5] However, its geographical location unsatisfactory political condition and border encroachments had increased British anxiety to have more satisfactory relations with it. But disputes over Sheoraj and Butwal and a few other territories rendered the achievement of this object almost impossible.

Of these two disputed territories, Sheoraj which was a part of Gorakhpur district and which originally belonged to the Nawab Vizier of Awadh, was captured by the Nepal Government in 1785[6] and Butwal belonged to the Raja of Palpa, a feudatory chief of the Nawab Vizier of Awadh. When on November 10, 1801,[7] the East India Company acquired sovereignty over the Nawab's three provinces, after the latter had signed a Treaty of subsidiary alliance in liquidation of his arrears of payments, it was alleged that Sheoraj and Butwal formed a part of the ceded territories. The former being already under *de facto* occupation of Nepal, Lord Wellesley did not raise the issue openly with the Government of Nepal. An attempt was, however, made by him to acquire overlordship of Butwal as the East India Company put forth the claim as the rightful heir to the Nawab in respect of the sovereignty. Immediately after the conclusion of the Treaty, a British officer was sent to Butwal with the purpose of forming a settlement with Prithi Pal Sein, the Raja of Palpa. But the latter was in confinement at Khatmandu. The negotiations were, therefore, conducted with Lal Run Bahadur Sein, the Raja's brother who in his absence governed his independent territory of Palpa. He executed a *Cabooliat* in December 1802 by which the British Government held Butwal on payment of Rs. 32, 000.00 per annum.[8] On being released from Khatmandu, when Raja Prithi Pal Sein arrived at Palpa in February 1804, he acknowledge the obligation of paying the revenue of these lands to the East India Company according to the terms of his *Cabooliat*.[9]

Soon after, the Raja of Palpa was implicated in the conspiracy which ended in the murder of Rana Run Bahadur Shah, the ruler of Nepal, and was seized and put to death by the Regent.[10] His lands were confiscated by the Nepal state which extended the sentence of confiscation to the district of Butwal. The pretensions of the Court of Nepal were resisted by Lord Wellesley.[11] But unwilling to involve his Government in a state of warfare upon the eve of his departure to England, he professed his readiness to enter into an amicable discussion of the claims in question, and proposed that Commissioners should be deputed on either side to investigate and adjust them. He also suggested that the Commissioners should at the same time determine other claims preferred by the Napalese to the revenues of the district of Sheoraj which was likewise situated within the limits of the ceded Provinces, but had been usurped by the Gorkhas before the date of the cession. The Court of Nepal refused to entertain the latter proposition and a vakeel was sent with this reply to Calcutta. No disposition was evinced to await the result of this mission, and a body of Gorkha troops took possession at once of more than two-thirds of Butwal.[12] Since then, a territorial dispute between the British Government and Nepal ensued over the issue of Butwal. The negotiations, which had been suspended by Wellesley's relinquishment of office, were resumed by Sir George Barlow who raised a strong protest against this aggrandizement. As a result of some correspondence, the Nepal Government offered to Sir George Barlow to hold the district of Butwal on payment of the annual rent, but this proposal was not acceptable to him as it would have been tantamount to the acceptance of Nepal's suzerainty over it. He, however, agreed to relinquish British rights on Sheoraj, since it was occupied by Nepal before 1801, when the provinces were ceded by the Nawab Vizier of Awadh, on condition that the Nepal Government evacuated Butwal forthwith.[13] But the proposal did not meet with the concurrence of the Nepal Government, and the non-interventionist Barlow showed dis-inclination to carry this dispute to a crisis point. The matter, therefore, remained unresolved.

Meanwhile, Amar Singh Thapa, the Commander-in-Chief of the Napalese forces, encouraged by Bhim Sein Thapa, the Prime Minister of Nepal engaged himself actively in extending and consolidating his hold over the hill-chieftains across the western boundary of Nepal. He defeated the Raja of Garhwal and annexed his kingdom in 1806. Continuing his march westward, he snatched eastern part of the Kangra valley from Raja Sansar Chand and laid siege to the Kangra Fort, the occupation of which would give him control over a great strategic point and command over the hilly tract upto the borders of Kashmir.[14] Unable to resist the Gorkha forces with his own limited resources, Raja Sansar Chand sought Ranjit Singh's help by offering him his fort of Kangra already besieged by the Gorkhas and coveted by the ambitious and powerful Sikh Chief who considered its occupation as means to dominate the hill-states between the Ravi and Sutlej.[15] He, therefore, gladly accepted this offer and helped Raja Sansar Chand in forcing the Gorkha troops to raise siege and retreat from the precincts of the fort on August 24, 1807. Amar Singh Thapa now devised other means of subjugating the Kangra Fort. He entered into negotiations with the Rajas of Kulu and Mandi who were inimically disposed to Raja Sansar Chand. But these diplomatic negotiations and secret military manoeuvres of the Gorkha Commander made Ranjit Singh apprehensive of his designs on his tributary hill-chieftains.[16] He, therefore, sought British help against the apprehended Nepalese incursions. But Lord Minto declined to enter into the disputes between Punjab and Nepal as he did not want to embroil his Government with Nepal and to aid Maharaja Ranjit Singh in becoming more powerful by the establishment of his control over the entire hilly terrain.[17] He also apprehended the gradual coming into closeness of the frontiers of the two military powerful states. Their mutual rivalry might endanger the peace of the neighbouring British dissects, and cooperation might result in a formidable anti-British combination of the two material communities, threatening British existence in India. This apprehension made Lord Minto watchful of the activities of the two powerful potentates north of the Delhi territories.

The outcome of these conflicts was the acquisition of the Kangra Fort by Ranjit Singh,[18] and the continuance of the Gorkha hold over a portion of the Kangra valley. Ranjit Singh's help could not prove to be of much avail to Raja Sansar Chand as he was more interested in the extension of his power than in the restoration of the authority of the ruler, he had supported. Raja Sansar Chand, therefore, demanded British help against both of his enemies who had usurped his territories.[19] But Lord Minto in reply stated that the British compliance with his request to assist him in repelling the Nepalese attack and in the restitution of his territories seized by the Lahore Chief would be 'tantamount to a predetermination on the part of the British Government at some future time to carry its army into the Punjab and to subjugate the Sikh Chiefs'. He also made it clear to him that relations of amity subsisted between the British Government and the state of Nepal, and would continue to subsist likewise in future.[20] He, thus, scrupulously avoided chances of a British conflict with Nepal which might have been the outcome of his help to Raja Sansar Chand. Whatever might have been his apprehension, he considered it prudent to observe complete neutrality in the military adventures of Nepal and Punjab in the Kangra valley. Neither the anticipated conflicts between Ranjit Singh and the Nepal Government, nor the entreaties of Raja Sansar Chand succeeded in effecting any deviation in the policy of the British Government towards Nepal in spite of the existing bitterness between the two Government on the issues of Sheoraj and Butwal.

In 1807, a fresh border dispute cropped up between the British Government and Nepal, when the Nepalese, posted at Morung. Crossed the border and forcibly dispossessed the British zamindar, Dooler Singh Chaudhuri of Bheemnagar, of his lands.[21] The protest made by the Magistarate of Purnea to the Nepalese officers at Morung brought no fruitful results. This dispute dragged on for two years; and during this period, the Nepal Government remained *de facto* occupant of the usurped territory. However, the relations between the two Governments remained more or less cordial as evidenced from the exchange of two friendly letters between them and the consequent grant of concession to the British to collect *fir* wood from the *terai* land under Nepal and to establish furnaces for the extraction of *tar* from it.[22]

Early in 1809, the British Government again took up the unresolved border dispute relating to villages focibly occupied by the Nepalese officers of Morung. For the fixation of the boundary in a spirit of harmony and friendship, the Governor-General suggested to the Raja Nepal to depute his representative to meet his British counterpart, and bring the border dispute to a satisfactory conclusion.[23] But as the Raja of Nepal appeared reluctant to part with the villages his officials had captured, the Company's Government decided to vindicate British right over the usurped villages and to restore them to the British subjects, the rightful claimants of these territories by employment of a military force without risking a major conflict. For this purpose, he gave necessary authority to the Magistrate of Purnea explaining clearly the British object and cautioning him against any overdoing.[24] In this project the British object was limited to the recovery of the usurped lands by the expulsion of the Gorkhas from there without committing any act of hostility against the Government of Nepal. The implied threat had the desired effect. The Nepal Government agreed to the British proposal and sent its representative, Guj Singh, to settle the matter amicably with Mr. Braddon, the officer deputed by the British Government. On the findings of the enquiry, the villages of Bheemnagar were restored to their rightful owner.[25]

Meanwhile certain new incidents created fresh complications between the Government of India and Nepal. One of them was the erection of a small military outpost at Kheri, within the British territory. Remonstrances made by the British local authorities to the officers of the Nepal Government brought no results. The Agent to the Governor-General in the Ceded Provinces also appealed to the Nepalese officials for withdrawal without pressing the issue to a breaking point.[26] His cautious approach in avoiding any measure that was likely to give offence to the Raja of Nepal was largely influenced by the success of Rutherford's commercial mission for the extraction of *tar* from *fir* tresss in

Nepal.[27] In view of the same considerations, the Governor-General-in-Council approved of the cautious step of his Agent in this affair and did not give much importance to this incident.[28]

Within a few months other complications arose. On June 27, 1811, 1600 sepoys of Bir Kishore Singh, the zamindar of Bettiah, entered the Nepalese Pargana of Routehat and committed depredations by killing Lochan Gir, a Tehsildar, Bhakta Ray and Bechoo Singh, the two zamindars and nine sepoys of that place and carrying away the State's property and treasure. The Raja of Nepal refrained from taking any action against the zamindar of Bettiah on accound of his friendly relations with the British Government and the assurances given to him by Hawkins, the Magistrate of Patna that he would be punished for his aggressive conduct. But in his letter to the Governor-General, he made a request to him either to punish Bir Kishore Singh for his outrageous conduct or to permit him to take action against him. Instead of taking any action, the Governor-General evaded by making a counter-complaint of frequent encroachments and aggressions of the Nepalese on the British territories, and referring to him the repeated representations made to him by the Magistrate of Saran.

The Raja of Nepal was annoyed at this reply of the Governor-General. He felt that the British Government put too much reliance on the unfounded representations made by Bir Kishore Singh, and emphatically charged the latter with the murder of the Tehsildar of Routehat. He informed the Governor-General that his officers had been subjected to several indignities for a long time by the British subjects and frankly stated that, if British Government were disposed to friendship, the Nepal Government would certainly reciprocate, but if its officers were out on all occasions to side with the aggressive elements, the friendship of the two States would be at stake and the Nepalese officers would not hesitate to punish the aggressor. But at the same time he expressed his desire for continued friendship with the Company's Government and again requested the Governor-General to take action against the zamindar of Bettiah.[29]

Having received no response from the British Government the Nepalese official reacted in an aggressive and retaliatory manner by crossing the East India Company's border and dispossessing Bir Kishore Singh of Bettiah of six villages, plundering the inhabitants and burning their houses.[30] On remonstrance of the British Government, the Nepal Government alleged that these villages belonged to their Pargana of Routehat, and this fact was acknowledged by Warren Hastings in 1781.[31] This event opened a fresh cause of Anglo-Nepalese dispute.

Under these circumstances, Lord Minto requested the Raja of Nepal to settle this dispute amicably by a conference of officials of the two Governments.[32] The Raja of Nepal accepted the proposal and deputed Kazee Randeep Singh, Sardar Parsu Ram Thapa and Raghunath Pandit for the task.[33] The Governor-General on his part appointed John Young; and the Magistrate of Saran issued necessary instructions to him for his guidance.[34]

During the course of investigation, the Nepalese officers committed another aggression by seizing forcibly sixteen other villages adjacent to the disputed villages, and asserted their claim on them on the same old plea that they were a part of the Pargana of Routehat, restored to them in 1781 by Warren Hastings.[35] This outrageous conduct of the Nepalese excited the annoyance and indignation of the British Government, and it was also made a subject of enquiry by the official of the two Governments.[36] Thus the enquiry was to be made into the alleged claim of the Nepalese Government over no less than twenty two border villages.[37]

During the progress of the investigation, the Nepalese Commissioners failed to substantiate the claims of their Government over the twenty-two disputed villages by submission of documentary evidences relating to Warren

Hastings' time. They could only prove that the Pargana of Routehat belonged to them, but could not produce a document which could conclusively indicate that the villages under dispute forcibly taken by their Government were a part of their pargana, as they claimed them to be. On the other hand, John Young advanced his contention that the villages in question were a part of the British pargana of Nunnore within the zamindari of the Raja of Bettiah, on the plea of their undisputed continuous occupation by his Government for thirty years.[38] He made it clear that they were never acknowledged by Warren Hastings to be a part of the Routehat pargana of Nepal.[39] Even if the Nepalese claim that they belonged to them in the remote past, were treated as true, about which he was not convinced in the absence of documentary evidence, the tacit acquiescence by the Nepal Government of allow these lands to go unclaimed for a period of thirty years was undoubtedly tantamount to a waiver. In view of these conflicting views unsupported by documents, the enquiry failed to produce any agreed solution, and the dispute remained unresolved.

On receipt of the report from John Young, the Persian Secretary to the Government of India addressed a letter to the Raja of Nepal on May 5, 1812 denouncing the violent, outrageous and unjustifiable seizure of the British villages as inconsistent with his professions of friendship with his Government, and conveying to him the expectations of his Government that he would preserve friendly relations unimpaired by admitting the equity and propriety of the demand for the evacuation of the 22 villages, over which he had no right, as a preliminary to any further probe into the matter.[40] In case of noncompliance, he threatened the use of force.[41]

This strong remonstrance had no effect on the Nepalese. Their incursions into the British territory continued as usual. They violently took possession of Tribeny Ghat in the zamindari of Bettiah had Sahpore, in the district of Gorakhpur and established their *thanas* at both the places, twelve miles deep inside the British territory.[42] This caused injury to the revenues of the zamindar of Bettiah who sought British help against the Nepalese and expressed his inability to pay the revenue of the lost villages to the East India Company, till they were restored to him.[43]

Some time after, the Nepalese committed further encroachments on Butwal, constituting the Northern forntier of Gorakhpur by forcibly seizing some villages in the thanas of Dhollia Bunder and Pallee, then under British possession.[44] They also made an incursion from Sheoraj into the adjoining estate of Debrooa, situated in the Pargana of Bansee, where they cut and carried off the rice crops and molested the inoffensive population. To resolve these new border disputes, the British Government suggested the immediate appointment of a joint commission on the frontier of Gorakhpur for a fair and amicable negotiation.[45]

In reply to this communication, the Raja of Nepal denied the allegations of border encroachments by his official and made counter-complaint of frontier violations by the British officers. He stated that the aforesaid lands had been in the possession of the Nepal Government several years prior to the cession of the district of Gorakhpur by the Nawab Vizier of Awadh to the Company's Government and that the had already enjoined upon his Commander-in-Chief, and other border officers to abstain from any encroachment on the Company's territory.[46] However, he pleaded for cordiality and good understanding with the British Government and, to achieve this purpose, he agreed with the Governor-General's proposal.[47]

Accordingly, Major Paris Bradshaw was appointed as the British representative to meet the Nepalese representatives, Raghunath Pandit, Pran Shah, Beer Bhunjan Pande and Parsu Ram Thapa on the frontiers of Gorakhpur in order to resolve the long-standing disputes relating to Sheoraj and Butwal.[48] Major Bradshaw was instructed to establish the British right to the sovereignty of Butwal by virtue of its cession to the

East India Company by the Nawab Vizier of Awadh in 1801 and to reject the Nepalese claim on Sheoraj by emphatic assertion that neither it was ever admitted nor was there any incontrovertible evidence to substantiate it except the plea of continuous usurpation for a long time.[49]

During the course of exploratory discussion, the Nepalese Commissioners persistently advanced their claims on the Pargana of Sheoraj on the ground that it had been in their possession since 1785, long before the acquisition of the Ceded Provinces by the East India Company from Awadh in 1801. Similarly, they based their claim on Butwal on the plea that it came into their possession by virtue of their suzerainty over the Raja of Palpa in 1796, when the latter was, in their custody at Khatmandu.[50] These claims, however, did not satisfy the British Commissioner, who stated that with the grant of the three provinces by the Nawab Vizier of Awadh to the Company's Government in 1801, Sheoraj and Butwal formed a part of the Ceded territories.[51] It appears that the two disputed territories originally belonged to Awadh; but Sheoraj was snatched by the Nepalese prior to the Ango-Awadh Treaty of 1801 and Butwal was captured by them in 1805 after the murder of Raja Prithi Pal Sein of Palpa. Under these circumstances when both the parties were adamant in advancing their claims which were not entirely baseless, adjustment of disputes by negotiations or their reasonable solution appeared to be quite difficult, if not impossible.

At one time the Nepalese Commissioners felt that these disputes could be set aside and other means of restoring friendly relations between the two Governments might be explored. With this end in view, they suggested renewal of the friendly commercial Treaty of 1801 which had virtually lapsed, but Major Paris Bradshaw refused to discuss it as it was not within his purview.[52] A hint also came from the Nepalese side that their Government might agree to relinquish the two disputed territories provided the East India Company was willing to farm out the entire *terai* region to it. But this suggestion was not entertained as that region was considered by the East India Company to be of great strategic importance to it.[53] Ultimately the conflicting findings of the Commissioners of the two sides were supported by their respective Government without any tendency to appreciate and concede the view-points of each other.

Hence in view of the conflicting claims rigidly adhered to by the two contestaints, the attempt to settle the ticklish disputes proved fruitless, just as the previous attempts to settle the dispute over the possession of the twenty-two villages were frustrated. Consequently, the relations between them worsened, and it appeared that the disputes might not be resolved without an exhibition of might as the only means left out to establish the questionable right. But Lord Minto was averse to pushing the matter to that extreme towards the end of his administration which was marked by an attitude of non-intervention. That is why his successor had to give top priority to this issue of settling for good the northern boundary of British India, and thereby acquiring several other much coveted advantages.

BURMA

Situated near the eastern frontiers of India, Burma, rich in natural resources and ports of strategic importance, was taken note by the British in the first half of the eighteenth century. With the growing Anglo-French commercial rivalry in the Indian Ocean, it began to enter into the Company's strategic calculations. Lord Wellesley attempted to secure commercial concessions and to establish political relations with Burma by the despatch of two missions under Captain Symes in 1802 and Lieutenant Canning in 1803. The first mission was both commercial and political, while the latter was exclusively political. The political object of both the missions was the exclusion of the French from Burma. Captain Symes succeeded in getting commercial concessions; but any discussion on political issues relating to the Mag refuges and the French activities, was carefully avoided by the Burmese Court. The canning mission was a total failure. It could not procure the elimination of the French from Burma.

When Lord Minto took over as Governor-General of India, relations between Burma and the Government of Bengal were not harmonious and good neighbourly. During his period, they were further strained due to certain unpleasant incidents. On March 1, 1808, the Burmese Government lodged a complaint that when a French ship, passing between the island of Cheduba and the Coast of Arakan, ran aground, the captain of a British ship nearby captured the French crew and carried them away on board his ship, and they took a very serious view of this unwarranted action by a foreign national in Burmese territory, tantamount to the violation of the laws of that country.[54] However, the Burmese authorities at Cheduba did not use force to oppose that measure as friendly relations subsisted between the two Governments.[55] To this, Lord Minto replied that Burmese law was violated not by the British, but by the French who first fired upon the English boat.[56] He also informed them that he had already restored restored the French crew to the Isle of France.[57] The matter ended there. Later on, the Governor-General conciliated the Burmese Government by permitting its agents to buy saltpetre and muskets in Calcutta.[58]

While these petty disputes were distracting the attention of British authorities in India, the Government of England issued an Order-in-Council on November 11, 1807 to frustrate the Continental System of Napoleon. Lord Minto feared that, by the rigid enforcement of this regulation, French trade with Burma would be severely curtailed and the commercial interests and its revenues would be adversely affected. The King of Burma might treat is as an act of hostility against his country and might seize the persons and property of British subjects, and prohibit their trade altogether in retaliation.[59]

With this apprehension in mind and in order to explain the new situation to the Kind of Burma, Lord Minto sent a mission under Captian Canning on July 20, 1809.[60] He was instructed to explain the guiding considerations motivating blockade of French trade with Burma and to assure the Burmese Government that these measures were not acts of hostility against it.[61] In case the Burmese Government took a different view of things, he was to take adequate steps to afford protection to the British subjects in Rangoon.[62] In view of the delicate situation, he was warned against proceeding beyond Rangoon, unless absolute necessity arose to go to the capital.[63]

On reaching Rangoon on October 1, 1809, Captain Canning was accorded a friendly reception by the Burmese Lieutenant-Governor to whom he explained the object of his mission, and received no adverse comments. Soon after, when he had an interview with the Viceroy of Pegu, he was well-received and, during the discussion, he was told that in view of the Ango-French struggle of gigantic dimensions, he could appreciate the blockade of the French Islands by the British navy.[64] From him, he came to know about the impending succession dispute between the King Bo-da-Pa-Ya's grandson and his uncles in the event of the King's death; and was sounded whether his Government would afford military help to the former against the latter and accept territorial reward in lieu of it. To this proposal Captain Canning gave a very cautious and non-committal reply that he was not authorized to discuss the matter officially, but the Viceroy could entertain some hope of British support.[65]

In this encouraging atmosphere, on receipt of summons from the capital, he reached Amarapura on February 9, 1810, where he found the royal court humming with intrigues.[66] On meeting the young heir-apparent, he expressed the same sentiments about the British attitude towards him in the disputed succession, as he had explained to the Viceroy of Pegu. In reply to the various enquiries of the Burmese minister regarding the principles and justification of blockade, he explained to them that the British measures were intended to frustrate the Continental System of Napoleon and were not directed against the interests of their country.[67] But thereafter, when he met the old king, he found him a man of different mettle. The king expressed his inability to negotiate with him as he was the representative of the Governor-General of India and not of the king of England. Hence nothing came out of this interview. However, he received an assurance from the heir-apparent that the Lieutenant-Governor of Rangoon would not grant any passport or protection of the Burmese flag to ships bound for the French Island.[68]

With this empty concession, Captain Canning returned to Calcutta. Lord Minto disapproved of his act of encouraging the heir-apparent of Burma to entertain the hope of British support for his succession[69] as it was inconsistent with his non-intervention policy. The Government of India could not know what reactions its anti-French naval activities in the Eastern seas created in the mind of the Burmese King; and it engaged itself in its task undeterredby any fear, till the intended object was achieved.

In 1811, the depredations of the Mag refugee leader, Kingbering, in Arakan created tense relations between the British and the Burmese. Having recruited an army of the Mags in the British territory and joined by a number of inhabitants of Arakan, he invaded Arakan from his base on the river Nauf, committed depredations and established his hold over its northern part. Conscious of the limitations of his resources for maintaining his authority permanently against the superior strength of the Government of Burma, he approached the British Government with a request to recognize his authority in North Arakan and accept him as a British tributary[70] Lord Minto rejected his request and instructed the Magistrate of Chittagong to arrest Kingbering and to prevent the Mag refugees from joining his standard. But no success was achieved in these attempts.[71]

The Burmese officials in Arakan took a very serious view of this intrusion by Kingbering, and ascribed it to the British instigations; and the Court of A V A accused the British

Government of encouraging and supporting rebellion against the Burmese authorities. The use British territory as a recruiting ground and base of Kingbering's operations in Arakan was undoubtedly a very serious political matter which created natural apprehension and irritation in Burmese minds. Fearing reprisals by the Burmese authorities against the British merchants in Rangoon, Lord Minto decided to despatch another mission under Captain Canning to the Court of A V A to explain the British position in relation to Kingbering's questionable activities in Arakan, and to patch up the differences between the two Governments, caused by his depredations.[72]

Canning reached Rangoon on October 21, 1811 with positive instructions to deny any British connection with Kingbering and his activities without being apologetic, and to afford protection to the British merchants in Rangoon against any reprisals. In the event of the seizure of their persons and property, he was to demand their release; and on its rejection, he was authorised to threaten a rupture between the two Governments. No military demonstration was, however, to be made without prior sanction.[73]

At Rangoon, Captain Canning found a very tense atmosphere.

The Viceroy of Pegu and all other Burmese officials entertained a strong suspicion of British complicity with Kingbering. They could not believe that the collection of a large number of Mag refugees under Kingbering at Chittagong and his invasion of Arakan was possible 'without the knowledge, participation and support of the British Government'.[74] All arguments of Canning to the contrary and his attempts to convince them of his Government's unconcern with the aggression of Kingbering appeared unconvincing and proved fruitless.[75] During Canning's period of stay at Rangoon, the Viceroy of Pegu had sent an envoy to Calcutta expressing his Government's displeasure at the encouragement, Kingbering and his associates had received in the British territories for their operations in Arakan and demanding an assurance that they would not be given shelter again; and in the event of their return, they would be seized and surrendered to the Burmese officials.[76] To this, Lord Minto expressed his readiness to expel them from the British territories, but refused to undertake the responsibility of surrendering them.[77]

In the mean time, Burmese troops defeated and pushed back Kingbering's forces which crossed river Nauf and took shelter in the British territory.[78] This created apprehension in the mind of the Magistrate of Chittagong that the Burmese troops also might enter into British territory in their pursuit. He, therefore, sent a detachment of troops to the southern frontier of Chittagong to check their apprehended incursion. In determining its policy towards the Mag refugees, the British Government divided them into three categories.[79] The first were the chiefs of whom Kingbering was the principal and by whom disturbances in Arakan were excited; the second were their followers who had tanen shelter in Chittagong and accompanied their chiefs, voluntarily or by compulsion in their expeditions into Arakan; and the third were those who had retired into Bengal owing to the violence and oppression of the Burmese. Lord Minto was unwilling to surrender the first category of refugees to the 'sanguinary vengeance' of the Burmese Government, although he was prepared to compel them to quit British territory. To the second category, he resolved to grant protection temporarily from the pursuit of the Burmese army and ultimately to induce them to retire from British territory. The third category of refugees were allowed to take shelter in Chittagong, but no definite decision was taken about their future fate.[80]

On February 21, 1812, the Raja of Arakan renewed the demand for the surrender of Kingbering and other chiefs and threatened to pursue them into British territory.[81] The Magistrate of Chittagong agreed to arrest them, but expressed his inability to surrender them without authority from his Government. Counselling him for friendly relations between the two Governments, he warned that the British Government will never allow any foreign state to invade its territory with impunity and 'it is well-prepared to resist such an undeserved act of aggression.[82] Accordingly, they were arrested at Chittagong and their surrender was pressed upon by the two vakeels of the Burmese Government especially deputed for this purpose. On refusal of this demand, they asked the Magistrate of Chittagong to encourage, permit and order the third category of refugees to return to Arakan.[83] It was agreed to on the Burmese assurance of their safety and freedom from molestation.

Notwithstanding these negotiations for amicable settlement of the refugee problem, a Burmese force of 500 crossed into British territory, and opened fire on British troops.[84] The Government of Bengal retaliated by reinforcement of troops to check the menace of possible invasion. Fearing that the life of Captain Canning might be in danger, a ship accompanied by a cruiser of 20 guns was sent there, and instructions were issued to him to remonstrate against the aggressive conduct of the Burmese forces on the Arakan frontier and to leave Rangoon in the event of insulting behaviour and threat of his life.[85]

Contrary to the apprehensions of Lord Minto, the Burmese Government wrote a conciliatory letter informing him that the movements of its troops on the frontier was intended to chastise the intruders, and no aggression against the British territory was in contemplation.[86] Lord Minto was satisfied with this reply and ordered the withdrawal of the British troops from the frontier[87] The border tension subsided for a while.

In this improved atmosphere, Captain Canning planned to proceed to A V A to accomplish the object of his mission. But within a short time, the arrival of two British war-ships— the 'Amboyna' and the 'Malabar', at Rangoon on March 18, 1812, created exaggerated fear and excited wide-spread alarm in the town about the British intentions. Many Burmese officials believed that war had already broken out on the

Arakan frontier, and the British war-ships intended to capture Rangoon.[88] The Viceroy of Pegu, therefore, invited Captain Canning and Captain Maxfield, the pilot of the 'Malabar' to a meeting to ascertain the British motive in sending the war-ships to Rangoon.[89] On hearing from the British pilot that he was cruising about the seas in search of enemy vessels in performance of his normal duties, and that his landing in the Rangoon port was intended to effect some necessary repairs and alterations in his vessels, the Viceroy promised to provide all facilities to him and advised him to leave the port soon after the repairs were completed.[90] Several other influential Burmese interviewed Captain Canning in their alarmed state of mind, and entreated him to send away the war-ships from their ports to remove apprehensions and to normalize the relations between the two Governments. Captain Canning replied that the visit of the British war-ships to Rangoon was not something unusual and extraordinary. In the past also when Colonel Syme visited Rangoon in 1802, a British cruizer, the 'Mornington' had stayed at Rangoon for eight months without any objection. This argument did not completely eliminate their fears. The Viceroy of Pegu, however, advised Captain Canning to proceed to Amarapura, where all disputes would be adjusted amicably[91] But in the absence of orders to that effect, he could not comply with this advice and stayed on in Rangoon awaiting orders from the Governor-General.[92]

In India, the Governor-General felt that in view of the explanation Captain Canning had given to the Viceroy of Pegu regarding the British attitude towards Kingbering and the consequent withdrawal of the Burmese troops from the Chittagong frontier, his stay in Rangoon was no longer necessary; and ordered him to return to Calcutta.[93] But before this order could reach him, certain unpleasant incidents in Rangoon, such as seizure of some tents of the British mission by the Burmese, demolition of some European tombs and monuments, including those of the graves of some 'respectable Europeans,' for utilizing their material for erecting fortifications, the sudden demand of the Viceroy of Pegu for the surrender of the Mag refugees and the exhibition of anti-British feelings causing insecurity to the British merchants, prolonged his stay in Rangoon.[94]

To resolve the refugee problem, Captain Canning even thought of proceeding to Amarapura in the belief that with the help of the friendly disposed heir-apparent, he might overcome all difficulties and bring the dispute to satisfactory conclusion by direct negotiations. But he could not proceed to Amarapura on account of the new border incursions by Kingbering which increased tension between the two Governments.[95] Kingbering and his chief adherents somehow escaped from the British custody, collected a large body of followers and made another bid. Taking advantage of the withdrawal of the Burmese army from Arakan, he crossed the river Nauf with about 500 followers and occupied a stockade at Maungdaw.[96] When the British Government came to know of his plan, Colonel Morgan was instructed to prevent his incursion into Arakan; and the magistrate of Chittagong was authorized to offer a reward of Rs. 5000.00 for the capture of Kingbering and his principal associates. A Proclamation was issued that assistance to them would be treated as an act of hostility to the British Government and the persons guilty of it would be punished according to law.[97]

This new development on the Arakan frontier created natural apprehensions in the British mind that it might furnish new sources of irritation and new grounds for 'arrogant demands' by the Court of A V A.[98] Hence instructions were issued to Captain Canning to wait at Rangoon instead of proceeding to Amarapura and to explain to the Viceroy of Pegu the measures adopted by the British authorities to prevent the Mag refugees from crossing the river Nauf and to assure British cooperation in quelling the insurrection headed by Kingbering without a commitment to surrender him in the event of his arrest.[99] He was, however, advised to retire from Rangoon in case the Burmese threatened him with insult or injury.[100]

Soon after the despatch of these instructions, news came from Arakan about the failure of Kingbering's expedition and his expulsion into British territory by the Burmese forces. This time the Burmese neither demanded the surrender of the rebels nor did they threaten to cross into the British territory in their pursuit.[101] Under these circumstances, the success of Captain Canning's mission appeared to be doubtful to Lord Minto. Therefore, Captain Canning returned to Calcutta on August 21, 1812 on instruction from him giving up his bid to make another attempt to resolve differences with the Burmese Government by proceeding to Amarapura.

The depredations of Kingbering, however, continued unabated. On December 26, 1812, another adventure of his also failed. This time 2000 Burmese troops entered the British territory to effect the seizure of the recalcitrant Mags.[102] Lieutenant Colonel Hall was despatched at the head of some troops to Rutnapullung with instructions to expel the Burmese forces from British territories.[103] But he did not find them in that part of the frontier. They were probably moving in the woods and hills on the frontier in search of Kingbering and the other insurgents.[104] In the meantime, on the demand made by the Governor of Arakan for British cooperation against the insurgents, the Magistrate of Chittagong promised to do the needful, provided an agreement was reached that the two parties would not cross into each other's territories without a 'specific invitation', and the Burmese Government disapproved of the encroachment already made by its troops.[105] In reply to these demands, the Governor of Arakan politely reiterated his request for the capture and surrender of the rebel Mags without offeing any apology for the violation of British territory by his troops.[106] Consequently, neither the British Government made any efforts to apprehend and surrender the Mags guilty of disturbing peace and tranquillity of Arakan from their base on the British side of the frontier, nor did the Buurmese Government excuse the British for their half-heartedness or reluctance in complying with their demands. The anti-Burmese Kingbering's activities therefore, continued to strain the Ango-Burmese relations throughout the period of the Governor-Generalship of Lord Minto, which was marked by want of firmness and consistency in this regard. By his attitude towards Kingbering and refusal to surrender him, he irritated the Court of A V A and the Burmese authorities in Arakan. It wan not the grant of shelter to the Mags in the British territories which was so much objectionable as were their anti-Burmese activities from their haunts across the Arakan border.

In the interest of peace, harmony and good neighbourly relations, Lord Minto should have taken effective measures to prevent Kingbering from invading Arakan. But his failure to do the needful was hardly justified, when he was not seriously involved in any difficulty in or outside India during 1811-13. The French menace to India was virtually removed by that time and danger of the French invasion had become far more remote than what it had been during 1807-9. Within the borders of India also, there was hardly any major danger of war. This was undoubtedly an excellent opportunity for Lord Minto to instil a conviction into the Burmese mind that the British Government would not harbour hostiles into its territory and would not tolerate their indulgence in anti-Burmese activities which might run the risk of being interpreted as their hostile action. But Lord Minto missed it and left for his successors a legacy of troubles on the eastern frontier, which ultimately led to a war soon after a decade of his retirement.

REFERENCES

1. Wright, Daniel, *History of Nepal*, p. 31.
2. Regmi, D. R., *Modern Nepal*, p. 204.
3. Aitchison, C. U. *op. cit.*, Vol. II, pp. 166-167.
4. *Ibid.*, pp. 168-171.
5. Lamb, Alastair, *Britain and Chinese Central Asia*, p. 36.
6. Chaudhuri, K. C. *Anglo-Nepalese Relations*, p. 150.

7. Aitchison, C. U. *op. cit.,*
8. Regmi, D. R. *op. cit.,* p. 114.
9. Report of the Persian Secy., dated nill, For. Deptt. Pol., Cons. June 12, 1812, Cons. 79.
10. Mill and Wilson, *op. cit.,* Vol. VIII, p. 7.
11. *Ibid.,*
12. *Ibid.,*
13. Chaudhuri, K. C. *op. cit.,*
14. Tucker, Francis, *Gorkha,* p. 63.
15. Sinha, N. K., *Ranjit Singh,* p. 72.
16. Ranjit Singh's hill tributaries were Rajas of Jasrota, Chamber, Basoli, Bhadu and Mankot.
17. Lord Minto to Raja Sansar Chand, Sept. 6, 1807, For. Deptt. Pol., Cons. Sept. 13, 1811, Cons. 56.
18. Sinha, N. K. *op. cit.,* p. 36, and Hutchison. J., *History of the Punjab Hill States,* Vol. I, p. 321.
19. Lord Minto to Raja Sansar Chand, Sept. 6, 1807, For. Deptt. Pol., Cons. Sept. 13, 1811, Cons. 56.
20. *Ibid.,*
21. Lord Minto to Raja of Nepal, June 5, 1809, For Deptt. Pol., Cons. June 13, 1809, Cons. 72.
22. Persian Secretary to Raja of Nepal, March 20, 1809, For. Deptt. Pol., Cons. April 10, 1809, Cons. 84 and Raja of Nepal to Lord Minto, Oct. 5, 1809, for. Deptt. Pol., Cons. Oct. 10, 1809, Cons. 47.
23. Lord Minto to Raja to Nepal, June 5, 1809, For. Deptt. Pol. Cons. June 13, 1809, Cons. 72.
24. Persian Secretary to Raja of Nepal, Now. 29, 1809, For Deptt. Pol, Cons. Dec. 5, 1809, Cons. 35.
25. *Ibid.*
26. Agent to Governor-General in Ceded Provinces to Edmonstone, April 8, 1811, For. Deptt. Pol., Cons., April 26, 1811, Cons 27.
27. *Ibid.*
28. Lord Minto to his Agent in Ceded Provinces, dated *nil,* For. Deptt. Pol. Cons, April, 26, 1811. Cons. 50.

29. Raja of Nepal to Vice-President-in-Council red. On Jan. 13, 1812, For Deptt. Secret, Cons. March 13, 1812, Cons. 39.
30. *Ibid.*
31. Persian Secretary to Raja of Nepal, Nov. 1, 1811, For. Deptt Pol., Cons. Nov. 8, 1811, Cons. 70.
32. *Ibid.*
33. Raja of Nepal to Lord Minto, January 3, 1812, For. Deptt. Secret, Cons. March 13, 1812, Cons. 38.
34. Magistrate of Saran to John Young, March 13, 1812, For. Deptt. Secret, Cons March 13, 1812. Cons. 42.
35. Report of Persian Secretary, May 5, 1812, For Deptt. Pol., Cons. June 12, 1812, Cons. 81.
36. *Ibid.*
37. *Ibid.*
38. John young to Magistrate of Saran, April 23, 1812, For. Deptt. Pol., Cons. Sept. 4, 1812, Cons. 51.
39. *Ibid.*
40. Persian Secretary to Raja of Nepal, May 5, 1812, For. Deptt. Pol, Cons June 12, 1812, Cons. 82.
41. *Ibid.*
42. Raja Bir Kishore Singh to magistrate of Saraff, May 26, 1812. For. Deptt. Pol., Cons. May 28, 1812, Cons. 84.
43. Raja Bir Kishore Singh to Magistrate of Saran, May 26, 1812, For. Deptt. Pol., Cons. May 28, 1812, Cons. 84.
44. Persian Secretary to Raja of Nepal, dated Nil, For. Deptt. Pol., Cons. June 12, 1812, Cons. 80.
45. *Ibid.*
46. Raja of Nepal to Persian Secretary, Sept. 28, 1812, For. Deptt. Pol., Cons. Jan. 15, 1813, Cons. 45.
47. *Ibid.*
48. Edmonstone to Major Paris Bradshaw, Jan., 13, 1813, For. Deptt. Pol. Cons. Jan. 15, 1813, Cons. 46.
49. Edmonstone to Major Paris Bradshaw, Jan. 13, 1813, For. Deptt. Pol., Cons. Jan. 15, 1813, Cons. 46.
50. Major Paris Bradshaw to Edmonstone, April 11, 1813 and April 8, 1813, For. Deptt. Pol., Cons. April 30, 1813, Cons. 32 and 40.

51. *Ibid.*
52. Edmonstone to Major Paris Bradshaw, June 18, 1813, Pol. Deptt. Secret, Cons. June 18, 1813. Cons. 23.
53. Major Paris Bradshaw to Edmonstone, received on April 9, 1813, For, Deptt. Secret Cons. June 23, 1813, Cons. 20.
54. Raja of Arakan to Lord Minto, March 1, 1808, For. Deptt. Pol., Cons. March 28, 1808, Cons. 55.
55. *Ibid.*
56. Lord Minto to Raja of Arakan, March 28, 1808, For. Deptt. Pol., Cons. March 28, 1808, Cons. 56.
57. *Ibid.*
58. Viceroy of Pegu to Lord Minto, March 6, 1809, For. Deptt. Pol., Cons April 29, 1809, Cons. 162, and Lord Minto to Viceroy of Pegu, April 12, 1809, For. Deptt. Pol, Cons. April 29, 1809, Cons. 163.
59. Edmonstone to Capt. Canning, July 20, 1809, For. Deptt. Pol., Cons. July 20, 1809, Cons. 11.
60. *Ibid.*
61. *Ibid.*
62. Pol. Letter to Court of Directors, Aug. 4, 1809.
63. *Ibid.*
64. Capt. Canning to Edmonstone, Oct. 2, 1809, For, Deptt. Pol., Cons. Nov. 14, 1809, Cons. 24.
65. Capt. Canning to Edmonstone, May 8, 1810, For, Deptt. Pol., Cons. May 29, 1810, Cons. 1.
66. *Ibid.*
67. *Ibid.*
68. *Ibid.*
69. Lord Minto to Capt, Canning, May 29, 1810, For, Deptt. Pol, Cons, May 29, 1810, Cons. 2.
70. Capt. Canning to Edmonstone, Oct., 24, 1811, For. Deptt. Pol., Cons. Nov. 22, 1811, Cons. 4.
71. *Ibid.*
72. Edmonstone to Capt. Canning, Sept. 6, 1811, For. Deptt. Pol., Cons. Sept. 6, 1811, Cons. 50.
73. *Ibid.*

74. Capt. Canning to Edmonstone, Oct. 25, 1811, For. Deptt. Pol., Cons. Nov. 22, 1811, Cons. 4.

75. Capt. Canning to Edmonstone, Nov. 28, 1811, For. Deptt. Pol., Cons. Dec. 6, 1811, Cons. 6.

76. Viceroy of Pegu to Edmonstone, Sept. 23, 1811, For. Deptt. Pol., Cons. Jan. 18, 1812, Cons. 63.

77. *Ibid.*

78. Edmonstone to Capt. Canning, Jan. 25, 1812, For. Deptt. Pol., Cons. Jan. 25, 1812, Cons. 53.

79. *Ibid.*

80. Edmonstone to Capt. Canning, Jan. 25, 1812, For. Deptt. Pol., Cons. Jan. 25, 1812. Cons. 53.

81. Raja of Arakan to Magistrate of Chittagong, Feb. 12 & Feb. 21. 1812, For. Deptt. Secret, Cons Feb. 21, 1812, Cons. 17 and 34.

82. Magistrate of Chittagong to Raja of Arakan, dated nil, For. Deptt. Secret, Cons. March 21, 1812, Cons, 22.

83. Col. Morgan to Magistrate of Chittagong, Feb. 25, 1812, For. Deptt. Secret. Cons. March 13, 1812, Cons. 13.

84. *Ibid.*

85. Magistrate of Chittagong to Raja of Arakan, Feb. 25, 1812, For. Deptt. Sectet, Cons. March 13, 1812, Cons. 6.

86. Raja of Arakan to Magistrate of Chittagong, Feb. 27, 1812, For, Deptt. Secret, Cons. March 13, 1812, Cons. 12.

87. Lord Minto to Magistrate of Chittagong April 17, 1812, For. Deptt. Secret, Cons. April 17, 1812, Cons. 59.

88. Capt. Canning to Edmonstone, April 9, 1812, For. Deptt. Secret, Cons. May 8, 1812, Cons. 23.

89. *Ibid.*

90. *Ibid.*

91. Capt. Canning to Edmonstone, April 9, 1812, For. Deptt. Secret, Cons. May 8, 1812, Cons. 23.

92. *Ibid.*

93. Edmonstone to Capt. Canning, May 8, 1812, For. Deptt. Secret, Cons. May 8, 1812, Cons. 25.

94. Capt. Canning to Edmonstone, May 20, 1812, For. Deptt. Secret, Cons. June 12, 1812, Cons. 22.

95. Capt. Canning to Edmonstone, May 23, 1817, For. Deptt. Secret, Cons. June 12, 1812, Cons. 24.

96. Magistrate of Chittagong to Edmonstone, June 4, 1812, For. Deptt. Secret, Cons. June 12, 1812, Cons. 19.

97. Proclamation of Governor-General-in-Council, dated nil, For. Deptt. Secret, Cons. July 4, 1812, Cons. 31.

98. Edmonstone to Capt. Canning, June 12, 1812, For. Deptt. Sevet, Cons. June 12, 1812, Cons. 25.

99. *Ibid.*

100. *Ibid.*

101. Edmonstone to Capt. Canning, June 25, 1812, For. Deptt. Secret, Cons June 25, 1812, Cons. 47.

102. Magistrate of Chittagong to Colonel Dick, Jan. 5, 1813, For. Deptt. Secret, Cons. Jan. 15, 1813, Cons. 31.

103. Magistrate of Chittagong to Edmonstone, Jan. 15, 1813, For. Deptt. Secret, Cons. Jan. 15, 1813, Cons. 34.

104. Magistrate of Chittagong to Edmonstone, Jan. 15, 1813. For, Deptt. Secret, Cons. Jan. 15, 1813, Cons. 35.

105. *Ibid.*

106. Governor of Arakan to Magistrate of Chattagong, Jan. 30, 1813, For. Deptt. Secret, Cons. Feb. 11, 1813, Cons. 17.

11

The Assessment

After completing the period of his office, Lord Minto left India on Oct. 1,1813. Before his departure for England, he won the plaudits of the Home authorities and the Government who acknowledged his services by advancing him a step in the peerage by which he became Earl Minto.

An active and ambitious man with scholastic tastes and closely associated with Burke, Fox and Sheridan, Lord Minto was a discerning politician and a skilful administrator. His administration was distinguished by moderation in his approach to Indian problem and his foreign policy was marked by considerable ability and energy which he had gained by his varied experience during his past career. He did well in India and devoted himself to consolidating British influence more by peaceful than aggressive methods, and outside India, he extended it by diplomatic and military activities to safeguard the Imperial interest from outside aggression, during the critical years created by the projects of Napoleon Bonaparte.

Though specifically pledged to follow the policy advocated by Cornwallis and endorsed by British Parliament, of non-aggression, non-interference in the affairs of Indian States and non-extension of British possession in India, Lord Minto found it difficult to pursue such a line of policy because of a new danger, threatening the Company's commercial and political interests. In assessing the reasons for a change in Indian policy he always kept in view the prevailing conditions in Europe and Asia, and the working of the minds of the Court of Directors and the Cabinet. On his arrival in India, the undisguised and ambitious projects of France threatened to interrupt the tranquillity and security of the British dominion in the East and the Francophobia of the terrified British mind had become an all-devouring megalomania. Napoleon's manoeuvres, designed to cripple Britain in Asia, aimed at moving men and munitions towards India, the focal point of their attention. The Directors were subject to commercial and parliamentary opinion as well as mindful of their profits abroad, and the ministers of the day were sensitive to public opinion and the changes on the international scene.

Within the framework of these circumstances, Lord Minto functioned in India. Keenly aware of the magnitude and consequences of the aggressive French designs and fully conscious of the prevailing situation in India, he viewed Napoleon a more pressing danger than the Marathas or pindaris. For a while, he put the Indian problems in cold storages until the French menace was successfully encountered. By his unified approach and concerted action at all levels, he wrecked Napoleonic decisive gibe. This slight departure from the dictates of the Court of Directors in his foreign policy yielded fruitful results without disturbing peace in India, which he maintained unbroken for six years and three months. His successful achievements in the Persian Gulf, Mauritius, Bourbon and the Eastern Archipelago by which he ensured the safety of the British Empire in the East, flowed unquestionable from the war-policy of the Cabinet which, unlike the Imperial policy of Lord Wellesley, was not subjected to vehement criticism and censure by the parliament.

In the diplomatic sphere too, Lord Minto was quite successful. In the Court of Lahore, Sind, Kabul and Teheran, his missions improved the 'defensive means' of his

Government. In this respect, he kept the Company's European enemies at a distance. This policy marked a significant epoch in the history of the East India Company. It widened the scope of Indian policy and enlarged the circle of British diplomatic influence beyond the Company's borders. It involved expenditure and some departure from the policy of non-intervention, but the Home authorities relaxed their attitude of strict economy and non-involvement when the justice of Minto's representations was realized.

This period was also distinguished by the conquest of the French and Dutch settlements in the Indian ocean, leaving England without a European rival in the East. The French free-booters at their haunts in the islands of Mauritius and Bourbon, were a serious menace to the British commerce and shipping with the East. In the trial of strength between the British and the French, the latter finally succumbed. The ease with which the islands were taken, formed a commentary on the negligence which had so many years procrastinated so needful a measure, Besides, the vigorous blockade of Java and the Spice Islands, the important trading centres in the Orient, led to a new phase of British expansion in the South East Asia, though only for a short period of four years. British naval influence assumed a new significance from the Cape of Good Hope to the Pacific Ocean. This policy, of course, smacked of British Imperialism, but there was no rebuff from the Court of Directors as it was necessitated by circumstances and served their country's interests.

In India, Lord Minto's hesitation in taking bold and decisive steps on several occasions may be attributed less to himself and more to the Leedenhall Street which guided and controlled his policies. The outrages of the Pindaris, the encroachments of the Gorkhas and the insolence of the Burmese attracted his attention, and he was willing to settle with them. But lack of encouragement and political support from Home prevented him from grappling with these problems. This policy may be ascribed to his principle of 'Constitutional Caution'.

In Bundelkhand and Haryana, the free-booters and refractory tribes created ugly situations. Their timely suppression and the restoration of peace and order in those regions reveal his firmness as an administrator. His other notable achievements were the timely suppression of the white mutiny in Madras and the rebellion in Travancore, and the signing of the Treaty to Amritsar with Maharaja Ranjit Singh. This Treaty established friendly relations with the Sikhs for about thirty-five years and converted the Sikh Chief, a source of potential danger on the Western Frontier, into a firm ally and bulwark against, the Afghans. By his interference in Travancore, peace was restored in the strategically situated friendly State, and dangers to British interests in that region were eliminated.

Internally, Lord Minto tightened up the administration, when it had become intolerably lax. But in doing so, there was no return to 'bullying arrogance' of Lord Wellesley. Quiet and unassuming by nature, he was firm, efficient and quick in decisions. He effected some useful reforms in revenue, judicial, police, customs and postal departments. He very well under-stood that if the machinery of the administration was not lubricated occasionally, the entire structure would come to a creaking grinding halt. He was instrumental in affording religious toleration to the British subjects in the Company's territory, and discouraged offensive propaganda of the Christian missionaries amongst Hindu and Muslims. Though a cautious administrator, he was not slow to act, whenever events threatened the Company's interests in India. Instances of this aspect of his administrative measures were not few in number.

As an administrator, Lord Minto set up a good example of sober industry, adventurous spirit and administrative drive. He did not lack in initiative and originality. Although he always endeavoured to obey the orders of the Court of Directors without weakening the prestige of the British in India, he was not a blind follower of directions. Within their framework, he exercised his free discretion. Where there were no definite directions, he could take initiative to suggest to the higher authorities the measures which he considered to be necessary without giving much consideration to their past views. His Minute on education recorded on March 6,1811 was a notable instance in point. Knowing that the Court of Directors were disinclined to incur expenditure on the enlightening of the minds of the Indian subjects through education, he had the courage and audacity to suggest a departure from the existing indifference to active interest in the encouragement of learning in India. In this respect, he could anticipate the responsibility that was thrust upon the unwilling Court of Directors two years later by the Charter Act. His recommendations for the opening of educational institutions of higher learning by the Company and earmarking of separate funds for this purpose was quite in line with the emerging liberal spirit and utilitarian ideology in England. His reaction on several other innovations introduced in the Charter Act could not be known owing to his demise on reaching the shores of England. He was decidedly more liberal than the Court of Directors on matters of Indian administration.

On the whole, Lord Minto's administration was moderate and pacific, which epitomized the essence of his policy. This policy gave a strength to Peshwa, Sindhia, Holkar and Bhonsla to consolidate their positions. The Peshwa was showing signs of restiveness against the inconvenient restrictions imposed upon him by the Treaty of Bassein. Central India was in a state of chronic disorder, made worse by the activities of the Pindaris who burst terror and dismay on the helpless population, committing every sort of violence and excess, torturing innocent people to extort money, murdering and burning in the defenseless village. They soon ventured to extend their depredations into British territories causing worry to the Company's administrators. The increase in the Pindari excesses was a distinct political problem requiring vigilance, circumspection and precautionary measures. Lord Minto was alive to this problem. He took the diplomatic and military measures to keep their operations restricted to the smallest inaccessible areas. His measures against them marked the beginning of the policy which was pursued more vigorously by his successor, the Earl of Moria.

The preservation of the British power in the East by the elimination of European rival was the crowning act of Lord Minto's Government-Generalship. The value of his work was to reduce the Company's commitments at a time when they could not be indefinitely extended or even maintained at their existing limits, and to accomplish it without provoking a war of major dimensions or encouraging the subordinate principalities to assert their power. Thus by all standards, he was a competent person, with a conspicuous ability to hold his own among the best on the India stage. His administration was in many showed no extension of the British frontiers, yet he did much to consolidate the influence of his Government as the master power of India.

Index

□□□